CITIZENSHIP IN THE 21ST CENTURY

CITIZENSHIP IN THE 21ST CENTURY

LESTER T. KANE AND MARYLYN R. POWELLER
EDITORS

PARK LEARNING CENTRE
UNIVERSITY OF GLOUCESTERSHIRE
PO Box 220, The Park
Cheltenham GL50 2RH
Tel: 01242 714333

Nova Science Publishers, Inc.
New York

NOTICE TO THE READER

The Publisher has taken reasonable care in the preparation of this book, but makes no expressed or implied warranty of any kind and assumes no responsibility for any errors or omissions. No liability is assumed for incidental or consequential damages in connection with or arising out of information contained in this book. The Publisher shall not be liable for any special, consequential, or exemplary damages resulting, in whole or in part, from the readers' use of, or reliance upon, this material. Any parts of this book based on government reports are so indicated and copyright is claimed for those parts to the extent applicable to compilations of such works.

Independent verification should be sought for any data, advice or recommendations contained in this book. In addition, no responsibility is assumed by the publisher for any injury and/or damage to persons or property arising from any methods, products, instructions, ideas or otherwise contained in this publication.

This publication is designed to provide accurate and authoritative information with regard to the subject matter covered herein. It is sold with the clear understanding that the Publisher is not engaged in rendering legal or any other professional services. If legal or any other expert assistance is required, the services of a competent person should be sought. FROM A DECLARATION OF PARTICIPANTS JOINTLY ADOPTED BY A COMMITTEE OF THE AMERICAN BAR ASSOCIATION AND A COMMITTEE OF PUBLISHERS.

LIBRARY OF CONGRESS CATALOGING-IN-PUBLICATION DATA

Citizenship in the 21st century / Lester T. Kane and Marylyn R. Poweller, (editor).
    p. cm.
  ISBN 978-1-60456-401-3 (hardcover)
 1. Citizenship--Cross-cultural studies. 2. Civil society--Cross-cultural studies. I. Kane, Lester T. II. Poweller, Marylyn R.
JF801.C57353 2008
323.6--dc22
                          2008002871

Published by Nova Science Publishers, Inc. ✦ New York

CONTENTS

PREFACE

Citizenship is membership in a political community (originally a city or town but now usually a country) and carries with it rights to political participation; a person having such membership is a citizen. It is largely coterminous with nationality, although it is possible to have a nationality without being a citizen (i.e., be legally subject to a state and entitled to its protection without having rights of political participation in it); it is also possible to have political rights without being a national of a state. In most nations, a non-citizen is a non-national and called either a foreigner or an alien. In the United States, because there is state citizenship, foreign is the legal term for someone not a citizen of the state, and alien is reserved for someone not a citizen of the United States. Thus New York insurance companies are foreign in New Jersey, while a Dutch insurer is alien. Citizenship is thus the political rights of an individual within a society. One can possess citizenship from one country and be a national of another country. Citizenship derives from a legal relationship with a state. Citizenship can be lost, as in denaturalization, and gained, as in naturalization. This new book presents an outstanding line-up of contributors offering in-depth analyses of this important issue.

Chapter 1 - This Australian Research Council funded research in partnership with Aboriginal Australians and the South Australian Department of Health tests out ideas with people who are to be at the receiving end of the policy decisions. The authors research the principle of subsidiarity and Ashby's Rule (1956) to achieve better matches between policy and practice. The aim is to develop the capacity of service providers to understand what enhances wellbeing and social inclusion, why and how by listening to and learning from the experiences of the service users and providers. The service users are the capacity builders, not the other way around. A holistic approach to wellbeing and social inclusion is understood as a central value of Neporendi Forum Inc. Confidentiality and respect for the rights of the participants is central. It strives to address ways to promote wellbeing through enabling people to be involved in shaping the decision making not just in their personal lives but in their public lives. The participants address Aboriginality, their perceptions of well-being and their concerns about meeting their needs. The holistic approach includes the range of things people choose to include when they consider what constitutes wellbeing. The findings a) address the complex human service problem of co-coordinating care for those experiencing more than one social problem and enhancing social inclusion in a systemic way; b) develop a critical systems computer tool for knowledge management that includes Indigenous-non-Indigenous discourse management; c) strengthen the community through collaborative, functional networks across sectors and disciplines; d) build the capacity of the workforce to solve complex problems systemically; e) build skills within the Indigenous and non-Indigenous academic community. By mapping expressed need, normative need and perceived need, referral traffic and the refusals the authors create a dynamic evaluation and management model.

The project was initiated at a time when Aboriginal politics was at a low ebb when ATSIC was abolished in June 2004 and the regional councils were abolished the following year in June 2005. The Aboriginal service users tell stories that are the basis for participatory design to help manage complex decision-making and to provide critical insights into the perceived a) definitions of wellbeing and b) social, cultural, political, economic and environmental factors that support and undermine wellbeing. The authors hope that this research could enable the process of democratic decision making to be more responsive to the fine grained stories of life chances and the factors that can support wellbeing and counter balance the effects of social exclusion and marginalisation that lead to complex needs and being overwhelmed by limited life chances and challenges. The research addresses the questions about the role of social structure and personal agency in achieving wellbeing.

Chapter 2 - Success is a desired expectation in the most diverse experiences of our lives. In this context, social intervention with multi-problem poor families becomes relevant because it has constantly been associated with failure in spite of the efforts of the professionals who work with these families, of the investment of the State in social policies in support of the most vulnerable members of society and of the efforts of families to solve their problems.

In the area of social and community intervention, success has been defined in terms of results, which is relatively simple when a family experiences a specific and localised problem: for example, if a member of the family is unemployed, the intervention is successful if they get a job. The characteristics of multi-problem poor families (for whom problems are severe and long-term and experienced in a context of scarce economic and emotional resources) pose specific challenges for intervention and do not permit a linear application of this definition.

This research aims to contribute to a better understanding of the definition of success and failure in social intervention with multi-problem poor families, adopting the perspective of the practitioner. In this way the authors hope to allow understanding of how these definitions may be contributing to failure becoming a common result and to reveal alternatives which may enable the improvement of the quality of life of these families.

The main results indicate that success is defined in terms of clients becoming autonomous of formal services and carrying out the instructions of professionals. This is paradoxical, since when one is autonomous, one makes one's own decisions. So this definition of success may be encouraging actions which promote dependency instead of promoting the desired autonomy. Failure is defined in terms of the client remaining dependent on formal services, not fulfilling the proposals of intervention and not being motivated for intervention and/or change. This definition places the responsibility for failure on clients, allowing professionals to maintain a passive stance in face of this situation.

However, their results reveal some reorientation of professionals towards more operational definitions which are more in tune with the specificities of these families: encouraging small changes; activating competences in specific areas (parenting, managing school and professional life); supporting social integration. This seems to be a more fruitful way of building a better quality of life for these families.

Chapter 3 - Current educational discourses about what school science students need to become citizens of the 21st century are focused on specific science content without any reference to what this science content will allow these future citizens to do. However, the "basics" that we are asked to return to by back-to-basics advocates, that is, many of the "scientific skills" students are subjected to today, may have been useful some 100 years ago, but are no longer found in modern research laboratories. More so, the skills students acquire in school science today have little use in coping with the demands of everyday life in a rapidly changing world—the massive prevalence of hand-held calculators makes it possible for students to get by without learning longhand division in the same way that the massive presence of high-level programming language allows computer scientists to get by without knowing machine code. If this is the case, we have to ask questions about the content of an education for this relatively new century. What form(s) of scientific literacy do the citizens of the 21st century need to master? What do student citizens need to be able to do not only for coping in a rapidly changing world but also to contribute to the way it continuously takes shape and reshapes itself? To begin a project of rethinking science education for the 21st century, the author presents a case study of one everyday situation where ordinary citizens have been involved in a struggle over access to the local water grid, which serves as a context for articulating aspects of scientific literacy in and for a democracy-to-come. The author then articulates a particular teaching experiment where seventh-grade students became involved in the environmental issues of the same municipality where the citizens simultaneously struggled for access to the local water grid.

Chapter 4 - In this chapter, the authors advance the idea that organizational citizenship behaviors (OCBs) are discretionary and, as a result, employees engage in decisional processes before acting. Emphasizing conceptual differences in affiliative OCBs, such as helping, compared to challenging OCBs, such as voice, they propose that voice is a function of more elaborate cognitive processes than helping. Extending this idea, the primary objective is to develop a conceptual model that explicates cognitive processes as antecedents to employee voice behavior. They draw on work in social psychology with an emphasis on dual process decision-making theories (e.g., systematic vs. heuristic processing: see Smith and DeCoster, 2000, for a review) to guide their model. The authors aim to stimulate research on voice and other comparatively neglected forms of challenging OCB (e.g., personal initiative, taking charge) as well as research on decision processes that should enhance the ability to predict and encourage these important citizenship behaviors.

Chapter 5 - In this chapter the authors set out to explore what may be described as part of a global paradox. On the one hand, democracy is triumphant throughout the world with new waves of democracy occurring in Eastern Europe, Latin America and Asia. But on the other hand, fewer citizens are willing to turn out and vote in many of these democracies, when electoral participation is essential for the operation of democratic politics. This decline in voting is seen very clearly in Britain where the 59% turnout in the 2001 general election was the lowest recorded in modern British history. This trend continued in 2005 with 61% turnout.

Against this background, there are increasing concerns about changes in society that are undermining the effectiveness of democratic institutions and weakening traditional conceptions of citizenship. These changes include a growing public cynicism about politics and a widespread disaffection with political institutions, a decline in the institutions that underpin civic society and democracy such as political parties; and the long-term decline in electoral turnout in the majority of democratic countries. This reduction in electoral engagement is most starkly represented among young first-time voters, with 63% of 18-24 year olds not voting in the 2005 British general election. Thus, this group, who can be said to constitute the future of democracy within Britain, are the focus of investigation for this chapter.

The authors begin with an in-depth review and analysis of youth voting behaviour within the UK, where evidence suggests that trust, cynicism, efficacy and alienation are key concepts in understanding youth electoral engagement. A discussion of the meaning of these concepts based on the extant literature follows. They then present the methodology employed in their unique, empirical large scale survey of 1134 British young people eligible to vote for the first time in the 2005 British general election. In presenting their results the authors concentrate on examining youth levels of interest in the election, their voting behaviour and their levels of trust, cynicism and efficacy in relation to politicians, political parties and the political process. In conclusion the authors discuss the emergence of an engaged critical citizenry – through the vector of political sophistication – which gives voice to young peoples' politicisation and could reflect a new form of youth citizenship and their judicious engagement with politics in the future.

Chapter 6 - This chapter focuses on the emergence as citizens of a group of people previously excluded from this qualification due to their perceived intellectual impairment. Using the United Kingdom as an example of trends across the developed world where people with intellectual disability, once the targets of policies of exclusion and dependency, have emerged at the advent of the twenty-first century [C21] as citizens in their own right. However, while it is possible to see this trend within a humanitarian perspective with the newly enlightened populace able and willing to accept into it's mist a group of people previously disenfranchised; this position somewhat underplays the significance of what has occurred and complex nature of the processes that underpin this shift. Drawing on range of theories of citizenship the discussion locates these developments within the 'governmentality thesis' originally described by the French Philosopher Michel Foucault. Reasons for choosing this perspective relate to the way that Foucault, in contrast with many other writers, focussed on how particular configurations of knowledge [discourse] and associated practices underpinned the management of populations. In this process, he highlighted the key role of social institutions, particularly those of health and social work. These institutions, which embed a range of professional expertise, have particular significance for people with intellectual disabilities as these institutions play a central role in both the management of this section of the population and consequentially in the realization of their citizenship.

A deal of space in the chapter is devoted to theoretical debates that identify citizenship as a complex, dynamic and contested idea that is subject to constant but subtle revision due to changes in social policy. Consequentially, individuals reliant upon a myriad of social supports to exercise citizenship are particularly vulnerable to any revisions particularly where these influence welfare provision. In addition, citizenship is a prominent idea in contemporary British social policy with notions of work, obligation, community and social inclusion providing core concepts in the dynamic relationship between the state and individuals. People with intellectual disability provide a special group within this process as previously they fell outside of entitlements as citizens rather; they held a secondary position as welfare subjects.

However, the turn of the C21 sees older discourses of care, support and normalisation rearticulated within a liberal discourse of citizenship. In turn, revising the social positions for individuals with intellectual disability who are no longer perceived as passive and dependent but constructed as having the capacity to make choices in a market orientated welfare system and therefore active citizens in their own right. However, this newly acquired status is conditional; citizenship rights bring responsibilities and obligations for individuals. In response, social provision deploys a range of risk management technologies to differentiate between individuals who can be 'empowered' to become responsible citizens and those who fail to meet these criteria. The latter, identified as 'risky' individuals and managed accordingly, thus providing different trajectories for those concerned.

There are four stages to this discussion. The first is to identify citizenship, as an ambiguous concept with changing and contested meanings while the second stage is to establish citizenship as a tactic of government through a discussion of Foucault's governmentality thesis. The third stage explores four themes linked to the citizenship of disabled people in general that also have significance for people with intellectual disabilities drawn from a thematic review of the literature and empirical work involving a range of providers of supports to people with intellectual disability. Themes of work, participation, community and consumption, suggest the principle discourses that underpin the citizenship of this section of the population. This is not to underplay the significance of standard social variables such as class, gender, race, ethnicity etc. that continue to cross cut the experience of individuals; rather it identifies the common experience of intellectual disability as the core variable. Evaluation of the interplay of these themes and the practices provides the final section, which highlights confusion over what citizenship entails and the observation that the organisations that provide support to people with intellectual disability continue to mediate their experience of citizenship.

Chapter 7 - For a dozen years now, organizational citizenship behaviour has been a subject of continually increasing interest in academic managerial literature. While most current research comes from the United States, several scholars have argued for the need for global data. As Podsakoff, MacKensie, Paine and Bachrach (2000, p. 556) insist, "cultural context may affect a) the forms of citizenship behaviour observed in organizations and b) the strengths of relationships between citizenship behaviour and its antecedents and consequences." To date, little research has been done in the French context and existing research does not sufficiently take conceptual advances into account in the French context. Furthermore, new targets of commitment (commitment to the supervisor and to the workgroup) have appeared. New forms of citizenship (civic virtue and sportsmanship) may be added to these. Empirical relations between various targets of commitment and these new forms of citizenship remain to be clarified in the French context. This chapter proposes to examine dimensionality of citizenship behaviour and explore empirical links between attitudes (targets of affective commitment to the organization, one's supervisor and colleagues), job satisfaction, and job involvement and citizenship oriented towards the organization and individuals to determine which attitude explains which forms of citizenship.

In: Citizenship in the 21ˢᵗ Century
Editors: L. T. Kane and M. R. Poweller, pp. 1-53

ISBN: 978-1-60456-401-3
© 2008 Nova Science Publishers, Inc.

Chapter 1

PARTICIPATORY DEMOCRACY BASED ON USER-CENTRIC POLICY DESIGN TO ADDRESS COMPLEX NEEDS

Janet McIntyre-Mills, D. De Vries and J. Deakin[1]
Flinders University, Adelaide, South Australia

"…The systems approach begins when first you see the world through the eyes of another." (C. West Churchman, 1979: 231-232).

1. BACKGROUND AND AREA OF CONCERN

This Australian Research Council funded research in partnership with Aboriginal Australians and the South Australian Department of Health tests out ideas with people who are to be at the receiving end of the policy decisions[2]. We research the principle of subsidiarity and Ashby's Rule (1956) to achieve better matches between policy and practice. The aim is to develop the capacity of service providers to understand what enhances

---

[1] The contributions of members of Neporendi Forum Inc, Teresa Francis, Daphne Rickett, Dr Doug Morgan, Bevin Wilson, Kim O'Donnell, Professor John Roddick, Dr Denise De Vries and Professor Anne Roche are gratefully acknowledged as co-researchers, as is the PhD work in progress by Jon Deakin on sections of the ARC funded project. Work in progress has been presented at conferences as indicated in the references. Some of the figures have been cited as indicated in Systemic Governance and Accountability. The overall study entitled: "User centric policy design to address complex needs", forthcoming.

[2] The collaboration spans the SA Health, Flinders University, University of South Australia and Neporendi Forum Inc and was formed in order to enable the service users to build the capacity of the service providers. The research used the process of drawing on complexity, encouraging service users to tell the details of their lives and to use yarning and picturing to enable people to explore their lives. The next step was to analyze the stories and pictures using qualitative data analysis to find themes which were then analyzed in recursive cycles to establish how to achieve wellbeing. The methodology we will use is a participatory design project that addresses the process of making social inclusion and joined up governance work through: Listening to stories shared by users and service providers. Exploring stories to understand what works. Matching of services to needs. Responding to social and cultural diversity through drawing on the 'wisdom of the people (Christakis 2004, Ramsden 2002).The process involves documenting what is said and also keeping a diary of the process, so that the context of data collection is recorded.

wellbeing and social inclusion, why and how by listening to and learning from the experiences of the service users and providers. The service users are the capacity builders, not the other way around. A holistic approach to wellbeing and social inclusion is understood as a central value of Neporendi Forum Inc. Confidentiality and respect for the rights of the participants is central. It strives to address ways to promote wellbeing through enabling people to be involved in shaping the decision making not just in their personal lives but in their public lives[3]. The participants address Aboriginality, their perceptions of well-being and their concerns about meeting their needs. The holistic approach (see Walsh 2002 and McIntyre-Mills 2003a, 2006b) includes the range of things people choose to include[4] when they consider what constitutes wellbeing. The findings a) address the complex human service problem of co-coordinating care for those experiencing more than one social problem and enhancing social inclusion in a systemic way; b) develop a critical systems computer tool for knowledge management that includes Indigenous-non-Indigenous discourse management; c) strengthen the community through collaborative, functional networks across sectors and disciplines; d) build the capacity of the workforce to solve complex problems systemically; e) build skills within the Indigenous and non-Indigenous academic community. By mapping expressed need, normative need and perceived need, referral traffic and the refusals we will create a dynamic evaluation and management model.

The project was initiated at a time when Aboriginal politics was at a low ebb when ATSIC was abolished in June 2004 and the regional councils were abolished the following year in June 2005. The Aboriginal service users tell stories that are the basis for participatory design to help manage complex decision-making and to provide critical insights into the perceived a) definitions of wellbeing and b)social, cultural, political, economic and environmental factors that support and undermine wellbeing. We hope that this research could enable the process of democratic decision making to be more responsive to the fine grained stories of life chances and the factors that can support wellbeing and counter balance the effects of social exclusion and marginalisation that lead to complex needs and being overwhelmed by limited life chances and challenges. The research addresses the questions about the role of social structure and personal agency in achieving wellbeing.

---

[3] The service users are the capacity builders, not the other way around. A holistic approach to wellbeing and social inclusion is understood as a central value of Neporendi Forum Inc. Confidentiality and respect for the rights of the participants is central. The findings a) address the complex human service problem of co-coordinating care for those experiencing more than one social problem and enhancing social inclusion in a systemic way; b) develop a critical systems computer tool for knowledge management that includes Indigenous-non-Indigenous discourse management; c) Strengthen the community through collaborative, functional networks across sectors and disciplines; d) Build the capacity of the workforce to solve complex problems systemically; e) Build skills within the Indigenous and non-Indigenous academic community. By mapping expressed need, normative need and perceived need, referral traffic and the refusals we will create a dynamic evaluation and management model. The project was initiated at a time when Aboriginal politics was at a low ebb when ATSIC was abolished in June 2004 and the regional councils were abolished the following year in June 2005. "ATSIC's national body was replaced by the National Indigenous Council (NIC), a government appointed body of 15 individuals. This new body has been criticized for a number of reasons including that the appointed representatives have no responsibility to represent broader Indigenous interests. The appointees are acting in an individual capacity are not accountable to the community whose interests their decisions will affect...ATSIC created a structure that linked a regional representative governance model with a national representative body, a governance structure that allowed for regional priorities too be set and met while at the same time providing an opportunity for a unified, and therefore more effective, voice at the federal level..." (Behrendt 2005:6-7).

[4] See Churchman (1979, 1983) on 'unfolding' and 'sweeping in' social, cultural, political and economic issues.

2. RATIONALE FOR THE RESEARCH

The idea is that testing should be done by those with lived experience and that the complexity of the decisions taken should match the complexity of the decision makers. This is a rule derived from cybernetics, called Ashby's Rule (1956 see C.West Churchman Legacy and Related Works Series 1-3).The discussion is premised on the idea that many bodies of knowledge exist and that the challenge is to ask questions that will enable the appropriate knowledge to be matched contextually to a task, challenge or problem (Aristotle in Nicomachean Ethics, Irwin, 1985). The three kinds of knowledge are *techne, episteme and phronesis* (based on the wisdom of matching the right kind of knowledge to context, based on dialogue and testing out ideas)[5].

Ethically decisions are better when those at the receiving end of the decisions are party to the process. It ensures that democracy is not debased by what Michels called the 'iron rule of oligarchy', or the notion that powerful stakeholders at the top of political parties can corrupt democratic decision making. Aboriginal Australians are arguably the most marginalized Australians with the most complex needs. The idea is that if we can get this research to work effectively, i.e. achieve better match between perceived policy needs and performance out comes, using a design that considers 'if then' scenarios and updates chosen responses, based on the ideas of the users then it could be applied more generally as a way to enable user centric design.

It is hoped that this research into participatory democracy will enable people to:

- make contributions based on their lived experiences,
- to work across conceptual and geographical boundaries and that they will be able to combine their ideas better.

Identities are shaped as personal narratives to make sense of life. Identities can be molar (fixed) or molecular (fluid) in response to social , cultural , political, economic and environmental circumstances . The emotions of desire and will play a role as do hopelessness and helplessness in the face of structural determinants (see Bogue 1989 and McIntyre-Mills 2006a).

2.1. Reconsidering the Boundaries

"Democracy, in its most basic sense of majority decision making, requires that those who decide be sufficiently alike that they will respect the will of the majority. Global-level decisions will inevitably have a highly restricted agenda, set by what the majority of

---

[5] The challenge is to balance individualism and collectivism. Bonds of connection need to be balanced by boundaries and norms (Elias and Lichterman, 2003). Paradoxically human beings are drawn to be individuals and to be part of a group. Also human beings perceive the world through the filters of 'religion, politics, morality and aesthetics' (West Churchman 1982). Representation and accountability are the twin challenges for both the enlightenment and democracy. Democracy is currently increasingly criticised for not representing the interests of citizens (Institute of Governance, 2005) or not taking into account the social justice and environmental concerns that span national boundaries (Singer, 2002). The enlightenment has been critiqued and post positivists (this is quite different from a postmodernist approach) have responded by expanding the process of falisification to include a wider range of tests .

the richest nations will tolerate and a very reduced role for the world's publics. The difficulties of global democracy should make us pause when considering the rhetoric about democracy at the national level, for that too, despite the belief that nations are relatively homogenous political communities, is subject to similar limitations as to both agenda and participation. The question is whether one needs to rethink some of the assumptions of democratic theory in order to find ways to widen the scope of accountable government by consent." (Hirst in Pierre, 2000, p.17).

On the 24th of August 2007 Julian Burnside engaged in an Australian Broadcasting Television Program entitled 'Difference of Opinion'. He made the point that Australia was losing civil liberties as a result of the response to the terrorism. His comments echoed the points raised by Gore in relation to the changes that had occurred in USA in relation to the rights to the individual. Similarly in Australia the centralized intervention by the military to address violence in Aboriginal communities has been linked with control of community areas and is thus seen as an erosion of land rights and self determination.[6]

Gore (2007) makes the case that money politics controls political agendas and that it is vital for democracy that open fora are available to the people. Those who can afford to buy time on TV can use it for one way communication:

> "Hebert Krugman, in experiments conducted for General Electric, seems to have been the first man to discover the relationship between television and the alpha state. Picture yourself sitting down for a nights viewing. You have had a days worth of analytical problems, whether you have been fixing the car or doing actuarial tables. You switch on the set. Almost immediately your left brain slides into a …neutral state, lulled by the dots flashing sequentially across the screen …But the right brain remains alert stimulated by the bright…images…and random movement…Freed from the restraints of the watch dog left, your mind is in a condition …for the non rational sell…" (McLuhan and Powers 1989: 87)

But the potential exists for technology to be used in more liberative ways to engage in dialogue. It is also possible to make greater use of the Internet to enable two –way dialogue. [7] The argument about the problems with democracy and the tendency for one-way communication does not eliminate space for improvements through participatory decision-making, not only by using the media creatively, but also working for change in a range of arenas. I am not arguing that democracy would be best served by a completely open and

---

[6] Atkinson, J. 2007 What I would do Australian Policy on Line http??www.apo.org/webboard/print-version.chtml? filename _num=154957 accessed 28/08/2007. Anderson, I 2007 Remote communities: unexplained differences Australian Policy on Line   http??www.apo.org/webboard/print-version.chtml? filename _num=161613 accessed 28/08/2007.

[7] One-way communication tends to dominate the world today. Derrida makes the point (Borradori, 2003: 122) that TV and not the Internet predominates as a medium of digital communication and that less than 5% of the world's population has access to the Internet and even in America only 50% of the population have access to it. Habermas in the same publication entitled *Philosophy in a Time of Terror*, stresses that the one-way communication in most consumerist advertising messages could have negative implications for democracy and world peace (not only for poorer nations and peoples) but also for the increasingly divided "haves" and "have-nots" in developed nations (see Chomsky, 2003; Pilger, 2002). One-way media communication within Western democracies and the rest of the world tends to dominate via TV today. Creating webs of shared meaning and appreciating areas of difference through communication is vital for sustainable democracy (McIntyre-Mills, 2000). Participatory democracy projects to design our shared future needs (according to Marx Hubbard, 2003) to use TV and other media in a responsible manner that supports public dialogue in many contexts (Banathy, 2000, 2003) to address some of the deep divides.

unstructured approach.[8]. In democracies government representatives have to make decisions and to draw a line whilst remaining open to suggestions for changes to laws and policies. Local people need to be able to work together to share their personal knowledge based on their own experience [9] and influence higher and wider levels of governance. Gore (2007) and Borradori (2003) in conversation with Habermas and Derrida engage in discussion on the importance of two –way dialogue in public spaces to keep democracy on track and to ensure that it is not taken over by money politics or sectarian interests.

Deepening democracy', to use Fung, Wright et al's phrase (2003) and improving co-learning needs to be based on detailed descriptions of what people think they need, why and how their needs could be addressed. This requires detailed, discursive description or "thick description", in the words of Clifford Geertz (1973) that supports "thick democracy", which is essential for social and economic wellbeing (see Edgar 2001) that will help to defuse the processes of projecting our own fears onto others and making policy according to stereotypes (McIntyre-Mills et al 2006 and McIntyre-Mills 2006, forthcoming).

Capacity building is needed in many arenas to enhance the ability of people to think holistically. A *Design of Inquiring Systems* could assist in this regard. The inquiring system (adapted from West Churchman, 1971) addresses many domains of knowledge, namely logic, empiricism, idealism, the dialectic (which addresses thesis, antithesis and synthesis of ideas) and an expanded pragmatism, based on thinking about the consequences of policy for all life in this generation and the next. To know is a process based on the senses, emotions and the contextual experience. It is not merely about representing reality "that is out there". Knowing is a potentially transformative experience. 'A Design of Inquiring Systems' strives to appreciate subjective, the objective and the intersubjective logic as domains. To learn and to know is transformative and recursive. It is not merely about representation, but about change. Thus learning and knowing is constructivist in nature. The process is not just about cause and effect, but about networks of feedback loops and the implications these have for us as researchers, practitioners and caretakers. C.West Churchman Legacy and Related Works Series (2006) on ways to enhance democracy and rescue the enlightenment from its failings by expanding the process of testing to include those who are to be at the receiving end of the decisions and with future generations in mind.

Accountability needs to be based on deliberation to achieve better decision making, based on testing out the ideas (not only by experts) but by people who have lived experience of issues (McIntyre-Mills, 2003, 2005a, 2006a, 2006b; Edgar, 1992; Polanyi, 1962). This is essential to address the interests of the less powerful, but also to ensure that the ideas of what works, why and how as far (as the principals are concerned) is addressed in the interests of environmental sustainability, accountability and socio-economic well-being (National Economic/ALGA, 2002, 2003; Edgar, 1992; Cox, 1995).

A process that helps to enhance connections is adapted from Ashby's Law (1956) of socio-cybernetics and the principle of subsidiarity (namely that policy needs to be made at the

---

[8] Ortegon-Montoy (2003) critiques the way in which chaos and complexity theory (as applied to management) stresses the value of self-organization and emergence. But according to Ortegon-Montoy managers who use this approach do not provide enough guidelines and boundaries (albeit open for revision) that are made by iterative decision processes. This is problematic in an organizational management context and even more so in an interorganisational governance context. Stretton (2001) when referring to the Australian context of development and planning stresses that space for diversity is not the same as an open slather approach or "anything goes"

[9] See Nonaka and Takeuchi 1995 and McIntyre-Mills 2006c for a discussion on ways to work with and share tacit learnings.

lowest level possible (without undermining the collective norms to sustain future generations) by those who are to be at the receiving end of the decision. (see McIntyre-Mills, 2005b, 2006b). To sum up, the complexity of the decision matches the complexity of the people who will be at the receiving end of the decision.

The elegance and simplicity of this argument is that it is based on systemic, feedback logic that tests out ideas in such a way that the experts are those who actually have lived experience of what works, why and how! This could be the way forward to enhance complex policy making. It is the subject of a current Australian Research Council Linkage Grant that has wider governance implications. Seeing the world in bounded conceptual (disciplinary), organisational and geographical silos supports limited, compartmentalised thinking and practice. According to Beck (1992, 1998). Once we are mindful that the consequences of our actions can not be quarantined we become systemic practitioners. We need to :

- Expand the boundaries of concern beyond the nation state and beyond the scope of this generation to address sustainable futures.
- Lobby to hold governments accountable is becoming more important than ever to ensure that the rights of the next generation of life are not jeopardised.

3. RESEARCH APPROACH

The aim of the project is to test out whether the match between service users and service providers can be better achieved by ensuring that service user's at the receiving end of the design are part of the design process to evaluate and to assess whether they think a range of factors, including the environment, supports their wellbeing.

Three data collection steps have been followed with the service users on what works, why and how. The first stage started with conversations that became increasingly focused on the issues that the informants raised as concerns and with the collaboration of De Vries, the pathways were considered more closely by using a proforma of more directed questions. In so doing the principles of participatory design and participatory action research were followed.

Our research addresses dualisms (as detailed by Petersen and Lupton 1996:176) right from the start, because service users are the designers. Thus the technocratic concerns that Habermas stresses are addressed at the outset and the notion of closed systems suggested by cybernetics is rejected, "as there is no such thing as a total or 'closed system', to use West Churchman's (1982) expression. All systems of meaning need to be open to revision as they are filtered by values that need to be considered carefully in context (Bausch 2006 in McIntyre-Mills 2006a). It addresses the notion of self/other, subject /object, service user/provider.[10] I was reminded at the outset of the research by the Aboriginal elders that the

---

[10] In designing the research the framing of questions was undertaken by members of Neporendi as co-researchers who draw on their own experiences. The research drew on existentialist ideas and from these diverse experiences to find patterns. But these patterns are not to be used to impose ideas, but as components to help decision making by adding their contextual ideas. As such it attempts to bridge the divide between universalist normative decisions that do not take into account individual experiences within cultural contexts and postmodern or cultural relativism which undermines social justice and makes sustainable environmental decisions difficult. It spans enlightenment representation and existentialist contextual narrative, by drawing on Aristotelian approach, namely phronesis or matching through dialogue and through a sense of systemic implications of policy decisions. The social environment shapes us and we shape the environment in recursive

colonizers had brought with them both the alcohol[11] and the enforced poverty through the loss of their lands and the creation of dependency through welfare (on this see Rowse 1998 and Atkinson).

Narratives from the users and the providers were complex, themes were identified and arranged as building blocks. These building blocks constituted typical patterns of response. But instead of imposing archetypes, the service users tell their own unique stories first to the service provider and then they use the opportunity to consider how similar or different their unique and personal story is to the typical narratives. These typical narratives will have building blocks arranged as:

- Characteristics to discard into the 'out basket'
- Their perceived ideas of what made their lives better or worse (turning points) including social, cultural, political, economic and environmental factors,
- Their perceived ideas of barriers including social, cultural, political, economic and environmental factors,
- Their perceived ideas, evaluations of services that helped them.

The data from iteration 1, 2 and 3 show that a range of factors spanning social cultural political economic and environmental dimensions are interrelated. It is also clear that for each individual, perceptions play a vital role in emotions of wellbeing and they are a result of both personal and public shapers. The NVivo generated map of the factors was shown to the participants in iteration 3. The participants were asked to add factors by positioning them appropriately and to provide synonyms (similar names for the factors and to draw pathways on the maps based on their stories)[12].

---

cycles. Awareness of systemic governance challenges becomes ever more important given the challenges to address social democratic (Held 2004) and environmental sustainability concerns (Singer 2002) that span boundaries and which require a reconsideration of the way in which we frame justice (Nussbaum 2006, McIntyre-Mills et al 2006) which needs to extend Rawls notion of citizenship and reciprocity within national boundaries and beyond to include caretaking. In this we can draw on Aboriginal cultural ideas about caretaking for those without a voice and for the environment. " As Foucault (1980) explains, science has been used not simply to 'explain' reality, but to produce, control and normalize it. One of the important insights of Foucault's work, and indeed of those scholarly writings that fall under the rubric of post structuralism, is in drawing attention to the interrelationship between discourses, knowledge's, practices and power relations when conducting sociopolitical analysis and critique. It is important that such representational practices of such hegemonic knowledges ...be laid open to scrutiny ....the self is discursively constructed" (Petersen and Lupton 1996 178).

[11] The use of alcohol by the grieving was discussed by Veverbrants (pers com 2002) an Aboriginal elder who lives and works as a healer in Alice Springs. For those who are without hope or direction, spirituality in a bottle or sharing a coolabah, passes time and enhances a sense of spiritual oneness with the land. This altered sense of consciousness that enables looking at an unbearable set of circumstances differently as a heightened state of spirituality   is a dimension of the history of structural violence and social exclusion and is supported by my early research with Indigenous healers and their use of maize beer (both nutritious and intoxicating) in South Africa during the Apartheid era. The use of alcohol and other drugs was raised as problematic if taken to extremes but also as a pleasurable lifestyle choice, if managed appropriately. The use of alcohol as a way to achieve forgetfulness or to cope with grief was clear. To prevent addiction, the promotion of other factors was essential.

[12] In critical path analysis the longest path is the critical path (Mukhi et al 1988: 521). Critical path and program evaluation and review techniques are : " network techniques for analyzing a system in terms of activities and events that must be completed in a specified sequence in order to achieve a goal. Some activities can be done concurrently, whereas others have precedence requirements. The activities are component tasks that take time and are designated by arrows (→) . Events are points in time that indicate that some activities have been

Starting with a basic map progressively more factors were added until saturation point was reached and the additional factors tended to be synonyms or closely related to what others had already explained in their personal stories. Some of the informants preferred to tell the researcher about the connections they thought were most important in stories. They said that they found most of the factors important, but that some were more central to their own experience than the other factors.

All the men and women who participated in this study had experienced poverty and the affects of interrelated problems of addictions, violence and homelessness. They stressed that their stories were drawn from their own experiences. Wellbeing and reconciliation go hand-in-hand with social inclusion and improved quality of life. In critical path analysis the longest path is the critical path (Mukhi et al 1988: 521). The data in this study show that addiction and poverty are two sides of one coin or more specifically they form a vicious cycle. Finding ways to break the cycle include listening to narratives as a first step for building relationships, understanding the context and addressing needs through matching responses based on the lived experience of others who have experienced similar circumstances.

The participatory approach involves all relevant parties in actively addressing the areas of concern (Wadsworth, 1998). The project develops an open *'Design of Inquiring Systems'* (West Churchman 1971, 1982) and ensures that the service users are part of *a community of inquiry and practice* together with service providers. The research is systemic in that the users tell the providers what works, why and how and they design a better way of doing things, thereby contributing to participatory democracy and governance(McIntyre –Mills 2003, 2004, 2005a, b). Complexity can be understood in stories and pictures and they form the basis for trying to model complex responses to needs. It is profoundly sad to tell a story and then not to receive a response. The aim is to:

- Identify the gaps in service delivery pertaining to social inclusion and complex problems.
- Provide a dialectical (Lind and Lind 2005) means of ensuring that knowledge management through networking supported by a computer system is empowering (Castells, 1996) to the workforce and the most marginalized Australians.
- Document tacit and explicit knowledge of Indigenous and non Indigenous Australians and to share it to help address the policy issues.
- Develop and pilot an integrated systemic management tool to enhance the workforce capacity to manage referrals and to ensure that user and service options can be better matched (Ulrich 1983, 2001).
- Build capacity across service users and providers to improve health, housing and welfare (to achieve greater social inclusion) requires a paradigm shift in the way social problems are understood and treated.
- Ensure that the availability of services can be updated.
- Make a contribution to theory and practice.
- Address problems systemically across sectors and disciplines.

---

completed and others may begin. They are sometimes called nodes and are designated by circles (O) A network diagram consists of the activities and events in their proper relationship…." " the path is critical because a delay in it means a delay in the project itself…" (Mukhi et al 1988: 522)

- Model complexity in perceptions, values and issues in 'what if' scenarios to improve strategic policy making decisions and predictions. This is the function of both the computer system and the civics process.
- Create iterative communication and action learning processes. Once the dreaming pathways have been created based on an analysis of their stories, the next step is to share the de-identified material in conversation with small groups of participants.

The social justice benefits of knowledge management to the organization; staff and service users are[13]:

"Responsiveness based on matching the needs of the user in terms of age, gender, cultural requirements for Indigenous and non Indigenous users and health needs and the service providers in a recursive feedback system, based on soft systems modelling.

Timeliness, the quick identification, contact and access to most or all appropriate service providers, (not to be confused with the capacity of the each service involved).

Minimum backtracking, the individual service pathway can be mapped out to ensure continuous progress towards desired outcomes.

Minimum staging, the client isn't moved from one service to another in sequential stages with needs evaluation processes (often duplicating previous similar processes) occurring at each stage.

Organizational data that can be analysed to determined network gaps or inefficiencies, patterns of use, social and operational costs".

The theory of sociocybernetics (Beer 1974) stresses that understanding non linear relationships is a first step to developing policy responses. The purpose of this research is to explore the relationships more deeply with service users and housing providers in the public and private sectors in order to build trust and mutual understanding to enhance the policy performance match between agents and principals (Warren, 1999, Uslaner 1999). The steps for undertaking the research are as follows:

1. Invitation to do action research with Neporendi, on basis of previous research.
2. Establishing rapport through participatory action research project on domestic violence funded through a small grant from Community Benefit SA. Participation as volunteer
3. Listening actively to narratives and not judging or passing judgmental comments. Narrative enables people to explore and reflect and make meaning
4. Identification of the area of concern with the participants and the formation of a partnership that built on previous research in South Australia and Central Australia with Aboriginal Australians.
5. An ethics approval process that involved all the partner organizations and the Aboriginal elders.
6. Developing relationships and trust based on past work, current continuity and availability and future commitment Narratives and response to 5 conversation

---

[13] The contribution made by David Corbett of Anglicare, to developing the aims of the research are gratefully acknowledged. Anglicare has contributed 'in kind' assistance to this project and has made it possible to consult with both service users and providers so as to provide a wider base for the research sample.

prompts/questions collected from service users and providers which explored the problems.

7. Data collection from observation, listening to 50 narratives from male and female service providers and 50 narratives from male and female service users. Analysis of rich pictures from participants.

8. Creating personal meaning maps through drawing soft systems maps.

9. Creating shared group maps and identifying archetypes in an iterative approach using PAR

10. Participants are encouraged to identify patterns for themselves and to learn from their experiences.

11. Testing the patterns of response by asking whether the users agree with them

12. Enabling comparison between their story and the typical stories from which they select on the basis of choosing the cluster of core factors that characterize particular narratives.

13. Construction of soft systems maps, coding and analysing the narratives and descriptions, giving weightings to the number of times items were mentioned.

14. Developing a proforma for the design of a knowledge base, based on the emergent themes to address solutions

15. Testing the design by using a walk through based on questions and ticking off factors from a map created by all the participants

16. Self selection of factors from the NVivo "factor map" of core building blocks will help to identify which archetype they are closest to. Personalising the factor map by adding factors by placing the new factor as close as possible to existing factors and describing the new factor. Conditional scenarios will enable participants to assess the implications for making changes in their lives.

4. THE KEY CONCEPTS

The key concepts are as follows:

- Aboriginality (according to the co-researchers is understood as family connections and a history of marginalization and disadvantage. But it is also about survival against the odds and a celebration of spirituality, creativity and life.
- Culture for the purpose of our research means how we make sense of the world. It comprises socialised living but also our ability to reshape or design our way of life.
- Consciousness is defined as 'making connections' and it is adapted14 from the work of Greenfield (2000: 13, 21) who stresses that emotions are the key to understanding

---

[14] Her work stresses that the brain is plastic and responsive to the environment. The title of her book *"The private life of the brain"* is unfortunate, because the brain is not private and it is the shaper and shaped by the world (Aleksander 2005. A better title would be: "The private and public life of the brain" as it would better suit her argument (as I have read it). Consciousness is not located in any one place according to her. It is also greater than the sum of the parts in the brain and the chemical connections and the social, historical and environmental stimuli, nevertheless the parts are important. Therefore it is possible as Cornelius (1996) suggests to integrate neurophysiological, Darwinian evolutionary theory about the similarities of all human beings, but also that all life is connected. Consciousness is a continuum, the more we can think about our thinking the more conscious we become (McIntyre-Mills Ed. 2006). Bodily aspects of thinking are important as Greenfield has suggested, but she also recognizes that

consciousness and our thinking. Nevertheless it is possible to think about the way our lives and life chances have been constructed (as a result of our culture and where we live and the level of education and income of our parents and whether or not they were given the vote). Our sense of control over our lives or sense of agency will be shaped by our experiences and emotions and the experiences and emotions of our family and friends, nevertheless we have the capacity to think about our situation and our emotions and to make connections across why our lives are the way they are. If we allow our emotions to dominate, we are likely to make very limited decisions. We can only moderate emotions and its impact on agency (hope) or helplessness, if we acknowledge the importance of emotion on consciousness. Greenfield (2000: 21) argues that emotions and feelings are the most basic aspects of consciousness. She calls them 'the building blocks' and that when we temper our emotions through thinking through implications of acting out passions we are able to become more mindful or conscious.

"Emotions are with us all the time, to a greater or lesser degree...I shall be arguing that you cannot understand consciousness without understanding emotion, and that consciousness is not purely rational or cognitive, as some particularly those working in artificial, computational systems have implied. .." (op cit).

Greenfield argues that the more connections[15] we can make, the more conscious and mindful we are and the more likely we are to make decisions that will promote our wellbeing. The most important contribution is that she stresses that consciousness cannot be located anywhere; it is about connections (across many neurons and perceived variables) and the number of connections that enhances consciousness and our ability to think and appreciate out situations. Drawing on and extending Cornelius (1996) it can be argued that emotion can be better understood from a systemic viewpoint that draws on many (not incommensurate theories of emotion). Awareness within context and responsive appraisal of many dimensions means that connections and interactions are the basis for human wellbeing. The brain is democratic and although it can think in hierarchies and divisions, it can also think in terms of connections and continuums and it is the latter capacity that enables us to be creative and more conscious. It is this dimension that is important for spiritual life and an area of interest

---

communication feedback loops to which we are exposed in our society, play a vital role as well to changing our consciousness. The more connections we make the more aware we become. The brain is able to make connections through experiential learning. The mind is not located in any one place it is the connections we make. Consciousness is a continuum, we can be more or less conscious depending on the number of connections made. So mindfulness is based on thinking about our thinking. Critical self awareness is essential for decision making and governance that supports wellbeing. The key to raising consciousness and self awareness is through greater understanding of the way that emotions cloud our thinking and limited our ability to make connections. The more we are able to understand the perceptions of others, the more connections we can make and the more conscious we become. Aboriginal understandings of wellbeing emphasize that wellbeing is about a sense of connection across self-other and the environment. Sharp (2005) has developed a powerful argument about consciousness and our connection to living creatures other than ourselves if we are prepared to accept that being gives rights. She argues that consciousness does not have to enable rational speech, just being.

[15] Consciousness is more than making neural connections. Although I take issue with Greenfield's construction of consciousness as 'a private life' of the brain, she does stress in many parts of her argument that the neural connections made are a result of thinking about emotions that are responsive to the environmental stimuli. Conscious decisions to think about our emotions and to control our emotions leads us to be able to expand our consciousness. Mindfulness is the basis for wellbeing.

to many Aboriginal informants on what constitutes wellbeing. Indigenous cultures have stressed the importance of connection with the land and nature (McIntyre-Mills et al, 2003, 2006c).

Compartmentalised thinking undermines accountability and risk management (Ackoff and Strumpfer 2003, Ackoff and Pourdehnad, 2001, Romm 2001, Wenger 1998, Wenger and Snyder 2000). Emotions are defined systemically by Cornelius (1996) who summarizes and combines four lenses for understanding different dimensions of emotion: a) Darwinian theory that stresses the similarity of emotions across people of all cultures. Darwin stressed the connection across all life. This continuum is supported by Greenfield's (2000) research into the neuroscience of consciousness The implications for social justice and for expanding notions of human rights are profound and have implications for cognitive capabilities, democracy, development and freedom (Nussbaum, 2001, 2006). The social constructions of difference across self and other impact on wellbeing.. b) Jamesian theory that stresses that emotions are bodily reactions and that we can influence emotions through changing our behavior. c) Cognitive approaches (drawing on Arnold 1960) stress that perceptions and emotion are mediated by appraisals and sense making and that our psychology can be changed by thinking. Cornelius stresses that cognitive approaches are predated by philosophers such as Aristotle (see Cornelius 1996 : 115) who stressed in Nichomachean ethics (see Irwin 1985)) that wellbeing is supported by being involved in decision making (see McIntyre-Mills 2007).

Cornelius (1996: 184-219) argues that these approaches are not incommensurable and that by combining them into an integrated approach we can gain greater insight into all the dimensions of emotion. He uses the analogies of the blind man and the elephant arguing that if one can only appreciated a limited part of a phenomenon in a limited way then one's understanding will remain partial. He also uses the example of eating (1996: 211) and that it can be understood in terms of many dimensions. His analysis includes biology, psychology and social relations, but it could be expanded to include political and economic dimensions more explicitly. This research extends social cognition by drawing on the emotional knowledge and intuitive wisdom within stories and other forms of expression such as mapping and drawing. The reason this is so important is that in enabled policy to be shaped by those who will be at the receiving end of the decision and not only by those who are elected. Liberal democracies work more effectively when the groups of people are small and not very diverse.

- Participatory democracy enables a closer match between the decisions and the decision makers through a process of ongoing dialogue between service users , policy makers and managers. Participation, social construction and valuing the experiences of those who are to be at the receiving end of decisions is important for wellbeing:

"But how does one attain deep, profound and lasting contentment? ....Although Aristotle mentions both wealth and political honour as candidates for eudaimonia, He denies that they are sufficient for eudaimonia. Rather, in order to become eudaimon, one must perfect the human function which, according to Aristotle is reasoning and thinking. Note that while practically all adults have reason and thought, few have perfected these abilities. According to Aristotle, it is only in the perfection of reasoning and thinking whereby a human being will achieve the profound happiness and contentment of which the human species is capable. Of course, many people disagree with Aristotle's view of the human good. Nevertheless his view that a human being is 'destined' by nature to think, rather than to spend money or rule over others is a profound and provocative view of human nature..." (May in O Grady ed 2005: 154).

- Systemic Governance (McIntyre-Mills et al 2006) which for the purpose of the research means ensuring all those who are at the receiving end of a decision are party to the decision making process (or well represented). Diversity is taken into account to the extent that it does not undermine the freedom of others. Subsidiarity (Schumacher 1973, Singer 2002) means for the purpose of the research that problems are best solved at the lowest level possible, in order to be able to draw on the lived experiences of people (see Polany1 1992, Wenger 1998 and Christakis with Bausch 2006 and the way these approaches are synthesised in McIntyre-Mills et al 2006).
- Ashby's (1956) Law of Requisite Variety asserted complex decisions need to reflect the complexity of the people and the system they will impact upon. Our research tests the principle of subsidiarity and Ashby's Rule to establish whether: a) Participation in the design process can ensure that service delivery is better matched with perceived need, so that organizations can become more responsive to people. b) The more the principle of empowerment is applied (people involved in the decision making at the level where the decision is to be implemented) c) The greater the match between the provider and the user and b) the level of wellbeing of the service user and the community.

5. DESIGNING THE ARCHITECTURE OF THE KNOWLEDGE BASE TO AID UNDERSTANDING BY BOTH SERVICE USERS AND PROVIDERS

5.1. Service Users and Service Providers Are Co-Designers

According to Roddick (2004) a generic computing algorithm for handling multi-variate and multi-dimensional resource allocation exists within the computing discipline and this will be adapted to enable an analysis to answer questions regarding the extent to which matrix team management can meet the needs of staff and service users and to establish where the gaps are in service delivery. Problems of organizational and social complexity occur in combination and are interconnected (see Rittel and Webber, 1984). Roddick (2004) stressed that information Technology has rarely, if ever, been applied successfully to such an area as meeting complex human needs. One outcome of the ARC Project will be to develop and evaluate a computing system that applies a concept called Mesodata that allows the domains of databases to be more complex (intelligent), learn from results, accommodate both hard (regulations) and soft (human preferences) constraints, be user friendly and provide options rather than single recommendations. The participants are assisted by the research team to develop an applied management tool that facilitates co-ordination of directed services and that is responsive to Indigenous discourses, models and processes. Knowledge management (KM) can be a process of working with different domains, discourses or areas of knowledge, rather than in specialized areas, in order to understand the ways in which problems are defined and perceived and to innovate ways to solve problems with the participants. It is more than information management using computers (Long 2002); it is based on understanding the value of diverse ways of knowing through narratives and drawing conceptual diagrams for problem solving with the stakeholders.

This version of KM strives to improve better communication and better understanding. Social cognition is about how individuals and groups perceive the world 'out there'. The computer design is based on the principles of subsidiarity (Schumacher 1973, Singer 2002) and Ashby's law (1956) of social cybernetics ensuring that those at the receiving end of a decision are party to the decision making process. Designing and developing a knowledge base of healing pathways or tracks based on experiences of those who have shared their wisdom. Participatory action research is used to set up the collaborative framework and to build existing relationships. The dynamic process of service delivery and referral will be modelled by means of the system. The system will ensure that only general data are made available and that confidentiality of service users will be preserved. Neporendi along with organisations with which it is closely linked have tested a paper-based version of the design and the testing and refinement process continues. Mapping is something that people already do when trying to explain the connections across a number of variables[16]. Some of the questions in the research conversations build on the research experience that the team brings from other projects. This research develops a means to enable people to engage in participatory government using digital technology to support two way communication.

The major findings from the research confirm that Maslow's hierarchy of needs as perceived by the service providers is not greatly different from the 5 axial themes highlighted by the service users, but an analysis of the rich data from their narratives on what works, why and how, made it clear that it was a combination of these 5 axial factors that made a difference and that they needed to be seen as interconnected pathways. Stories from co-researchers (both service users and providers) reveal the following dimensions of wellbeing:

Table 1.

Dimensions of wellbeing	Indicators
Physical health	Safe housing (free of violence) in a safe community, regular meals, household goods to support wellbeing (stove, fridge and washing machine, furniture), clothing, dental health and , healthy body free of diabetes.
Mental health	Good interpersonal skills, a sense of respect and belonging, trust in a network of people and confidence

---

[16] Rich pictures were built up based on data collected from the informants using the Neporendi services. In summary the soft systems map the way in which service users and providers understand a problem. It includes the many variables they think are relevant and it includes their perceptions on why they think the variables are relevant (Fonow and Cook, 1991; Stanley and Wise, 1993).

Table 1. Continued

Dimensions of wellbeing	Indicators
Socio –cultural	Routine roles to maintain a household and connections with a community Access services such as health and education
Political	Engaged in decision making outside the private sphere, Sense of rights and responsibilities
Economic	Access to employment Learning literacy, numeracy and computer skills.
Environmental and spiritual	Establishing connections with 'country'

The words of the informants will be used to summarise each theme. Six typologies to represent typical (but not fixed archetypical) approaches (life in balance, rebuilding, making a transition, keeping it together, not coping and at rock bottom). These typologies are seen as overlapping domains that change over time as the lives of the men and women change. Changes from one domain to another are summarized as 6 dimensions (in baskets, out baskets, barriers, turning points and services that worked for them). The entry point for the user is as follows:

- Step one, please tell narrative. Then see which of the stories based on the above typologies is closest to you. Select a story and explore and discuss with the service provider which story resonates and why.
- Add more information as data to enrich the knowledge base and to help the next service user.
- Walk through the interconnected and overlapping pathways and collect items for basket (based on the drawings and stories) and select items to discard (based on the drawings and stories).
- Identify the barriers on the pathway and give them a name.

Based on an analysis of the data, wellbeing for service users can be understood as a state that can be interpreted in many ways, it has many domains. For some it is:

1. '*Being employed*' and 'able to help others', because their 'life is in balance'.
2. '*Rebuilding*'
3. '*Making a transition*' by using a combination of services[17]
4. '*Keeping it together*' after leaving a violent situation and trying to control drug and alcohol misuse – use cigarettes extensively
5. '*Making the break*' *from* an unsatisfactory way of life
6. '*Not coping*' and unable to leave or repeatedly returning to a violent situation.

Instead of using a flat continuum from 1-6, we modelled a series of overlapping spirals spanning holistic, integrated service delivery to fragmented and compartmentalised delivery of services as options with many variants in between (See Downes 2006: 36). Those who are most in need require the most integrated services and the most participation in decision

---

[17] Using CDEP, ASK job network, Neporendi and Cultural ties.

making. Those who are least in need require the least integrated services and are able to draw together services for themselves and act as facilitators for others, volunteers in service delivery or act as service providers for others. The challenge is to map the turning points for the a) better or b) worse that lead to changes in life and to c) identify the barriers from the point of view of both service providers and users.

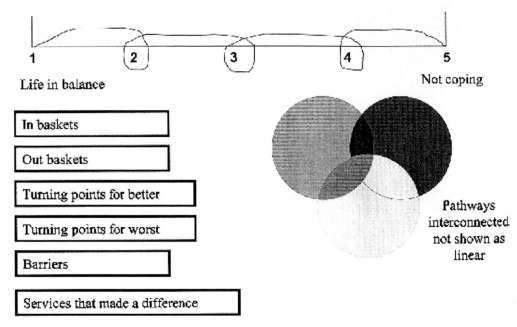

Source : Figure 10.5. McIntyre-Mills et al 2006:287.
These patterns are drawn from analysing the stories of women and men.
The overarching architecture for the knowledge base in this model as illustrated below:

Figure 1. Healing Pathways.

6. OUTCOMES FOR SERVICE USERS

- Pattern recognition and meaning making is vital for making sense the trauma and losses they have experienced
- Taking an active, constructive step away from the problem to wards co-creating a solution.
- The service users become participants in designing solutions and they take control of their healing.

6.1. In Basket

It enables a realization that all healing is self healing and that passivity that is a legacy of the colonial past, of structural violence, intergenerational family violence and community violence is one of the greatest barriers.

Realizing that change occurs when individuals take control of their lives and this can require moving away from abusive people and places.

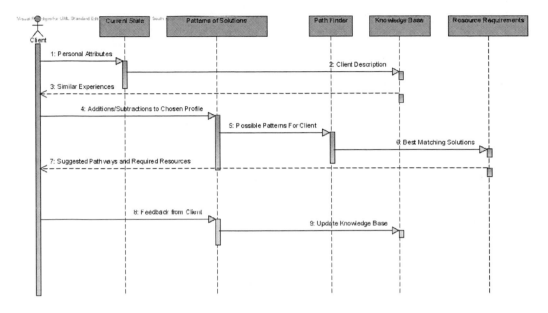

Figure 2. Sequence Diagram of System, De Vries 2006.[18]

6.2. Out Basket

Sense of shame needs to be recognized and then set aside. Using alcohol to self medicate grief and shame is one of the great challenges.

6.3. Barriers

Paradoxically abusers are often close family members. As stressed by Atkinson (2002), the shame and the silence lead to rage, depression, hopelessness and suicide. The Aboriginal cultural norm not to 'dob in' family is a barrier as is the notion that 'custom' can be held up as a justification for abusing younger children and women.

Fear of change and inability to leave abusive situations can be likened to the hostage syndrome, according to Atkinson, where the victim identifies with the aggressors, added to which is the cultural learning that:

"They know that in turning against their family they violate one of the first and most basic tenets: 'that country and people take care of their own': They turn against their families because they feel that ….. " their lives, bodies and wills have been controlled by others for others purposes and they have not been protected, defined and nurtured in return. Through violence, young people turn outwards, testing, in a manner that is

---

[18] Cited, in McIntyre-Mills 2007a

guaranteed to fail, whether others really do care for them (Rose 2000: 182-3 cited by Atkinson 2002: 226).

"In some Aboriginal families and communities, psychic prisons have been built and people have become simultaneously prisoner and warden and even executioner" (Baker 1983: 40 cited in Atkinson: 226).

6.4. Turning Points

The key turning point is the realization that rights and responsibility go hand in hand and that self determination comes with a sense of self worth and recognizing that "shame" is a learned reaction to abuse and social exclusion.

Building relationships is crucial for healing. Those who leave family and place to escape violence build new community networks over time. But when these relationships fail (as evidenced in many conversations and stories) it became clear that the sense of identity fragmentation and loss is heightened. Being aware of being an outsider and not being a local meant that some informants stressed that they needed to be "careful about what they said" and avoid "putting themselves forward". The interface will be designed as detailed in Figure 3 below.

These patterns are drawn from analysing the stories of women and men. Wellbeing can be seen as a function of the following:

Combinations of 5 axial factors appear important at this stage of the analysis:

- Home safety (and being free of violence)
- Health (physical and mental health – appearance, energy)
- Purpose (Formal Employment or preparation for employment /profession employment/CDEP / training /education)
- Connection/belonging (people and place), volunteering, community leadership and cultural spirituality
- Self respect and confidence, feeling good about oneself which is linked with being able to access services, work, study, maintain a stable home for children.

The inference from the analysis of the data so far is that by providing a combination of factors (safe housing, meeting basic physical needs then accessing education and employment) wellbeing becomes possible.

To overcome barriers in accessing services, it is vital that service providers in mainstream and specific services are welcoming to ensure that the confidence of service users is built. The role played by holistic or (one –stop shop outreach) is important in this context as it enables rapport and relationships to be formed. Also a quickly negotiated pathway to ensure that the above mentioned axial themes are addressed effectively and efficiently would enable better outcomes. Once a preliminary analysis of the data was undertaken a series of iterative workshops were held to explore the map of factors with the participants using the following answer sheet. Question 3, asks for a linear response and it is a reflection of the construction made by De Vries, but the informants considered each of the factors equally important. But were in agreement that the 5 axial factors together made a difference to wellbeing. Their contribution to the research was to stress the need for combinations of intervention to occur simultaneously. These were considered core factors that needed to be considered contextually in a friendly conversation.

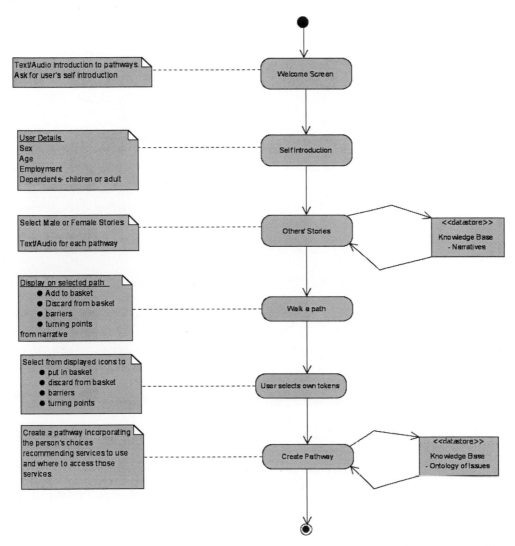

Source: Figure 9.4: Activity diagram for Pathway Creation, De Vries, 2006 in McIntyre-Mills et al 2006 :297.

Figure 3. Activity diagram for Pathway Creation.

Service providers tended to refer to Maslow's (1943) hierarchy of needs that span: "Physical needs such as food, housing, Safety, Belonging, Esteem and Self Actualization". Narratives from participants stress that their experiences and perceptions are what matters. They did not think in terms of an a *priori* list, based on Western culture. Basic needs are essential but they can only be identified by understanding personal stories. For example safety is a priority, but safety can be the casualty if women and children continue to remain in a situation, because they fear reprisals or that they will be unable to cope alone. Respect and knowledge about rights is one of the most important dimensions of wellbeing.

Source: Cited in McIntyre-Mills 2007a and McIntyre-Mills, 2008 forthcoming[19] .

Figure 4. Map for the proforma.

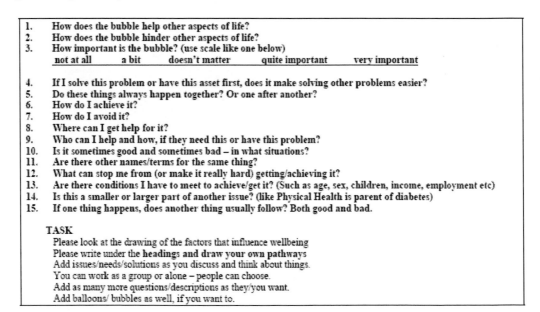

Figure 5. Second Proforma for Data Acquisition (De Vries 2006)[20]

[19] User Centric Policy Design to Meet Complex Needs, Nova Science, New York.

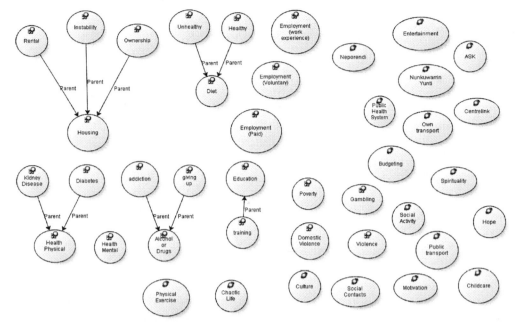

Source: Cited in McIntyre-Mills 2007a[21].

Figure 6. Pathways based on the identified factors.

The first NVivo maps were developed iteratively for discussion with the male and female service users and Aboriginal service providers who formed part of the reference group and later with a wider group of non Aboriginal commentators at a workshop hosted with co-researchers and corrections were made, for example. The aim is to find the shortest pathway approach to achieving wellbeing outcomes. But the pathways are based on the perceived lived experiences of the service users as to what constitutes successful, integrated outcomes.

6.5. Lessons from the Research

The key finding *from the service users* is that self respect and respect from others is vital for achieving a sense of rights and responsibilities. Having just a few supportive people, makes a difference to life chances and can help people to recover. Women said they need to have self esteem to insist on their own rights to safety. For the women pathways to wellbeing are relationships, role models and alternatives to their existing situation.

For the men, pathways to wellbeing are through activities that build positive relationships and self esteem. Once they "feel good about themselves" they are willing to take time to reflect on the personal and public barriers they have had to overcome. The experience of unemployment needs to be understood within the context the history of dispossession and marginalisation and the impact this has had on their life chances and choices. Opportunities

---

[20] Cited in McIntyre-Mills 2007a and User Centric Policy Design to Meet Complex Needs, Nova Science, New York.

[21] See mcintyre-Mills, 2008 forthcoming : "User Centric Policy Design to Meet Complex Needs", Nova Science, New York for further details.

for men to engage with others in relationship building and healing through shared activities at the were perceived by the participants to be limited by the lack of communal facilities for wood work or metal work that could support bonding and bridging activities with other men and service providers.

For both men and women, making the connections and understanding is all important. This sense of being able to engage with trusted service providers is achieved through active listening and providing continuity (see Atkinson 2002). People who are 'overwhelmed' (Deakin 2007) can achieve change if they are able to make connections with supportive networks. Being able to make sense of challenges and construct alternatives is the most important factor for wellbeing. The means for achieving this is through dialogue and listening and so access to supportive networks is vital for this process. The personal and the social are supported by the environment or undermined by the environment[22]. If health is not just about physical bodies, but about relationships then the suggestions made by the elders about social inclusion and wellbeing relate directly to this systemic orientation:

> "The holistic approach directs its attention at an 'environment' that includes not only the material world, but also social, economic and political aspects, incorporating human relationships and their spatial, temporal, emotional, psychological and social dimensions. The approach regards humans as placed at risk not simply from their material surroundings bit also from other humans. The social therefore is viewed as an important subset of a more general conceptualization of 'the environment'. Kickbusch has described this perspective as emerging from a 'new understanding of ourselves and our bodies....bodies are not just biological but social entities (1986: 34) ....including social class; the economy, culture, political, legal and administrative frameworks and institutions, health services; and lifestyles (Marmot and Morris 1984) ... (Petersen and Lupton 1996: 108). [23]

7. MEANING MAKING

To sum up, it is clear that we are able to use mapping only as an aid to decision making in context, not as a means to represent reality.

The key finding *for the service providers* is that mainstream services can be used effectively by many, but that a small group of people take up the most time and in a sense use up resources, because they are not appropriately handled by the mainstream or compartmentalized departmental system. The solution is to ensure close and carefully

---

[22] Macintyre et al (1993) pose the question: " ..should we be focusing on places or people?" . This research has attempted to make a contribution to this challenge and demonstrates the importance of integrated responses to complex problems of health, housing and social inclusion. " this approach to the environment ...ecological or holistic ...seeks to incorporate humans into nature rather than constructing them as separate. Thus humans are taken from their 'outside' stance as the ...destroyers of nature and placed within the ecosystem ...sharing the results f environmental change....traditional Australian Aboriginal or Native American cultures, as though systems that are deemed more sensitive to and aware of the subtle and spiritual relationship between the land, its non human inhabitants and humanity. The emphasis is placed on the interconnectedness of all things ...." (Petersen and Lupton 1996: 105).

[23] Petersen and Lupton 1996: 108 cite the work of Hawks et al in the American Journal of Health promotion that stresses the importance of spirituality for wellbeing. Participation for wellbeing is a theme that Petersen and Lupton 1996 : 154) take up as being vital for empowerment, but that participation needs to be done

targeted services and case management of those most in need. According to Deakin's (2007) findings:

"For service providers the issues of concern pertaining to,
Social health were, culture, discrimination, the effects of domestic violence and addiction on family and grief.
Economic health were, income, opportunity (education and employment), the addictions and discriminations that detract from them.
Physical health were, housing, lifestyle choices and the burden of disadvantage that leads to chronic disease, and depression.
Mental health were, the lack of self esteem and motivation, substance abuse and violence that perpetuated a cycle of crisis".

According to Deakin (2007)[24]:

"The analysis of the data demonstrates the systemic nature of Aboriginal disadvantage, in that education and employment delivers: a) income, b) housing, a c) good life style, d) physical health and e) wellbeing.
That family, community, culture, delivers social inclusion and wellbeing. However it also demonstrates that frustration, depression delivers poor mental health, low self esteem, a lack of motivation, addiction and anger. This again, in respect to improving Aboriginal wellbeing, is evidence of the existence of positive cycles being balanced by negative cycles of addiction, frustration and violence associated with mental health.
Changes such as choosing between abstinence and alcoholism are supported by a combination of factors. Changes in life chances are both a result of personal and social intervention and that the social, economic, physical and mental health domains act in a cyclical fashion to reinforce wellbeing. Mental health and depression were identified as a reinforcing cycle affecting other health domains. For those in crisis who are overwhelmed and lacking personal capacity it was demonstrated that social support networks are needed".

An argument can be made to support the existence of mainstream services for the majority and for specific targeted service delivery for the following reasons:

- Firstly, it ensures that those who are most in need are given case work support to ensure an integrated response which is more effective for those who are isolated and who need to build self esteem and trust, in order to extend their networks and to develop a sense of agency.
- Secondly, if the computer system is used in such a way that the service user and service provider sit side by side and after listening to the story are able to identify what their needs are by comparing their lives with the typical narratives of others, then they can be better matched with services (in the mainstream) and better still supported by specialized agencies or targeted services. This could ensure that they do not get into a revolving cycle of returning to services that do not meet their needs.

---

effectively, they cite criticisms of healthy city projects (see Tsouros 1990a : 61) for not enabling participation that draws on the lived experience and community knowledge.

[24] PhD thesis submitted April 2008 to Flinders Institute of Public Policy and Management, entitled: " Addressing Indigenous complex health, housing and social inclusion issues through critical systems approaches to build workforce capacity". This is the title of an Australian Research Council Grant lead by McIntyre-Mills.

This is a form of triage or computer aided assessment, where the user and provider work together to assess perceived need and to find the services and interventions that best meet their needs. Governance needs to be guided by responsive process rules and performance results. By this we mean the following:

- Process rules, based on a priori norms and ideals of governance and regulations to ensure accountability and the public good based on values pertaining to social, cultural, political, economic and environmental concerns.

- Performance results, based on a posteriori assessment of performance, in other words the consequences of governance decisions, in terms of outputs (measured by quantitative indicators) and outcomes (measured by qualitative indicators) based on consequences of actions by managers and service providers. Policy makers and service providers could address the needs of the marginalised who by virtue of age, gender, culture, race, level of income, for example are discriminated against by enabling *goodness of fit* and a sense of the *public good.* To sum up this is not a tool for making reductionist decisions but for informing better matches between service users and providers using ' if then' scenarios, not for excluding contextual choices. Our praxis strives to enable so-called joined up governance to work effectively and to apply the rule of subsidiarity as a way to address cross cultural and intercultural philosophies for governance. Change needs to be two-way and respectful, what can we learn from one another? When making policy we need to listen and to be open to innovation. The notion of experts making decisions on behalf of others undermines wellbeing. Our research makes recommendations that are very different from the narrow pragmatism of new public management approaches critiqued (see Minogue et al 1998) for their undermining of the public good. The research gives insights into more inclusive and systemic approaches to policy design (McIntyre-Mills 2003, 2006) and accountable governance (Colebatch 2006) and holds lessons for the future.

Context is all important to the design as the perceptions expressed are based on specific experiences which will be developed into conditional scenarios to guide action.[25]

The knowledge base will be updated as different users contribute and this will be achieved by positioning the factors (that the service users perceive to be important) as synonyms in response to contextual scenarios. We will test the program to establish if it enables:

- Greater self knowledge and learning from others.
- Better decisions, based on pattern recognition that could also help to make sense of the trauma and losses they have experienced.

---

[25] These suggestions are however, only meant to guide decisions made by service users together with a service provider, who could sit side by side and use the computer program to help identify which narratives resonate with their own experiences and explore the choices made by others and then to consider their own possible responses that could be added to the program. As each service user works with the program they will add items that they perceive to be valuable for the 'in baskets', items that need to be discarded. They will identify the turning points they have experienced for the better and the worse and the barriers (De Crespigny et al 2002) they have experienced.

- Participating in an active, constructive way in designing alternatives.

Being 'shamed' by service providers was discussed as being one of the greatest barriers (on this see Atkinson, 2002) to healing as it creates a sense of victimhood and leads to mistrust. The diagram below was drawn whilst telling a narrative about how users perceived relationships with service providers.[26] In the diagram below the story teller explained that she was made to "feel small" and to "feel shamed" in the way the service providers communicated, because they do not communicate respectfully in the way that women ideally communicate in groups. She explained that when people sit in a circle and each person's contribution is listened to carefully, people feel better about themselves. If the dynamics make you feel disrespected, it undermines opportunities to build connections and pathways to wellbeing. The emotions felt by those who are turned away from service providers who do not understand their needs were expressed graphically in the picture below as an unfriendly interaction with a service provider - depicted as tall, intimidating and unsmiling, next to a pictures of what works- a circle of women talking as equals. This is supported by the work of Ainsworth and Bowlby (1991), Brewer and Hewstone (2004), Atkinson (2002) as well as Greenfield (2000) all of whom stress the importance of engagement and making connections. The data from two men's focus groups and from two combined focus groups with men and women service users stress the importance of not only respectful communication and interactions, but warmth and friendliness. Borradori, Habermas and Derrida (2003) take up this issue and stress the implications of the quality of communication for democracy. Respect is not enough, warmth and the quality of the engagement matters. This requires building rapport through "two-way communication". Gore (2007) argues that one way communication raises many problems for democracy. Importantly Gore writes about the way in which two way communication is vital for building relationships and creating attachments (Ainsworth and Bowlby 1991, Bretherton, 1992) between people at the individual level and also at the societal level[27].

"As Miller and Ferroggiaro (1996) have pointed out 'respect and self respect are central components of an enlarged concept of citizenship...Respect affects how we are treated, what help from others is likely, what economic arrangements others are willing to

---

[26] The legacy of racism, loss of land and generations of social exclusion provide the lens through which the service users view their life chances and evaluate the services. Poverty and a lack of resources, combined with a lack of self respect associated with violence, abuse and alcohol misuse are part of the systemically linked web of problems. This is why a sociocybernetics approach is needed to explore the complex, recursive interrelationships so that a web of interventions can be provided.

[27] Democracy is currently increasingly criticized for not representing the interests of diverse citizens and for not taking into account the social justice and environmental concerns that span national boundaries(Beer 1974,1994), Habermas, Derrida, and Borradori, 2003, Pape 2005, Devji 2005, Singer 2002 and McIntyre-Mills 2003, 2006a,b,c). As Savage (2005: 330) argues, there are many kinds of bureaucracy and current democratic forms are in need of an overhaul. Revitalizing democracy (Putnam 1995) and democratic institutions by finding new ways to engage the marginalized is the challenge (highlighted by Savage 2005) to which this research is addressed. Florini (2003: 83) sums up the challenge as follows: "...when decision making reaches the rarefied level of intergovernmental organizations or even informal multilateral rule making, the threads of democratic accountability can be stretched very thin. It is often hard to see such decision making systems as a means by which the people of the world, through the instrument of their freely chosen governments, resolve their common problems. ... Accountability to the general public is at best indirect, and often, for all intents and purposes, it does not exist at all ...[The] mechanisms we have put in place to deal with large scale collective action problems seem so thoroughly inadequate when matched up against the scale of the problems...".

engage in ..., when reciprocity is to be expected'. Respect acts as a resource for individuals, and should be considered a component of the norms of reciprocity, trust, and social obligation that are essential for minimising the risks of poor physical, psychological, or social health (Aday1994)[28]. Indeed, mutual respect and the avoidance of inflicting humiliation on people is the central concept of Margalit's 'decent society' (Margalit 1996). ...honour and shame are soc crucial to human relations and may often become issues of life and death has long been recognised...." (Wilkinson 1998: 594).

The data *from service users* has produced very specific recommendations about a) meeting safety concerns that go beyond just physical housing and b) the importance of social networks to support those who have complex needs. c) Throughout the very detailed stories, supported by pictures and vignettes, the informants have stressed the value of respectful interactions from service providers.

---

[28] Aday, L.A. 1994. The health status of vulnerable populations. *Annual Review of Public Health.* 15. 487-509.

Example of Meaning Making

Typologies	Life in balance A and B	Rebuilding and making a transition	Keeping it together	Not coping	Rock Bottom
Cross cultural storying and picturing	Self reflection on what is the case?	Self reflection what is the case?	Self reflection what is the case?.	Self reflection what is the case?	Self reflection what is the case?
	The in basket is filled with confidence and a sense of agency which has enabled health, education, employment and housing needs to be met with the help of strong community networks and trust in a circle of friends.	The in basket is filled with a sense of agency, 'can do' attitude to achieve life goals.	The in basket is filled with confidence to use service providers effectively and to build an extensive and inclusive community network. Trust in others is enhanced through relationships. Through participating in a family wellbeing course and through use of services participants are able to make sense of the problems in their lives and work out strategies to address the barriers.	The in basket is mostly empty in that she does not have a safe home, physical strength, good nutrition, training, self confidence or employment	The in basket is mostly empty in that she does not have a stable home, physical strength, good nutrition, training, self confidence or employment.
	The out basket contains alcohol misuse, time wasting and sense of hopelessness	The out basket is filled with a wider range of harmful life choices than A, self blame and hopelessness	The out basket contains fear, self blame and hopelessness	The out basket is empty, because she has not discarded harmful life choices such as alcohol misuse or left her abusive partner	The out basket is empty, because she has not discarded harmful life choices such as alcohol misuse

Example of Meaning Making (Continued).

Typologies	Life in balance A and B	Rebuilding and making a transition	Keeping it together	Not coping	Rock Bottom
	Turning points for the better include owning a home after successfully finding safe accommodation that provides the base from which to work, educate themselves and give their own children a supportive home environment.	Turning points for the better includes successfully finding safe accommodation that provides the base from which to work, educate themselves and give their own children a supportive home environment	Turning point for the better include safe accommodation, accessing friendly Aboriginal services such as kindergarten, Nunkawarrin Yunti, Noarlunga Health and Neporendi, for example that provide an environment where bonds can be built with others within the Aboriginal community and bridges with those beyond the Aboriginal community can be built at lunches and woman's days where service providers meet service users whilst engaged in an activity. This is the first step to creating links with others who can help to create a sense of belonging and a sense of purpose.		A turning point for the better ought to be will power to overcome fear and drawing on supportive carers to bolster hope and determination Barriers Fear at this stage is the greatest barrier to overcome and a sense of hopelessness. Turning points for the better are supported through spirituality, faith, hope and determination . This is possible with supportive networks.
	Turning points for the worse are addressed through determination, faith in themselves and good use of services both mainstream and Aboriginal.	Turning points for the worse are addressed through careful use of services, both mainstream and Aboriginal.	Turning points for the worse are addressed through careful use of services, both mainstream and Aboriginal. Barriers include racism, unfriendliness, difficult procedures at Centrelink	Turning points for the worse are fighting with members of the Aboriginal community and choosing to live with an abusive partner and being unable to muster the courage to leave with her son.	Turning points for the worse are increased used of alcohol to address her fear of kidney failure and the dialysis treatment.

Typologies	Life in balance A and B	Rebuilding and making a transition	Keeping it together	Not coping	Rock Bottom
	Barriers exist but they are addressed through mobilising personal and public resources to address issues.	Barriers include racism, unfriendliness, difficult procedures at Centrelink	Barriers include racism, unfriendliness, difficult procedures at Centrelink	Barriers such as racism and exclusion ought to be addressed through finding alternative pathways and then through lobbying through community and political organisations	Barriers Fear at this stage is the greatest barrier to overcome and a sense of hopelessness.
	Self reflection on what ought to be the case? Determination to continue to continue to live a life in balance by ensuring that turning points and barriers are addressed through making sense of the problem, recognising what to do to address the challenge.	Self reflection on what ought to be the case? Determination to continue to have a sense of agency.	Self reflection on what ought to be the case? The in basket needs to be filled with determination to continue 'keeping it together' and where possible and appropriate to add some training and part time employment, but this depends on health and caring commitments which are primary	Self reflection on what ought to be the case? The In basket needs to be filled with the security of safe housing and connections with a mentor , case worker or community organisation who can build her confidence to think about what is best for herself and her son. Support networks are vital for creating a sense of safety, belonging, purpose and self esteem. Out basket needs contain alcoholism, fighting and abusive relationships	

Example of Meaning Making (Continued).

Typologies	Life in balance A and B	Rebuilding and making a transition	Keeping it together	Not coping	Rock Bottom
Context			By using services effectively problems such as mental illness and chronic physical problems can be managed. Stages in life where single mother needs to look after babies, pre school and young children is primary concern.	A cycle of returning to an abusive partner who is not part of the Aboriginal community. He is called "white trash" by a judgmental aunt who is Aboriginal. She visits for a few weeks to recover and then returns to her partner. This has continued for many years. The aunt disrespects her chosen way of life. She does not have close family or friends in the non Aboriginal community other than her son and her abusive partner. She chose to move away from the Aboriginal community and returns from time to time to her 'aunt'. As a result she is caught between two communities and does not feel accepted in either. She has made enemies in the Aboriginal community and was hospitalised after a fight with 'an old enemy' whom she met by chance in the city.	A cycle of drinking to the extent that kidney failure has occurred. Whilst preparing for dialysis she continued to drink as she was frightened. She lost hope for a while, but her mother's partner who had been on dialysis for a while provided support. She separated from her partner and her children were looked after by her mother.

Typologies	Life in balance A and B	Rebuilding and making a transition	Keeping it together	Not coping	Rock Bottom
Problem			Physical and mental ill health such as schizophrenia, diabetes and heart problems. Time of life when need to concentrate on caring for children, the elderly, those with disabilities and or illnesses.	Violence and domestic violence associated with alcohol Lack of trust and lack of strong rapport and support networks. She finds Centrelink difficult and struggles to fill out the forms.	Alcohol use a way of life learned from the previous generation, linked with social exclusion and intergenerational unemployment
Solution in the context			Build trust and confidence to use services. Enable participants to recognise patterns	Needs confidence to move away from a violent relationship and needs supportive networks, Co-ordinated case work and support from a helpful case worker to find a safe home. Parenting allowances, training and access to school for son.	Alleviation of depression based on an understanding that colonisation,dispossession and marginalisation have created generational health problems. The fault is not personal, it is also a legacy of public issues. Personal wellbeing can be achieved through making changes that are personal and political. Willpower supported by spirituality , hope and determination to deal with the challenges.

7.2. Interactive Modelling Process

The interactive modelling process could support matching services to need as long as it is seen as an aid to decision making and an aid to e-democracy- not as a means to predict and control. It could also be used to enable accountability by making the pathways of choices transparent to users and providers. The mapping process enables participants to have a say in shaping the direction for the future. The goal is to achieve more effective matches of services to perceived need and to develop a generic tool to support participatory decision making.

- The narratives and pictures (both abstract and concrete representations) were used to develop metaphors of weaving together strands of experience into baskets that could be used to: Tell their unique personal history shaped by a range of social, economic and environmental circumstances.
- Explore how it has been shaped by their experiences, for example of violence at home, homelessness, or unsafe neighbourhoods and limited networks.
- Identify with a story that others have told and explain how it is different and similar
- Assess positive life lessons and identify assets that they have and need for their in baskets
- Discard the problem areas from their lives by taking personal responsibility and
- Seek assistance to address identified needs that have been prioritized through considering their specific circumstances.
- The research process aims to enable:
- social inclusion (building on Carson et al 2007: 113, Bourdieu 1986 and a critical reading of Putnam 1995).
- connecting with others who are from the same background (bonding), make connections with those who are different (bridging) and create links horizontally and vertically to bring about change strategically.

The value of matching is enmeshed in the process of engaging those who have lived experience in social life. The engagement is in itself important for democracy, personal and public accountability and for wellbeing.

8. The Process Is the Message: Democracy, Participation, Friendliness and Wellbeing

"Democratization theories were initially dominated by the modernization approach that searched for the structural prerequisites of democracy. Governance in democratization theory is this, in a sense, metapolicy making: it refers to the setting of rules that guide rule making. .. " (Kjaer 2004: 194).

"There has never been a serious attempt to focus on the institutional interface between Indigenous people and governments in Australia. To construct an interface that creates greater parity and mutual accountability (and true shared responsibility) would require governments to agree to limitations on their existing powers and prerogatives and to make accountability a two –way street rather than the existing one-way street. ...[29]

A decade ago McLuhan and Powers (1989) argued that digital technology would change the world, because of the way in which passive watchers of TV use their right brain which is stimulated by the flashing movements, rather than their analytical left brain. Clearly digital technology can be used for one way communication and to play on the emotions, but it can also be used to stimulate debate and analysis. It depends on the way it is used. Participation is a means and an end to support wellbeing in democratic societies: The process is the message (to adapt McLuhan and Powers (1989) phrase! What is needed is two –way communication, supported if possible by digital technology to enable analysis and greater awareness of issues (Christakis and Bausch 2006, Gore, 2007). Thus testing out ideas with people is both a means to an end, namely better decisions and a sense of being citizens with rights and responsibilities to 'have a say' and 'have a fair go'. Wellbeing is based on involvement in decision making (see chapter 2 on implications for democracy). Contemporary debates centre on the role of digital communication in globalisation and the implications for the way in which technology can be used, either to promote two-way communication through e – governance (see McIntyre-Mills, 2000, 2006b) or to promote one-way communication. This theme has been explored by Borradori (2003) in conversation with Habermas and Derrida. They raised concerns about the need for respectful versus hospitable dialogue and recently by Al Gore in his new book *"The Assault on Reason"* (2007), where he argues that one way communication raises many problems for democracy.

Emotions are common to all people, but contextual circumstances will shape the way in which we name these emotions (see Kleinman and Good 1985: 8). Importantly Gore writes about the way in which two way communication is vital for building relationships and creating attachments between people at the individual level and also at the societal level. When people are faced with the exigencies of life they can respond to their emotions with mindfulness so as to transcend the pain of loss (see Obeysekere in Kleinman and Good 1985) and accept them as part of life. Buddhism was regarded with interest by some of the participant service users in this research who faced difficulties and wished to gain a sense of inner peace. Being able to think about thinking is a step towards enlightenment. Another step is to be able to engage with others in hospitable dialogue about both family matters and matters pertaining to public life. Participation is inextricably bound to wellbeing and democracy. This research supports the idea that meanings and values need to be placed centre stage when addressing complex needs. The process of engaging stakeholders is all important to addressing wellbeing which is a complex, interrelated concept based on perceptions and values along with the meeting of core basic needs, it requires respect and a sense of being connected with the community in which one lives.

This research argues that structural barriers influence life chances up to a point, but that people are able to overcome the barriers in certain contexts. What works, why and how was the subject of the research, based on the people's perceptions and narratives.

People need to be able to reflect on their lived experience and the way in which they live. Clusters of factors make a difference and they span all the levels of the Dhalgren and Whitehead Model (1991)[30] and impact as personal troubles and public issues (Mills 1975).

---

[29] Pearson, N. 2007. A structure for empowerment. *The Weekend Australian Inquirer*. June 16-17

Davey Smith et al. (1997, 1998) found that fine grain detail is important to understand how people achieve "income, occupational advantage or prestige with different life histories behind them…Those with the greatest accumulation of 'bio-material' advantages are likely to have experienced optimal combinations of events from childhood onwards. Hence the fine grain- the two cars and the rather larger house- are serving to indicate that bit more financial security …' (Bartley et al. 1998: 573).

But this research shows that even though wellbeing is linked with having material needs met, it is also about feeling respected and identifying strongly with others through a community network. For those who feel overwhelmed and who have little sense of control over their destiny, violence is a frequent event. According to Wilkinson et al. (1998: 594):

> "the violence associated with income inequality serves as an indicator of the psychosocial impact of wider income differences. …the most pressing aspect of relative deprivation and low relative income is less the shortage of material goods which others have, as the low social status and the desperate lack of sources of self esteem which usually goes with it. If social cohesion matters to health, then perhaps the component of it which matters most is that people have positions and roles in society which accord them dignity and respect…violence …seems above all to express a lack of adequate internal and external sources of self esteem, dignity and social status…"

'Control of destiny' through being able to shape one's life has been highlighted in this research and supports the findings of Tsey et al. (2003) who argue that wellbeing can be enhanced through the empowerment of men, women and children through teaching different ways to relate to one another. Relationships in the workplace, family and in civil society are central to wellbeing. Having poor health is not only the result of poverty, but the result of having a low status and feeling marginalised and alienated. Tsey cites the British Whitehall studies which show that civil servants who are respected have better health than those who are lower in the pecking order, even if they are of the same professional status. Tsey argues that being part of social network where one feels respected and in control is important for wellbeing:

> " …it is the level of control an individual has within their environment that determines whether the demands and stresses they experience have neural, positive or negative consequences in terms of health. Research indicates that the pathways that link low levels of control and poor health have a neuroendocrine basis and that : ' the things which really affect most people's health over the long periods of time are not dramatic life events, but are really the day to day problems, the wear and tear that we all experience in one degree or another, and …these effects may accumulate over months and years to cause problems…Central to this 'wear and tear' is relative powerlessness resulting from social class position. According to Syme : " the higher social classes have, from their earliest years, been given more training, opportunity, resources and skills to deal with life's problems; the lower the person's position in the social hierarchy, the less likely he or she is to have received these benefits' (494) he identifies …being able to traverse life's difficulties and solve everyday problems so that they do not overwhelm us…The skills are non specific, analytical and reflective problem-solving abilities that

---

[30] Dahlgren, G. and Whitehead,M. 1991 *Policies and Strategies to Promote Social Equity in Health*. Stockholm : Institute for Future Studies.

enable people to ' problem –solve' and can be applied in different contexts ..." (Tsey et al. 2003: 36)

The processes of healing is assisted by :

- Actively listening and affirming the person's story.
- Conversation a) one-to- one, b) in separate gender groups associated with a range of activities. c) Conversations with men and women were also held in combined focus groups of people who identified that they were happy to meet together, because they knew and trusted each other and because the shared conversations were to evaluate the analysis of the data and to test out the design.
- Individual stories were developed into typical stories along an overlapping continuum of wellbeing states and associated responses to life challenges.

The research confirms the argument made in "Trauma Trails" by Judy Atkinson (2002), an Aboriginal Academic who gave evidence to the Aboriginal and Torres Strait Islander Women's Task Force (2000). A pathway to recovery is weaving together the strands of experience to ensure that the individual experiencing the personal trouble understands that it is part of a public issue on domestic violence, poverty and addiction including the misuse of alcohol and other drugs. These are vicious problems in that they are both causes and effects (on this see Stafford Beer 1974). This research explored the argument made in *Critical Systemic Praxis* (McIntyre –Mills, 2003 Diagram 1.5, page 14 called : 'Breaking the cycle through participatory governance and developing citizenship rights and responsibilities') and the work of Atkinson (2002). The elders made the point that by flying the Aboriginal flag bullying at school could be reduced and the next generation would have a sense of their rights and responsibilities as Australian citizens (see chapter 4).

The elders, service users and many Aboriginal service providers stressed the importance of 'yarning' and using this interactive process to make sense of public and private issues to raise awareness and to prevent silencing. This research supports the argument by Atkins (2002) and Gore (2007) that discursive democracy and participation enhances wellbeing.

Our approach has been to take knowledge management and build in ontologies, meanings and perceptions which tap into people's emotions. The service providers stressed that frustration and anger is caused when people who are 'overwhelmed' do not get targeted care (Deakin 2007). Our research makes a strong case for better linkages and pathways to support a section of the service users and thus to triage the users (as per David Calvert 2005). Pathways converge on the importance of a) active participation in the process of healing and b), building strong networks and c) respectful and friendly communication as a means and an end for wellbeing. Participants agree that achieving safety (physical wellbeing) is dependent on having self esteem and confidence based on knowledge of one's rights and responsibilities.

Social, cognitive, emotional and spiritual wellbeing rests on access to alternatives which participants learn about through role models, mentors and service providers who can work closely with service users to ensure holistic and specialised care can be provided.

The mainstream delivery of services is appropriate for some, but not all service users. Those with the least confidence and the most limited social support networks need to be given additional assistance to negotiate and combine services and social, cultural, political, economic and environmental resources to support wellbeing. Provision and availability of a service or a resource is not the issue. The issue is ability of service users to access services, the ability of service providers to match and combine services effectively and contextually on the basis of need, in order to prevent social exclusion caused by bureaucratic mismatches and lack of accountability that can lead to hardships (ACOSS 2001).

New approaches to communication within and across organizations to support good governance requires working with many variables and considering not merely linear cause and effect but instead considering communication feedback loops(See Christakis and Bausch 2006, McIntyre-Mills et al. 2006a,b and Van Gigch with McIntyre Mills 2006).

Those who work in terms of categories of cause and effect can argue as does Encarnacion (2006) that civil society needs to be reconsidered, because a state can be undermined by civil society. This misses the point. Diversity and freedom need to be encouraged to the extent that they are not undermined. Yes, the state is needed to provide the context for democracy to flourish, but the state also needs democracy to keep it democratic. The mutual testing is the sine qua non of both democracy and new science. The 'iron rule of oligarchy' (Michels 1915) should not be forgotten. The argument being that democratic organizations become increasingly structured, hierarchical and bureaucratic and the leaders control access to information and resources and are consequently more powerful than those at the bottom of the hierarchy as a result. The processes for dealing with complex situations are streamlined in democracies and the less powerful voices are silenced which undermines social inclusion opportunities for wellbeing.

Michels argues that he did not want to try to solve the problem of democracy because it was unsolvable. He described it as a law: "Democracy leads to oligarchy, and necessarily contains an oligarchical nucleus" (Michel's 1915 translated by E. and C. Paul 2001: 6). This is a problematic argument in that it is assumed that social systems are governed by laws, rather than understood in terms of probabilities.

Nevertheless the comment about the potential for rigidity in bureaucracies and the potential of states to represent the interests of the powerful is well taken. Secondly his argument about the ability of organizations to respond to complexity is also well taken. Fortunately with new forms of technology and with the development of socio-cybernetics it is possible to reconstruct the way in which organizations operate so that they do not undermine democratic principles. A potential way forward is by enabling more accountable communication on an ongoing basis, in order to make the Third Way (Giddens 1998) less market oriented and more participatory. Our research does not strive to undermine bureaucracy per se, but to enable the public sector to become more responsive and thus live up to the ideal of serving the public good.

8.1. Closing the Circle: Getting the Match Right through Respectful 'I-Thou' Communication

Whilst the assumption underpinning this research is that we can and do construct our own identity (albeit in conditions not always of our own choosing)[31] and that we can be harmed by the way we are treated by others, because lack of respect can be a core reason for a lack of

---

[31] See Popay et al 1998 Theorizing inequalities in health : the place of lay knowledge. *Sociology of Health and Illness* Vol. 20: No 5 : 640.

wellbeing, it is possible to reflect on lived experience as a means to remake or reconstruct the way people perceive situations. Telling narratives and making sense of situations can be a positive step in enhancing a sense of agency and control through taking control of " the social construction of identity"(Somers 1994: 605, Atkinson 2002), it is also a way to ensure that democracy is not just for the powerful (Buck, 2005).

> "While being black has been the powerful social attribution in my life, it is only one of a number of governing narratives or presiding dictions by which I am constantly reconfiguring myself in the world. Gender is another, along with ecology, pacifism, my particular brand of colloquial English...all describe and impose boundary in my life, even as they confound one another in unfolding spirals of confrontation, deflection, and dream...." (Williams, The Alchemy of Race and Rights, 256-257 cited by Somers 1994: 605-606).

A perception that identity is shaped by many factors exists when people are self actualized. When they are overwhelmed they may see themselves first and foremost as disadvantaged by colonization, disrespected by racists and socially marginalized.

Sharing a narrative with others requires trust and a willingness to make oneself vulnerable to others. Confidentiality and respect for culture were central concerns raised by participant service users and providers. These concerns need to be addressed through understanding the importance of Buber's (1947) I-thou approach to communication that supports relationship building as a basis for learning and healing.

When people feel that engaging with others is unlikely to lead to positive responses, they disengage, become helpless and hopeless. This is expressed by depression, anxiety or violence. According to Gore:

> " Attachment theory is an interesting new branch of developmental psychology that sheds light on the importance of consistent, appropriate and responsive two-way communication and why it is essential for an individual's feeling empowered...First developed by John Bowlby..., attachment theory was developed by Ainsworth... Although it applies to individuals, attachment theory is, in my view, a metaphor that illuminates the significance of authentic free flowing communication in any relationship that requires trust...." (Gore 2007: 246).

This is as important within nation states as it is to communication across nation states[32] The ethical imperative to consider ideals and the public good can be supplemented by an

---

[32] This supports the arguments made by Devji (2005), Pape (2005) and Borradori in conversation with Derrida and Habermas (2003). In democracies diverse interest groups need to be represented and need to feel as if they are being included in decision making. The challenge outlined cogently by Fishkin (2000) is to avoid filtering in a bid to achieve greater representation that achieves a balance between mob rule and mirroring without analysis based on discursive review to find the best route. McLuhan and Powers (1989) made the point that "the medium is the message" and that communication technology can have many unexpected impacts, such as dumbing down thinking, because watching TV can be a very passive experience that does not require conceptualisation through reading and thinking. Alternative ways of using communication technology (including TV) in a more interactive way are raised by Banathy (2000). The boundaries of concern beyond the nation state raise questions about the value of limited nationalism (see McIntyre-Mills 2000, 2006, a,b, 2007). Nussbaum (2006) in her recent book 'Frontiers of Justice' poses questions about the extent to which current forms of democracy can meet the needs of those who are not protected within the boundaries of the nation state, such as the disabled and those who are unable to speak for themselves. McIntyre-Mills (2006b) raises

inquiring system that enables considering perceptions and connections across services. It is important that audit trails are set up, so as to ensure that time and effort are used effectively and efficiently. By using this approach service user and service provider perceptions and values are taken into consideration when addressing complex wicked problems. Most importantly the stories told by people need to be acknowledged with respect and people need to be given time. Once their story has been told the listener should be able to help with case work through ensuring better connectedness across organizations. Making connections and creating rapport are the most essential aspects of healing. Even if organizations are large they should be organized in such a way that people do not feel that they are being 'fobbed off' to another person or section. From the moment a person enters an organization the potential to promote or undermine wellbeing exists. A friendly welcome, well organized spaces equipped to educate and inform make a difference to the way people feel.

Organizations need to strive towards the ideal of promoting the public good, whilst mindful of the consequences of their choices in day to day operations. This research addresses the dialectic of thesis, antithesis and synthesis. Two –way dialogue is the basis of Aristotelian notions of wisdom (which he called phronesis in Nichomachean ethics),which Marxist and critical theorists have re-worked and which Aboriginal Australians have always used as a basis for spirituality, healing and governance, summed up by the symbol of the boomerang.

9. CONCLUDING THOUGHTS

Wellbeing is a state of mind based on our perceived values (social, cultural, political, economic and environmental) within specific contexts. For some it can be achieved through religious transcendence, for others through relationships, a sense of belonging, accessing a range of services or through personal agency. People at the receiving end of decisions need to be part of the decision making process or be well represented (McIntyre-Mills, 2005). Unlike Herbert Simon, Churchman believed in using *thinking about thinking* as a way to escape the closed or "total systems" approach. Instead of "Thinking like a computer" (Schmaltz 2006), this research enables the soft ware to be designed creatively by those with lived experience and thus could enable 'if then scenarios' to be considered by both the service user and the provider as a tool for self knowledge. The tool is not intended to mirror or represent reality. Blind spots will always exist. There is no such thing as a "total system", according to West Churchman (1979, 1982) who argues that the so-called enemies of a total system are: " religion, politics, morality and aesthetics". These provide our values, but they also filter the way we see the world. They will impact on the way we construct any model and they will influence our interpretations. This is why we need to be see all systems as open approximations, not as 'the truth'.

Life is a process based on communication and relationships (adapted from Bausch 2001, Rosen 1991). Emotions and respectful two-way communication are vital for wellbeing. Wellbeing is a state of mind based on our perceived values (social, cultural, political, economic and environmental) within specific contexts For some it can be achieved through religious transcendence, for others through relationships, a sense of belonging , accessing a

---

this question in relation to all those who are powerless including young people, asylum seekers, the disabled and sentient beings.

range of services or through personal agency. People at the receiving end of decisions need to be part of the decision making process or be well represented (McIntyre-Mills, 2005). This is vital for promoting wellbeing and for addressing complex or interrelated problems associated with social exclusion.

REFERENCES

[1]   Ainsworth, M.D. and Bowlby, J. 1991. An Ethological Approach to Personality Development. *American Psychologist.* Vol.. 46. 333-341.

[2]   Aleksander, I. 2005. The World in my mind, my Mind in the world: key mechanisms of consciousness in people, animals and machines. Imprint Academic. Exeter.

[3]   Armstrong, R. and Van Der Weyden 2005 Indigenous Partners in *Healing Medical Journal of Australia.* 182 (10) 498-499.

[4]   Ashby, W.R., 1956, An introduction to Cybernetics, Chapman and Hall, London.

[5]   Atkinson, J. 2002. Trauma trails, recreating song lines: the transgenerational effects of trauma in Indigenous Australia. Spinifex. Melbourne.

[6]   Atkinson, J. 2007 A national crisis: What John Howard is not doing. *ALAR Journal Volume.* 12 No 1 87-91.

[7]   Australian Bureau of Statistics (ABS) 2001 Census of Population and Housing.

[8]   Australian Bureau of Statistics 2005 The Health and Welfare of Australia's Aboriginal and Torres Strait Islander People's Report 4704.0.

[9]   Australian Institute of Health and Welfare 2006 Alcohol and other drugs treatment services in South Australia 2004-2005: findings from the National Minimum Data Set (NMDS).

[10]   Australian Institute of Health and Welfare 2006 *Australia's Health* ISSN 1032.

[11]   Banathy, B., 1996, Designing Social Systems in a Changing World, Plenum, New York.

[12]   Banathy, B., 2000, Guided Evolution of Society: A Systems View, Kluwer/Plenum, London.

[13]   Banathy, B., 2001a, Self-guided evolution of society: the challenge: the self guided evolution of ISSS 45th International Conference for the Systems Sciences. July 8th-13th.

[14]   Banathy, B., 2003, Self-Guiding Evolution of Civilisation, *Systems Research and Behavioural Science*, 20:4309-323.

[15]   Bartley, M. Blane, D, Davey Smith, G. 1998. Introduction: beyond the Black report. *Sociology of Health and Illness.* Vol.20 No 5 : 563-577.

[16]   Barton, J, Emery, M., Flood, R.L., Selensky, J. and Wolstenholme, 2004. A maturing of systems thinking? Evidence from three perspectives, *Systemic Practice and Action Research,* 17(1): 3-36.

[17]   Baruma, I. and Margalit, A.2004.*Occidentalism: The West in the Eyes of its Enemies*, Penguin, New York.

[18]   Bateson, G.1972. Steps to ecology of mind: a revolutionary approach to man's understanding of himself. New York: Ballantine.

[19] Baum, F, Ziersch A, Zhang, G. Putland, C. Palmer, C. MacDonald, C. O'Dwyer, L. and Coveney, J. 2007. *People and places: urban location, social capital and health.* NH and MRC project 229913 and 324724 .

[20] Baum, F., Bush, R., Modra, C. and Murray, C., 2000, "Epidemiology of participation: an Australian community study", *Journal of Epidemiology and Community Health,* 54(6):414-426.

[21] Baum, F., Cooke, R., Crowe, K., Traynor, M. and Clarke, B., 1990, *Healthy Cities Noarlunga Pilot Project Evaluation,* Southern Community Health Research Unit.

[22] Baum, Scott, Stimson, Robert, Mullins, Patrick, and O'Connor, Kevin, 2000, "Welfare dependency in communities within Australia's metropolitan regions", *People and Place,* 8(3).

[23] Bausch, K., 2001, The Emerging Consensus in Social Systems Theory, Kluwer/Plenum.

[24] Bausch, K., 2006, 'Be your enemy : The Contributions of West Churchman to Doing Better Governance and International Relations" in McIntyre-Mills, J., *Rescuing the Enlightenment from Itself: Critical and Systemic Implications for Democracy,* C.West Churchman Series, Vol. 1, Springer, New York, Boston, London.

[25] Beck, U., 1992, Risk Society Towards a New Modernity, Sage, London.

[26] Beck, U., 1998, *Democracy Without Enemies*, Polity, Cambridge.

[27] Beer, S., 1974, *Designing Freedom,* Wiley, London.

[28] Beer, S., 1994, Beyond Dispute. The Invention of Team Syntegrity, Wiley. New York.

[29] Behrendt, L. 2005. The abolition of ATSIC- implications for democracy. *Democratic Audit of Australia.* http://democratic.audit.anu.edu.au/ accessed 4/01/2006

[30] Berger, P., 1976, Pyramids of Sacrifice: Political Ethics and Social Change, Penguin, Harmonsworth.

[31] Berger, P.L., 1977, *Facing Up to Modernity,* Penguin, Harmondsworth.

[32] Bevir, M. and Rhodes, R.A.W., 2003b, "Traditions of governance interpreting the changing role of the public sector", *Public Administration,* 81(1):1-17.

[33] Bhabha, H.K. 1994 *The location of culture.* Routledge, London.

[34] Bishop, P. and Davis, G., 2001, *"Mapping public participation choices",* APSA Conference, Brisbane. Unpublished paper cited in Public Sector Management Guide 120, Managing Out.

[35] Bogue, R., 1989, *Deleuze and Guattari,* Routledge, London.

[36] Borradori, G., 2003, *Philosophy in a Time of Terror Dialogues with Jurgen Habermas and Jacques Derrida* interviewed by Borradori Giovanna, University of Chicago Press, Chicago.

[37] Bourdieu, P., 1986, The forms of capital. Reprinted from Richardson, J. in: *Education, Culture, Economy and Society*, A.H. Halsey, ed., 1997, Oxford University Press, Oxford.

[38] Bourke, C. 1989.Cross –cultural communication and professional education: an aboriginal perspective. *Paper presented to Multicultural Communication Conference* 25th Sept.

[39] Bowden, B. 2006. Civil Society, the State, and the limits to Global Civil Society *Global Society* vol. 20 No 2 April.

[40] Bradley, R. 2001. Bits and logans: information processing and communication in social systems. *Abstracts: International Systems Sciences Conference, Asilomar.*

[41] Brady, M 1991 The health of young Aborigines: a report on the health of Aborigines aged 12-25 years, Hobart, national Clearinghouse for Youth Services.

[42] Bretherton, I. 1992. The origins of attachment theory. *Developmental Psychology*. No 28: 759-775.

[43] Brewer, M. and Hewstone, M. 2004.Eds *Social cognition*. Blackwell, Oxford.

[44] Bridgman,P. and Davis, G. 2004 *The Australian Policy Handbook*, 3 ed Allen and Unwin Crows Nest.

[45] Brubaker, R. 2004. Loveman, M. and Stamatov, P. Ethnicity as cognition. *Theory and Society*. 33: 31 –64.

[46] Brubaker, R. and Cooper, F., 2000, "Beyond Identity", Theory and Society. 29(1-47).

[47] Brubaker, R., Loveman, M. and Stamatov, P., 2004, "Ethnicity as cognition", Theory and Society, 33:31–64.

[48] Buber, M., 1947, *Between Man and Man*, Collins. London.

[49] Buck, A.R. and Wright, N. 2005 *The poor man : law and satire in 19th Century New South Wales*. Australian Scholarly. Melbourne.

[50] Burrell, G. and Morgan, G, Sociological Paradigms and Organizational Analysis. Heinemann, London.

[51] Carter, D. ed. 2003. Housing and health. Building for the future. British Medical Association. Housing report 43937. http://209.85.165.104/ search?q=cache: Zxz0s9zu _XwJ:www.bma.org.uk/ap.nsf/Attac... 12/04/2007.

[52] Castells, M. 1996. *The rise of network society*. Oxford: Blackwell.

[53] Chambers, R., 1983, *Rural Development: Putting the Last First*, Wiley and Sons, New York.

[54] Chambers, R., 1997, Whose Reality Counts: Putting the First Last, ITDG, Bath.

[55] Checkland, P. and Scholes, J.1990. *Soft Systems Methodology in Action*. Chichester: Wiley.

[56] Chesterman, J. and Galligan, B., 1997, *Citizens Without Rights: Aborigines and Australian Citizenship*, Cambridge University Press.

[57] Chomsky, N., 2003, Hegemony or Survival: America's Quest for Global Dominance, Allen and Unwin, Crows Nest, NSW.

[58] Christakis, A. 2004. Wisdom of the People *Systems Research and Behavioural Science* Volume 21 No 5 479-488.

[59] Christakis, A. and Bausch, K. 2006. How people harness their collective wisdom and power to construct the future in co-laboratories of democracy Information Age. Greewich.

[60] Christakis, A. and Brahms, S., 2003, "Boundary spanning dialogue for the 21st century agoras", *Systems Research and Behavioural Science*. 20:371-382.

[61] Churchman, C. West, 1979a, *The Systems Approach*, Delta, New York.

[62] Churchman, C. West, 1979b, *The Systems Approach and its Enemies*, Basic Books, New York.

[63] Churchman, C. West, 1982, *Thought and Wisdom*, Intersystems Publications, California.

[64] Churchman, C. West., 1971, The Design of Inquiring Systems. Basic Concepts of Systems and Organization, Basic Books, New York.

[65] Colebatch, H.K. 2006. Accounting for Policy in Australia Public Policy. Public Policy Vol 1 No 137-51.

[66] Collard, K.S., D.Antoine, H., Eggington, D. Henry, B, R. Martine, C. and Mooney, G. 2005 Can Mutual Obligation in Indigenous Health: can shared responsibility agreements be truly mutual? *Medical Journal of Australia* 182 (10) 502-504.

[67] Connolly, W. 1969. The Bias of Pluralism Atherton, New York.

[68] Cornelius, R. 1996, The science of emotion: The research and tradition in the psychology of emotion. Prentice Hall. New Jersey.

[69] Cox, E., 1995, *A Truly Civil Society, Boyer Lectures,* ABC Books, Sydney, NSW.

[70] Crispin, S. and Meixner, S. 2003, 'Boiling Mad', *Far Eastern Economic Review*, 13 February 2003, (online), Available:

[71] Crocker, D. 1995. Functioning and Capability: The Foundations of Sen's and Nussbaum's Development Ethic, Part 2 in Nussbaum, M, and Glover, J. Women, Culture and Development: A study of Human Capabilities. Oxford. Clarendon Press.

[72] Davey Smith,G. Hart,C. Blane,D. Gillis,C. and Hawthorne,V. 1997. Lifetime socioeconomic position and mortality": prospective observational study. *British Medical Journal.,* 314: 547-552.

[73] Davey Smith, G. Neaton, J.D., Wentworth, D. and Stamler, R. 1998 Mortality differences between black and white men in the USA: contribution of income and other risk factors among men screened for the MRFIT. *Lancet.* 351: 934-9

[74] Davies, J. and Kelly, M. 1993. *Healthy Cities: research and practice.* London: Routledge de Crespigny, C. Groenkjaet, M. and Casey, W. Murray, H. and Parfoot, W. 2002 Breaking down the barriers: Urban Aboriginal Women: drinking and licensed Premises in the Southern Metropolitan Region of South Australia. School of Nursing and Midwifery, Flinders University of SA and Aboriginal Drug and Alcohol Council (SA) Inc.

[75] De Tocqueville, A. 1945. *Democracy in America.* New York. Knopf.

[76] De Vries, D. (2006). *Mesodata: Engineering Domains for Attribute Evolution and Data Integration.* School of Informatics and Engineering. Adelaide, South Australia, Flinders University.

[77] De Vries, D. and J. Roddick (2004). Facilitating Database Attribute Domain Evolution Using Mesodata. 3rd *International Workshop on Evolution and Change in Data Management.*

[78] De Vries, D., S. Rice, et al. (2004). In Support of Mesodata in Database Management Systems. 15th *International Conference on Database and Expert Systems Applications* ({DEXA} 2004), Zaragoza, Spain, Springer Verlag.

[79] Denzin, N. and Lincoln, Y.1994. *Handbook of qualitative research.* London: Sage.

[80] Devji, F. 2005. Landscapes of the Jihad: militancy, morality and modernity. London. Hurst and Company.

[81] Dewey, J., 1997, "Democracy and education", Simon and Schuster: *A Journal of Australian Social Policy,* VCOSS, 27:3-10.

[82] Dewey, J., 1997, *How We Think*, Ontario, Dover.

[83] Dey, I., 1993, Qualitative Data Analysis: A User-Friendly Guide for Social Scientists, Routledge, London.

[84] Dixon, J. and Scheurell,R. 1995. *Social Welfare with Indigenous Peoples* . Routledge. London.

[85] Douglas, M., 1978, Purity and Danger: An Analysis of the Concepts of Pollution and Taboo, Routledge and Kegan Paul, London.

[86] Downes,P. Newtonian Space: The blind Spot in Newell and Simon's Information Processing paradigm *Cybernetics and Human Knowing*. Vo 13, no 3-4 27-57.

[87] Dryzek, J. 1999 Democratizing rationality in Discursive Democracy. Cambridge.

[88] Dryzek, J. 2000. Deliberative democracy and beyond: liberals, critics, contestations. Oxford University Press.

[89] Du Gay, P., 1998, "Office as vocation: bureaucracy but not as we know it", *Cultural Policy Paper No 4, Institute for Cultural Policy Studies*. http://www.gu.edu.au/centre/cmp/du_gay2.html.

[90] Du Gay, P.2002a How responsive is 'responsive' government? *Economy and Society* Vol. 31 Number 3: 461-482.

[91] Du Gay, P.2002b A common power to keep them all in awe: A comment on governance. *Cultural values* Vol. 6 Number 1: 11-27.

[92] Duhl, L. 2002. Systems and Services. *Systems Research and Behavioural Science*. 19. 391-397.

[93] Du Gay 2005. Bureaucracy and Liberty: State, Authority, and Freedom by du Gay in *The values of democracy*. Oxford University Press.

[94] Edgar, D., 2001, The Patchwork Nation: Rethinking Government-Rebuilding Community, Harper, Sydney.

[95] Edgar, D., 2001, The Patchwork Nation: Rethinking Government-Rebuilding Community, Harper, Sydney.

[96] Edwards, M. and Gaventa, J., 2001, *Global Citizen Action*, Boulder, Colorado.

[97] Edwards. and Gaventa, J., 2001, *Global Citizen Action*, Colorado, Boulder.

[98] Eisenstein, Z. Against Empire: feminisms, racism and the west. Spinifex Press.

[99] Elias, N and Lichterman, P. 2003. Culture in interaction. *The American Journal of Sociology* 108. 4: 735-794.

[100] Elias, N. and Lichterman, P., 2003, "Culture in interaction", *The American Journal of Sociology*, 108(4):735-794.

[101] Elkington, J., 1997, *Cannibals with Forks*, Capstone, Oxford.

[102] Ellis C. and Bochner, A., 2000, "Autoethnography. Personal narrative, reflexivity: researcher as subject", in: *Handbook of Qualitative Research*, 2nd. ed., N. Denzin and Y. Lincoln, Sage, London.

[103] Encarnacion, O. G. 2006 Civil Society Reconsidered *Comparative Politics* : 257-273.

[104] Espejo, R. 2006. Reflections on Power, Democracy and Communications *Cybernetics and Human Knowing* vol. 13, 3-4, 144-152

[105] Espejo, R., 2002, "Self-construction and restricted conversations", *Systems Research and Behavioural Science*, 19(6):517-529.

[106] Esponosa, A. and Mejia, A., 2003, "Team syntegrity as a learning process: some considerations about its capacity to develop critical active learners", *47th Annual Conference of the International Society of the Systems Sciences,* Hersonissos, Crete.

[107] Estrella, M., 2000, *Learning from Change, Issues and Experience in Participatory Monitoring and Evaluation*, Participation in Development Series, Intermediate Technology Publications, International Development Research Centre, UK.

[108] Fals-Borda, O. and Rathman, M.A., 1991, Action and Knowledge: Breaking the Monopoly with Participatory Action Research, Intermediate Technology, London.

[109] Fishkin, J. 2000 The Filter, the Mirror and the Mob: reflections on deliberative democracy. Paper presented at " Deliberating about Deliberative Democracy. February

4-6, University of Texas at Austin. http://scholar.google.com/scholar?q= Fishkin%2C+J.S+2000+The+filter%2C+the+mirror+and+the+mob and hl=en and lr= and btnG=Search accessed 20 /03/2007.

[110] Fishkin and Laslett 2003 *Debating deliberative democracy*. Blackwell Publishing.

[111] Flood, R. and Carson, R. 1993. Dealing with complexity: An introduction to the theory and application of Systems Science. Plenum. London.

[112] Flood, R. and Carson, E., 1998, Dealing with Complexity: An Introduction to the Theory and application of Systems Science, 2nd. ed., Plenum, London.

[113] Flood, R. and Romm, N., 1996, *Diversity Management: Triple Loop Learning*, John Wiley and Sons, New York.

[114] Flood, R.L., 2001, "The relationship of 'systems thinking' to action research" in: Handbook of Action Research: Participative Inquiry and Practice, P. Reason and H. Bradbury, Sage, London.

[115] Florini, Ann, 2003, The Coming Democracy: New Rules for Running a New World, Island Press.

[116] Foley, D., 2002, Indigenous standpoint theory, *Sharing the Space Conference*, Flinders University.

[117] Foley, D., 2003, An examination of indigenous Australian entrepreneurs. *Journal of Developmental Entrepreneurship*, 8(2).

[118] Fonow, M. and Cook, J. 1991. Beyond Methodology. *Feminist Scholarship as lived research*. Bloomington: Indiana University Press.

[119] Forrester, J. 2000.Conservative epistemology, reductive ethics, far too narrow politics: some clarifications in response to Yiftachel and Huxley *International journal of Urban and Regional Research*. Vol. 24. Vol. 4: 914-916.

[120] Forrester, J., 1999, The Deliberative Practitioner: Encouraging Deliberative Planning Processes, Massachusetts Institute of Technology, Cambridge.

[121] Foucault, M. and Gordon, C. eds., 1980, Power/Knowledge: Selected Interviews and Other Writings 1972- 1977, Harvester, Brighton.

[122] Freire, P., 1982, Creating alternative research methods: learning to do it, in: Creating Knowledge: a monopoly? Society for participatory research in Asia, B. Hall, A. Gillette and R. Tandon, New Delhi: 29-37 in: *The Action Research Reader*, Deakin University publication, Victoria.

[123] Frey, J. and Fontana, A., 1993, "Interviewing: the art of science", in: A Source Book of Qualitative Research Methods, N. Denzin, and Y. Lincoln, Sage, London.

[124] Fukuyama, F., 1992, *The End of History and the Last Man*, Free Press, Simon and Schuster.

[125] Fukuyama, F., 2004, *State Building: Governance and World Order in the 21st Century*, Cornell University Press, New York, Ithaca.

[126] Fung, A. and Wright, E.O., 2003, Deepening Democracy. Institutional innovations in Empowered Participatory Governance. The Real Utopias Project 1V. Verso, London.

[127] Fung, A. and Wright, E.O., 2003, *Deepening Democracy*. Institutional innovations in Empowered Participatory Governance. The Real Utopias Project 1V, Verso, London.

[128] Gallhofer, S. and Chew, A., 2000, Introduction: accounting and indigenous peoples, *Accounting, Auditing and Accountability Journal*, 13(3): 256-267.

[129] Gao, F. and Yoshiteru, N. 2001. Systems thinking on knowledge and its management 45th *International Conference for the Systems Sciences, Asilomar, USA*.

[130] Gaventa, J. and Cornwell, A. 2001, Power and Knowledge, *Handbook of Action Research,* P. Reason and H. Bradbury, eds., Sage, London.

[131] Gaventa, J. and Valderrama, C., 1999, Participation, citizenship and local governance: background note for workshop on *"Strengthening Participation in Local Governance",* Institute of Development Studies, June.

[132] Gaventa, J., 2001, Towards participatory local governance: six propositions for discussion, Paper presented to the *Ford Foundation, LOGO Program with the Institute of Development Studies,* June.

[133] Geertz, C., 1973, Thick description: towards an interpretive theory of culture, in: *The Interpretation of Cultures. Selected Essays,* C. Geertz, Basic Books, New York, pp.3-32

[134] Gibbons, M., Limonges, C., Nowotny, H., Schwartzman, S., Scott, P. and Trow, M., The New Productions of Knowledge: The Dynamics of Science and Research in Contemporary Societies. London: Sage.

[135] Giddens, A. 1991. Modernity and self identity; Self and society in the Late modern age. California. Stanford.

[136] Giddens, A., 1998, The Third Way: The Social Renewal of Democracy, Polity, Cambridge.

[137] Giddens, A., 2001, The Global Thirdway Debate, Polity, Blackwell.

[138] Golding, S. Gramsci's Democratic theory. Contributions to a post liberal democracy. University of Toronto. London.

[139] Goldstein, M. 2006, Subjective Bayesian Analysis: Principles and Practice, *Bayesian Analysis* 1(3): 403--420.

[140] Gore,Al 2007. *Assault on Reason.* Bloomsbury.London.

[141] Gouldner, A.W., 1971, *The Coming Crisis of Western* Sociology, Heinemann, London.

[142] Greenfield, S, 2000, The private life of the brain: emotions, consciousness and the secret of the self. Wiley.Canada.

[143] Grugel, J., 1999, Democracy Without Borders. Transnationalization and Conditionality in New Democracies, Routledge, London.

[144] Guddemi, P. 2006 Breaking the Concept of Power (and redescribing its Domain) Batesonian and Autopoetic Perspectives *Cybernetics and Human Knowing* vol. 13, 3-4, 144-152.

[145] Habermas, J., 1984, The theory of communicative action: reason and the rationalization of society. Beacon: Boston.

[146] Habermas, J., 1995, Reconciliation through the public use of reason: remarks on John Rawls's political liberalism, *The Journal of Philosophy,* XC11 (3): 109-131.

[147] Habermas, J., Derrida, J. and Borradori, H.2003, *Philosophy in a Time of Terror Dialogues with Jurgen Habermas and Jacques Derrida* interviewed by Borradori Giovanna, University of Chicago Press, Chicago.

[148] Haggerty, R. 2005 Ending homelessness in South Australia www.thinkers.sa.gov.au

[149] Hampden-Turner, C., 1981, *Maps of the Mind*, Macmillan, London.

[150] Harris, L. and Wasilewski, J. 2004 Indigeneity, an alternative worldview- four R's (relationship, responsibility, reciprocity, redistribution0 versus Two P's (power and profit). Sharing the journey towards conscious evolution. *Systems Research and Behavioural Science.* Vol. 21 no 5 489-505.

[151] Harris, L. and Wasilewski, J. 2004 Indigenous wisdom of the people forum: strategies for expanding a web of transnational Indigenous interactions Systems *Research and Behavioural Science*. Vol. 21 no 5 489-505.

[152] Hassim,A. Heywood,M and Berger,J. 2007. Health Democracy: a guide to human rights, health law and policy in post apartheid South Africa. SyberInk.CapeTown.

[153] Held, D. 2004. Global covenant: The social democratic alternative to the Washington consensus . Polity. Cambridge.

[154] Helman, C.G.1990., *Culture, Health and Illness* second edition. Wright, London.

[155] Hildebrand, D. 2005. Pragmatism, Neopragmatism and Public administration. *Administration and Society*. Vol. 37. No 3. 345-359.

[156] Hillier, J, Fisher, C. And Tonts, M.2002. Rural Housing, regional; Development and Policy Integration: An Evaluation of Alternative Policy Responses to regional disadvantage. *IHURI Final Report* ISBN 1877005398.

[157] Hobbs, H. 1994 City Hall Goes Abroad: the foreign policy of local politics, Sage. London.

[158] Hobbs, H. Ed 2000. Pondering Post Internationalism. A paradigm for the twenty first Century? State University of New York Press.

[159] Hopkins, M. Couture,C., and Moore,E. 2001. Moving from Heroic to the everyday: Lessons learned from leading horizontal projects, CCMD roundtable on the management of horizontal initiatives, chaired by James Lahey, Canadian Centre for management Development http://www.apsc.gov.au/mac/connectingabstracts.htm http://www.feer.com/articles/2003/0302_13/p018region.html (10 July 2003).

[160] Institute of Governance 2005 *The Democratic Deficit, Citizens Engagement and Consultation: a roundtable report*. Otawa, Canada see www.iog.ca.

[161] Irwin, T. 1985 *Aristotle Nicomachean Ethics* translated with Introduction and notes Hackett. Cambridge.

[162] Jackson, M., 2000, *Systems Approaches to Management*, Plenum, London.

[163] Jackson, M.C. 2006, Knowledge management in the ERP Era. *Systems Research and Behavioural Science* vol. 23.No 2.

[164] Jamrozik, A., 2001, Social Policy in the Post Welfare State: Australians on the Threshold of the 21st Century, Longman, NSW.

[165] Jung, C.J., 1972, Translated by Hull, R., Mandala Symbolism from the Collected Works of Jung, C.G. Bollingen Series, Princeton University Press.

[166] Kavanagh, D. and Richards, D. 2000. Can Joined-Up Government be a Reality? *Paper presented at the Australian Political Studies Association 2000 Conference,* Australian National University, Canberra 4-6 October, 2000.

[167] Keeffe, K., 1988, "Aboriginality: Resistance and Persistence", *Australian Aboriginal Studies,* 1:67-81.

[168] Keel, M. 2004. Family violence and sexual assault in Indigenous communities "Walking the Talk" *Australian Institute of Family Studies*.

[169] Keene, I., 1988, Being Black: Aboriginal Cultures in 'Settled' Australia, Aboriginal Press, Canberra.

[170] Kelly, L. 1993 . Reconciliation and the Implications for a Sovereign Aboriginal Nation. Aboriginal Law Bulletin. http://bar.austlii.edu.au/au/journals/Aboriginal LB/1993/11.html accessed 21/03/2007.

[171] Kjaer, A.N. 2004, *Governance*, Polity Press, Cambridge.

[172] Klineman, A. and Good, B. eds 1985. Culture and Depression: Studies in the Anthropology and Cross Cultural Psychiatry of Affect and Disorder. University of California Press. Berkley.

[173] Kulvicki, J. 2004. Isomorphism in information carrying systems. *Pacific Philosophical Quarterly* 85, 380-395.

[174] Langford, J. and Edwards, M. 2002, Boundary spanning and public sector reform, in Edwards, M. and Langford, J. (editors), New Players, Partners, Processes: A Public Sector without Boundaries, National Institute for Governance, ACT.

[175] Lindstrom,B and Eriksson, M. Salutogenesis 2005. *Journal of Epidemiology and Community Health*, 59: 440-442.

[176] Macintyre, S. Maciver, S. and Sooman, A. 1993. Area, class and health: should we be focussing on places or people? *Journal of Social Policy* 22(1) 213-234.

[177] Management Advisory Committee, 2004, Connecting Government- Whole of Government responses to Australia's Priority Challenges, APSC, Canberra.

[178] March, C., Smythe, I. and Mukhopadhyay, 1999, *A Guide to Gender-Analysis Frameworks*, Oxfam, Oxford. Margalit,A. 1966. *The Decent Society*. Harvard. Harvard University Press.

[179] Martin, D. 2005 Rethinking Aboriginal Community Governance. In Smyth, P., Reddel, T. and Jones, A. *Community and Local Governance in Australia.* Sydney. UNSW Press.

[180] Maslowe,A.H. 1943. A theory of human motivation. *Psychological Review*, 50: 370-396.

[181] McCline, R.L., Bhat, S. and Baj, P., 2000, Opportunity recognition: an exploratory investigation of a component of the entrepreneurial process in the context of the health care industry, *Entrepreneurship Theory and Practice*, Winter.

[182] McDonald, C. and Marston, G., 2003, Fixing the niche? Rhetorics of the community sector in the neo liberal welfare regime, *Just Policy: A Journal of Australian Public Policy*. 27 August, VCOSS, pp. 3-10.

[183] McIntyre-Mills, J., 2000, Global Citizenship and Social Movements: Creating Transcultural Webs of Meaning for the New Millennium, Harwood. Netherlands.

[184] McIntyre, J., 2002a, A community of practice approach to knowledge management and evaluation re-conceptualised and owned by Indigenous stakeholders, *Evaluation Journal of Australasia*, 2(2): 57-60.

[185] McIntyre, J .2002b. Critical Systemic Practice for Social and Environmental Justice: a case study of management, governance and policy. *Systemic Practice and Action Research. Vol. 15(1) 3-35.*

[186] McIntyre, J. 2002c, "Yeperenye dreaming in conceptual, geographical and cyberspace: a participatory action research approach to address local governance within an Australian Indigenous Housing Association", *Systemic Practice and Action Research,* 16(5), 309-338, 2002.

[187] McIntyre-Mills, J., 2003a, Critical Systemic Praxis for Social and Environmental Justice: Participatory Policy Design and Governance for a Global Age, Kluwer, London

[188] McIntyre, J. 2003b Participatory democracy: drawing on C.West Churchman's thinking when making public policy. *Systems Research and Behavioural Science*. Volume 20, 489-498.

[189] McIntyre, J. 2003c. Participatory Design: The Community of Practice (COP) Approach and its relevance to Strategic Management and Ethical Governance. *Journal of Sociocybernetics*. Vol. 4, No 1, 1-23.

[190] McIntyre, J. 2004. Facilitating critical systemic praxis (CSP) by means of Experiential learning and conceptual tools. *Systems Research and Behavioural Science*. Vol. 21, 37-61.

[191] McIntyre, J. 2005a Working and re-working the conceptual and geographical boundaries of governance and international relations *Systemic Practice and Action Research*. Vol. 18, No 2 157- 220.

[192] McIntyre, J. 2005b Participatory planning: computer design and strategic partnerships to address complex health, housing and social inclusion issues with Aboriginal Australians theses' International Society for the Systems Sciences 49th Annual Meeting, July, Cancun, Mexico, published in proceedings ISBN 0-9740735-5-5.

[193] McIntyre, J 2005c. "Critical and systemic practice to address fixed and fluid identity and politics at the local, national and international level", *Systemic Practice and Action Research*, 18, No. 3 223-258.

[194] .McIntyre-Mills, J. et al . 2006a *Rescuing the Enlightenment from Itself: Critical and Systemic Implications for Democracy*. Springer. London, Boston. Vol. 1 of C.West Churchman Series.

[195] McIntyre–Mills, J., 2006a, 'Molar and Molecular Identity and Politics', in Van Gigch, J., with McIntyre-Mills, J., *Wisdom, knowledge and management,* Vol. 2, Springer, New York, Boston, London.

[196] McIntyre, J. 2006b Rescuing the Enlightenment from Itself: implications for addressing democracy and the enemies within. A summary of volumes 1-3 of the C.West Churchman Series. RC 10 International Sociological Association Congress of Sociology, Durban South Africa 23-29 July.

[197] McIntyre-Mills, J. et al 2006c Systemic Governance and Accountability: working and reworking conceptual and spatial boundaries, Springer. London, Boston, Vol. 3 of C. West Churchman Series.

[198] McIntyre, J. 2006d. Healing pathways: implications for addressing democracy through improved collaboration and knowledge management. RC 51 *International Sociological Association Congress of Sociology*, Durban South Africa 23-29 July.

[199] McIntyre-Mills, J. 2007a. Challenging economic and religious fundamentalisms: implications for the state, the market and ' the enemies within' *International Journal of Applied Systemic Studies*. Vol. 1 No 1 49-67.

[200] McIntyre-Mills J,2007b Systemic wellbeing based on user centric design and experiential learning: making new meanings through identification of patterns. Proceedings of the 51st Annual Conference of the International Society of the Systems Sciences: Integrated Systems Sciences: Systems Thinking, Modeling and Practice, Tokyo Institute of Technology, Japan. August5-10 ISBN 0 974073571.

[201] McIntyre, (sic –Mills) J 2007 Participation as a means and an end to support wellbeing in democratic societies . *ALAR Journal*. Volume 12. No 1 81-86.

[202] McLuhan, M and Powers, B. 1989. The Global Village. Transformations in world life and media in the 21st Century. Oxford University Press. Oxford..

[203] Meadows, G. Burgess,P. Fossey,E. and Harvey,C. 2000 Perceived need for mental health care, findings from the Australian National Survey of Mental Health and Well-being. *Psychological Medicine*. 30 645-656.

[204] Michels, R. 1915 Political Parties: A sociological study of the oligarchical tendencies of Modern Democracy. Translated by Eden and Cedar Paul, 2001 Batoche Books: Kitchener.

[205] Michels, R. 1915 Political Parties: A sociological study of the oligarchical tendencies of Modern Democracy. Translated by Eden and Cedar Paul, 2001 Batoche Books: Kitchener.

[206] Midgley, G. 2000. Systemic Intervention: Philosophy, methodology, and practice. New York: Kluwer.

[207] Midgley, G. and Ochoa-Arias, A., 2001, Unfolding a theory of systemic intervention, *Systemic Praxis and Action Research*, 14(5): 615-649.

[208] Midgley, G., 1997, Dealing with coercion: critical systems heuristics and beyond, *Systems Practice*, 10(1): 37-57.

[209] Minogue,M., Polidano,C and Hulme eds 1998. Beyond the new Public Management: Changing ideas and Practices in Governance. Edward Elgar. Northhampton.

[210] Moser, C.O., 1993, Gender Planning and Development: Theory, Practice and Training, Routledge, London.

[211] National Economic/ALGA, 2002, *State of the Regions Report,* by P. Brain, National Economic Director and C. Shepl, ALGA, published by Australian Local Government Association.

[212] Negroponte, N., 1995, *Being Digital*, Vintage, New York.

[213] Norris, P. 1999 Critical citizens: global support for democratic governance. Oxford University Press.

[214] Nonaka, I. and Takeuchi, H., 1995, The Knowledge Creating Company: How Japanese Companies Create the Dynamics of Innovation, Oxford University Press, Oxford.

[215] Nussbaum, M. 2001 Upheavals of thought: the intelligence of emotions. Cambridge University Press.

[216] Nussbaum, M 1995 Women. Culture and Development: A study of human capabilities. Oxford, Claredon.

[217] Nussbaum, M. 2006. Frontiers of justice, disability, nationality and species membership. Harvard University Press. London.

[218] O'Grady,P. 2005. Meet the philosophers of ancient Greece. Ashgate. Aldershot.

[219] O'Reilly, B. and Townsend, J. 1999. *Young people and substance use.* Darwin: Territory Health Services.

[220] Ogawa, H. 2000. Lessons learned from regional experiences: Healthy Cities in the Western Pacific Region. Regional Advisor in Environmental Health, WHO Western Pacific Regional Office, Key Note Address, Australian Pacific Healthy Cities Conference June 2000.

[221] Pape, R.A. 2005. Dying to win. The strategic logic of suicide terrorism. Random House. New York.

[222] Pearson, N .1999. Positive and negative welfare and Australia's Indigenous Communities *Australian Institute of Family Studies in Family Matters.* No 54. Springs/Summer.

[223] Pearson, N., 1999, Positive and negative welfare and Australia's Indigenous Communities, *Australian Institute of Family Studies in Family Matters*, 54(Spring/Summer).

[224] Peters, P. and Savoie. 2000 *Governance in the Twenty-First Century: Revitalising the Public Service*, McGill-Queen's University Press, Montreal.

[225] Petersen, A and Lupton, D. 1996. *The new public health: health and self in the age of risk* . Allen and Unwin. St Leonards,NSW.

[226] Pierre, J. and Peters, B.G, 2000, *Governance, Politics and the State*, Macmillan, Hampshire.

[227] Pierre, J., ed., 2000, *Debating Governance*: *Authority, Steering and Democracy*, University Press, Oxford.

[228] Pierre, J., ed., 2000, Debating Governance: Authority, Steering and Democracy, University Press, Oxford.

[229] Pike, K., 1967, Language in Relation to a Unified Theory of the Structure of Human Behaviour, Mouton, The Hague.

[230] Pilger, J., 2002, *The New Rulers of the World*, Verso, London.

[231] Polanyi, M., 1962, *Personal Knowledge*, Routledge and Kegan Paul, London.

[232] Popay, J. Williams, G. Thomas,C. and Gatrell, A. 1998. Theorising inequalities in health: the place of lay knowledge. *Sociology of Health and Illness*. Vol. 20.No 5. 619-644.

[233] Popper, K., 1968, *The Logic of Scientific Discovery*, Hutchinson, London.

[234] Putnam, R., 1995, "Bowling alone", *Journal of Democracy*, 6(1):65-78.

[235] Ramsden. I. M. 2002*Cultural Safety and Nursing Education in Aotearoa and Te Waipounamu* A thesis submitted to the Victoria University of Wellington in fulfilment of the requirements for the degree of Doctor of Philosophy in Nursing, Victoria University of Wellington.

[236] Rawls, J., 1993, *Political Liberalism*, Columbia University Press, New York.

[237] Rawls, J., 1995, "Reply to Habermas", *The Journal of Philosophy*, XC11 (3):132-180.

[238] Rawls, J., 1999, *The Law of Peoples with the Idea of Public Reason Revisited*, Harvard University Press, London.Pilger, J., 2002, *The New Rulers of the World*, Verso, London.

[239] Reason, P. 1991. Power and conflict in multidisciplinary collaboration. *Complementary Medical Research* 5(3).

[240] Reason, P. and Bradbury, H., 2001, Handbook of Action Research: Participative Inquiry and Practice, Sage, London.

[241] Reason, P., 1988, *Human Inquiry in Action*, Sage, London.

[242] Reason, P., 2002, 'Justice, sustainability and participation. Inaugural lecture', *Concepts and Transformations*, 7(1):7-29.

[243] Renton, A. and Macintosh, A. 2007. Computer Supported Maps as a Policy Memory *Information Society* 23 : 125-133.

[244] Rhodes, RAW, 1997, Understanding Governance. Policy networks, governance, reflexivity and accountability, Open University Press, Maidenhead.

[245] Rittel, H. and Webber, M. 1984. Planning problems are wicked problems *Developments in Design Methodology*. New York: Wiley.

[246] Robbins, J. 2005. Life after ATSIC: Indigenous citizenship in an era of mutual obligation. *Paper presented at APSA Conference*, University of Otago, Dunedin, NZ. September.

[247] Roberts,D. Hugo,G., Bradley,H.Coffee,N. and Gollan,S. 2005. The Emerging Housing Needs of Indigenous Australians. Australian Housing and Urban Research Centre. Southern Research Centre. Government of South Australia. Department for Families and Communities. ISBN 0975782312.

[248] Roche, A. and McDonald 2001. Systems, settings, people: workforce development challenges for the alcohol and other drugs field. Commonwealth Department of Health and Aged Care.

[249] Romm, N., 2001b, Accountability in Social Research: Issues and Debates. Romm, N., 1996, Inquiry-and intervention in Systems planning: probing methodological rationalities, World Futures, 47:25-36.

[250] Romm, N., 2002, "A trusting constructivist view of systems thinking in a knowledge age", in: Systems Theory and Practice in a Knowledge Age, G. Ragsdell, et. al., Plenum, New York.

[251] Romm, N., 2002, A trusting constructivist view of systems thinking in a knowledge age, in: Systems Theory and Practice in a Knowledge Age, Ragsdell et al, Plenum, New York.

[252] Rosen, R. Life itself: a comprehensive inquiry into the nature, origin and fabrication of life. Complexity in Ecological Systems Series. Columbia University Press, New York.

[253] Rowse, T., 1998a, "Nugget Coombs and the contradictions of self determination", in: For Central Land Council Taking Power Like this Old Man Here, A.Wright, IAD Press.

[254] Rowse, T., 1998b, White Flour: White Power: From Rations to Citizenship, Cambridge: University Press.

[255] Runcie and Bailie. 2002. *Evaluation of Environmental Health Survey on Housing.* Menzies School of Health School of Health

[256] Sakurai,Y. and Smith,R.G. 2003.*Gambling as a motivation for the commission of crime* Australian Institute of Criminology.

[257] Savage, M. 2005 The Popularity of Bureaucracy: Involvement in Voluntary Associations in du Gay in *The values of democracy*. Oxford University Press.

[258] Schaffer K and Smith S. 2004. *Human Rights and Narrated Lives, The Ethics of Recognition*. Published by Palgrave .New York.

[259] Schmaltz, D. 2006 Thinking like a Computer. *Cybernetics and Human Knowing*. Vol. 13, No 2 105-108.

[260] Schoeny, M. and Warfield, W. 2000 Reconnecting systems Maintenance with Social Justice: A Critical Role for Conflict Resolution. *Negotiation Journal*. 254-268.

[261] Schumacher, E.F. 1973. Small is beautiful: economics as if people mattered. New York. Harper.

[262] Scott, J., 1998, *Seeing Like a State*, Yale, London.

[263] Sen, A., 2000, *Development as Freedom*, Knopf, New York.

[264] Senge, P., 1990, *The Fifth Dimension*, Doubleday, New York.

[265] Senge, P., Kleiner, A., Roberts, R., Roth, R. and Smith, G., 1999, *The Dance of Change: The Challenges of Sustaining the Momentum in Learning Organizations*, Nicholas Brealey, London.

[266] Shields, P. 2003. The Community of Inquiry: Classical Pragmatism and Public *Administration. Administration and Society*. Vol. 35. No 5. 510-538.

[267] Singer, P., 2002, *One World: The Ethics of Globalisation*, The Text Publishers, Melbourne.

[268] Somers, M. 1994. The Narrative Constitution of Identity: A relational and Network Approach *Theory and Society*. Vol 23 No 5 605-649.

[269] Spiegelhalter, D. J., A. P. Dawid, et al., 1993. Bayesian Analysis in Expert Systems. *Statistical Science* 8(3): 219--283.

[270] Spoehr, J. ed. 2005. *State of South Australia: trends and issues* Australian Institute for Social Research., University of Adelaide. Wakefield Press.

[271] Stanley, L. and Wise, S. 1993. Breaking out Again. *Feminist Ontology and Epistemology*. London: Routledge.

[272] Steering Committee for the Review of Government Service Provision 2005. *Overcoming Indigenous Disadvantage*. Key Indicators 2005.

[273] Stringer, E. and Genat, W.J. 2004. *Action Research in Health*. Pearson –Merril. New Jersey.

[274] Syme, L. 1998 Social and economic disparities in health: thoughts about intervention. *The Milbank Quarterly* : 76: 493-502.

[275] Szreter,S. 2002. The state of social capital: bringing back in power, politics and history. *Theory and Society* 31 573-621.

[276] Tsey,K. 2003. Social determinants of health, the 'control facto' and the family wellbeing empowerment program. *Australian Psychiatry.* vol 11 Supplement 34-39.

[277] Tsey,K. Patterson,D, Whiteside, M. Baird,L. and Baird,B,. 2002 Indigenous Men taking the rightful place in society? A preliminary analysis of a participatory action research process with Yarrabah Men's Health group. *Australian Journal Rural Health*, 10 : 278-284.

[278] Ulrich, W. 2001. The quest for competence in systemic research and practice. *Systems Research and Behavioural Science* 18: 3-28.

[279] Ulrich, W., 2001, 'The quest for competence in systemic research and practice', *Systems Research and Behavioural Science*, 18:3-28.

[280] Ulrich, W., 2001, "The quest for competence in systemic research and practice", *Systems Research and Behavioural Science*, 18:3-28.

[281] Uslaner, E., 1999, Democracy and social capital, in: *Democracy and Trust,* M. Warren, Cambridge University Press, Cambridge.

[282] Van Gigch, J. in collaboration with McIntyre-Mills, J. 2006. *Wisdom, Knowledge and Management*. C.West Churchman Legacy and Related Works, vol. 2. Kluwer, Springer.

[283] Van Gigch, J.P. 1991. System design, modelling and metamodeling. London. Plenum.

[284] Van Gigch, J.P. 2002. Comparing the epistemologies of scientific disciplines in two distinct domains: modern physics versus social sciences. Part 1: the Epistemology and knowledge characteristics of the physical sciences. *Systems Research and Behavioural Science Vol.* 19, No 3: 199-210.

[285] Vickers, G., 1983, *Human Systems are Different*, Harper and Row, London.

[286] Von Foerster, H. 1995. *Cybernetics of cybernetics*. Second edition. Future Systems, Inc. Minneapolis.

[287] Wadsworth, Y., 1991, *Everyday Evaluation on the Run*, Action Research Issues Associated.

[288] Wadsworth, Y., 2001, "The Mirror, the magnifying glass, the compass and the map: facilitating participatory action research", in: *Handbook of Action Research*, P. Reason and H. Bradbury, Sage, London.

[289] Walsh, F and Paul Mitchell 2002. Planning for country: cross cultural approaches to decision-making on Aboriginal lands. Alice Springs .IAD press.

[290] Warren, E., 1999, *Democratic Theory and Trust*, Cambridge University Press, Cambridge.

[291] Warren, L., 2004, A systemic approach to entrepreneurial learning: an exploration using storytelling, *Systems Research Behavioural Science*, 21.

[292] Webb, S.P. 1998. Knowledge management: linchpin of change The Association for information management. London: ASLIB.

[293] Weil, S., 1998, "Reflexive turns in paradigm dialogues; tensions and challenges in transcending different domains for knowledge generation", *14th World Congress of Sociology*, Montreal.

[294] Wenger, E., 1998, Communities of Practice: Learning, Meaning and Identity, Cambridge University Press.

[295] White, L., 2001, "Effective governance: through complexity thinking and management science", *Systems Research and Behavioural Science*, 18(3):241-257.

[296] White, L., 2002, "Connection matters: exploring the implications of social capital and social networks for social policy", *Systems Research and Behavioural Science*, 19(2):255-270.

[297] Wilkinson,R.G., Kawachi,I., Kennedy,B. 1998. Mortality, the social environment, crime and violence. *Sociology of Health and Illness*. Vol. 20.No 5: 578-597.

[298] Wilson,G. 1993. Users and providers: Different Perspectives on Community care services. *Journal of Social Policy*. 507-526.

[299] Young,J. McIntyre,J. Drummond,M. 2007 forthcoming "Overlapping identities in 'white Anglo' PRE WW2 (South) Australia: lessons for 21st century Australia. *People and Place*. Vol.15, No 3: 42-52

In: Citizenship in the 21st Century
Editors: L. T. Kane and M. R. Poweller, pp.55-91

ISBN: 978-1-60456-401-3
© 2008 Nova Science Publishers, Inc.

Chapter 2

PROMOTING SUCCESS IN SOCIAL INTERVENTION WITH MULTI-PROBLEM POOR FAMILIES

Liliana Sousa[*,1] *and Sofia Rodrigues*[2]

[1] Department of Health Sciences;University of Aveiro, 3810-193 Aveiro, Portugal; PhD, Auxiliary Professor at the University of Aveiro
[2] Department of Health Sciences; University of Aveiro, 3810-193 Aveiro, Portugal; Psychologist, Research Assistant at the University of Aveiro

ABSTRACT

Success is a desired expectation in the most diverse experiences of our lives. In this context, social intervention with multi-problem poor families becomes relevant because it has constantly been associated with failure in spite of the efforts of the professionals who work with these families, of the investment of the State in social policies in support of the most vulnerable members of society and of the efforts of families to solve their problems.

In the area of social and community intervention, success has been defined in terms of results, which is relatively simple when a family experiences a specific and localised problem: for example, if a member of the family is unemployed, the intervention is successful if they get a job. The characteristics of multi-problem poor families (for whom problems are severe and long-term and experienced in a context of scarce economic and emotional resources) pose specific challenges for intervention and do not permit a linear application of this definition.

This research aims to contribute to a better understanding of the definition of success and failure in social intervention with multi-problem poor families, adopting the perspective of the practitioner. In this way we hope to understand how these definitions may be contributing to failure becoming a common result and to reveal alternatives which may enable the improvement of the quality of life of these families.

The main results indicate that success is defined in terms of clients becoming autonomous of formal services and carrying out the instructions of professionals. This is paradoxical, since when one is autonomous, one makes one's own decisions. So this definition of success may be encouraging actions which promote dependency instead of

[*] Liliana Sousa, PhD; Department of Health Sciences; Auxiliary Professor at the University of Aveiro, 3810-193 Aveiro, Portugal; Phone: +351234372440; Fax: +351234401597; E.mail: lilianax@cs.ua.pt

promoting the desired autonomy. Failure is defined in terms of the client remaining dependent on formal services, not fulfilling the proposals of intervention and not being motivated for intervention and/or change. This definition places the responsibility for failure on clients, allowing professionals to maintain a passive stance in face of this situation.

However, our results reveal some reorientation of professionals towards more operational definitions which are more in tune with the specificities of these families: encouraging small changes; activating competences in specific areas (parenting, managing school and professional life); supporting social integration. This seems to be a more fruitful way of building a better quality of life for these families.

INTRODUCTION

Success is a desired expectation in different experiences of our lives. In contrast, the lack of success (or failure) is undesired, even when it is recognised that the mistakes or failings have learning and development potential. The word success is in common usage, being associated with diverse activities in individual, family and social life, such as (e.g. Hiebert and Taylor, 1994; Sorensen *et al.*, 1998; Perkins, 2001): economics (e.g. Botswana is an example of success in Africa), education (e.g. the promotion of school success), health (e.g. certain operations reveal high success rates).

In this context, determining factors and indicators of success/failure, as well as strategies for promoting success have been implemented and assessed (e.g. Reppucci, Woolard and Fried, 1999; Cunningham and Henggeler, 1999; Chambless and Ollendick, 2001). The conceptualisation, definition and meaning of success/failure differ according to the areas under consideration and/or the tasks in hand: for example, in sport, success is associated with being better than everyone else in the competition; in health, success is related to promoting the health of people and of populations.

In social intervention (e.g. family, support groups, public health and community action) success and failure have been studied essentially through the results of intervention, the processes of evolution/change, and the satisfaction of the clients (individuals, families, groups and communities) (e.g. Kazdin, 1986; Hogue, Liddle and Rowe, 1996; Hampson and Beavers, 1996; Perkins, 1996).

Intervention with multi-problem poor families (which face multiple, severe and long-term problems in a context of scarce economic resources) is frequently associated with failure (e.g. Summers, Templeton-McMann and Fuger, 1997; Krumer-Nevo, Slonim-Nevo and Hirshenzon-Segev, 2006; Sousa, Ribeiro and Rodrigues, 2007). Besides, when facing an isolated problem (e.g. unemployment), success can be defined in a relatively simple way (e.g. getting a job), but when there is a family with diverse problems, whether in way of functioning, or in its members, it is more difficult to define success.

This study aims to contribute to a better understanding of the definitions of success and failure in social intervention with multi-problem poor families, focussing on the perspective of the practitioners. To this end, 15 practitioners with professional experience of intervention with multi-problem poor families were interviewed.

1. THE IMPORTANCE OF DEFINING SUCCESS AND FAILURE IN SOCIAL INTERVENTION

Success and failure appear to be very intuitive concepts and for this reason, the attempt to define them may seem, in a first attempt, to be practically useless. But, there are some questions which deserve attention: What do we mean when we characterise an intervention as being a failure or a success? Are we judging a particular process or model of intervention? Are we referring to the way in which the intervention was planned or to the way in which it was carried out by the practitioners? Do we pay attention to the way in which the client made an effort in the process? Are we referring to the effects on the client? Or are we only focussing on a problem or a symptom of the client? But the fundamental question is: How do we know whether the intervention was a success or a failure?

Assessing the success/failure of any intervention demands the clarification of these concepts. For example, when intervention with aggressors (e.g. domestic violence) is analysed, it is the conceptualisation which determines success or failure: some researchers use the significant reduction of physical violence as an indicator in order to justify the success of a programme (Neidig, 1986); others consider that the transformation only occurs when the aggressor is prepared to act socially against domestic violence (Gondolf, 1987). Thus, different social actors can have different perspectives on success/failure; for example, with multi-problem poor families different practitioners are involved in the intervention, as well as various family members, the informal network and the community. Multiple viewpoints can easily emerge; a health professional may emphasize the reduction of the symptoms, political actors may be more concerned about the crime rates and the communities about the disruption a person with mental health problems can cause to social life.

In essence, the success or failure of an intervention should be defined in ethical terms (what we are doing and what effects are we getting), in scientific terms (getting better results) and in practical terms (adjusting the processes of intervention and expectations).

From an ethical perspective, it is crucial to ensure the promotion of the well-being of the clients, respecting their values and guaranteeing the best use of resources (e.g. Minow, 1994; Neher, 1988). Besides this, some ethical questions are essential when the criteria of success/failure are being discussed: for example, euthanasia may be a sick person's wish, and for this reason, achieving it constitutes success for them; but, for a doctor who defines his/her mission as saving lives, attending to the wish of the client represents a failure. So the criteria of success need to be discussed and some choices need to be made, such as (e.g. Perkins, 2001): who should or has the right to define the desired success/failure (the client, society, the practitioner or someone else).

The scientific process should contribute to the improvement of social conditions, providing credible information to legitimate the action of social agents relative to the success/failure of the interventions which seek social benefits (Lipsey and Cordray, 2000). The discussion and the conceptualisation of the success/failure of the intervention is fundamental to the improvement of programmes and the provision of guidance for practitioners in order to develop, improve or adapt the processes of intervention to the needs of clients and communities. In this way, learning about success/failure requires that we know what makes it possible and in what contexts, and also has an impact on social expectations: for example, practitioners who work with multi-problem poor families indicate that communities expect them to exercise social control and normalise these families in short periods of time, identifying these circumstances with success.

In practice, different fields of intervention have come to emphasise more and more the importance of developing programmes with empirical validation, because this allows us (Santisteban *et al.*, 2006): to minimize the use of intervention processes with low impact or which may have adverse effects; to facilitate professional development and the implementation of intervention; to influence those responsible for the policies of financing and support of intervention based on the evaluation of success.

Etymologically, the word "success" derives from the Latin *successu*, which means to have success, realise and/or complete. The evaluation of success/failure and its promotion are present in different domains of human activity. Let us look at some examples.

The Food and Nutrition Service (FNS - USA) decided to measure the success and effectiveness of its programme (Doner, 1997). Consequently it began to incorporate components of nutritional education in order to provide better nutritional support and make better use of their limited resources. The success or failure, causes and conditions of humanitarian military intervention have come to be increasingly debated. This type of intervention is controversial, being based on the premise that it is only justified when it is reasonably certain that this option will do more good than harm (Seybolt, 2007). In public health, intervention with the population for the prevention of illnesses is based on the reduction of risk behaviours, and are developed and implemented in such a way as to restrain the conditions which contribute to these illnesses (Sorensen *et al.*, 1998). Success is defined by the decrease in risk behaviours, and, consequently, in the incidence of illness in the greater number of individuals who make up the target public. Market failure is the term used to describe the situation in which markets do not distribute goods and services efficiently (Bowles, 2004). For economists, the term would be applied in situations of dramatic inefficacy, or when institutions which do not belong to the market (such as, the police or fire brigade) are more efficient than the market solutions. However, this term is also used to describe situations in which market forces do not serve the public interest. Besides these examples, there are many other areas in which success and failure are studied, such as: education, domestic violence, crime.

This transversal interest in success/failure reveals complementary meanings and perceptions. Although the concepts are different, always present is the idea of *doing the best that can be done*, even if it is not the ideal, to promote the quality of life of everybody, family and community, make the best use of resource, promote benefits (despite the possibility of some ill-effects being inevitable) and reduce risk.

The definition of success/failure can probably be based on some general guidelines, which will have to be adapted to each circumstance. Besides this, there will always have to be a balance between the ideal and the possible; in other words, success is sometimes only that which can be achieved in the context. In some cases, success/failure is not in an outcome which lasts, but in a process which unfolds, going through the best and the worst moments.

2. DEFINITION OF INTERVENTION AND IMPLICATIONS FOR THE DEFINITION OF SUCCESS /FAILURE

In general, intervention is a deliberate process by which it is hoped change will be introduced in the lives of people, families or communities. But conceptualisations of intervention have evolved through epistemological change.

The conception of typical modernist/positivist (traditional) intervention, embodied in the medical model, is characterised as: individualist (centred on a symptomatic subject) and pathologising (the symptom is conceived as an intra-psychic pathology). In this approach, the one who has the pathology is the individual, isolated from the context, with no influence from the surrounding cultural and social environment. The solution is in the hands of a specialist, extraneous to the system (neutral and non-participating), who masters interventional techniques and is thus in possession of the power of decision and resolution. The objective of the intervention is the cure, and this develops out of the exhaustive diagnosis which characterises the pathology and categorises it in systems of classification (like the DSM). In this way, the causes of the pathology are identified and the solution lies in eliminating the causes; if this is impossible, the subject is considered irrecuperable, and can be supported by compensatory measures (Sousa *et al.*, 2007).

At the beginning of the 20th Century, this method was found to be insufficient. The systemic revolution occurred in the United States of America, with the slogan *Meet to Understand* (Rosnay, 1977). The systemic model has evolved, and a significant revolution noted: from 1st Cybernetics (corresponding to the classical developments originating in the fields of engineering and informatics) to 2nd Cybernetics (influenced by Biology and Chemistry). The epistemological changes in this turn focus on two aspects (Sluzki, cited in Benoit *et al.*, 1988): from the homeostatic model to the evolutive model, from observed to "observing" or "self-observing" systems.

The 1st cybernetics, as the initial moment of a new paradigm, retains some remnants of the previous paradigm but evolution in relation to modernism is accentuated, essentially in the substitution of a linear with a circular causality, implying that it is impossible to isolate the individual from their environment, since both co-evolve; and because, the relationships and the whole assume greater importance vis-à-vis the parts. (Relvas, 1999). In this more classic formulation, a series of deep alterations in ways of acting can be outlined in relation to the medical model. The conception of mental illness changes, since the symptoms come to be understood as a logical behaviour (message), coherent and with a role in the family; in other words, it is a part of the relational game, which in the circular interaction, has the aim of maintaining stability (homeostatic mechanism). The concept of pathology becomes inexact, being substituted by dysfunctionality, indicating that the symptomatic subject is only one of the links in the dysfunctional interactive chain, coming to be called the identified patient (IP), since he/she is not *the sick person*, but the carrier of the dysfunctionality of family relations.

The 2nd Cybernetics developed in particular through the work of Humberto Maturana and Francisco Varela (biologists of the Santiago School) and Ilya Prigogine (Chemistry Nobel Prize – 1977). The two biologists presented a theory on the organisation of living systems, in which they demonstrate how the external world of facts and objects is not directly accessible, but is (re)created through each cognitive act (Maturana and Varela, 1980). The key concept is autopoiesis (autonomy or self-organisation), according to which the system has autonomy to keep itself organised in spite of external disturbances; in other words, it is not directed from outside, since the communicational exchange (informational openness) is accompanied by organisational autonomy (operational closure). Prigogine (1980) shows that equilibrium is never static, but permanently dynamic, although the direction of change is unpredictable from a point of bifurcation (degree of greater distance from the previous equilibrium). The work of these authors has decisive implications for the processes of systemic intervention: if systems are autonomous they follow their own rules and make their own choices. Therefore they cannot be regulated from outside (self-competence for change). If the world of facts is recreated then the observer participates actively in what he/she observes (observing systems); if change is unpredictable (there are no general rules), it is not directed from the outside but occurs within the system, which maintains its organisation, altering the structure (self-reference); stability and change coexist in systems, so the family is not a context of stability but also of change (evolutive model).

In this way of thinking, the value of the symptom is found in the (dysfunctional) interaction of the identified patient with the family and/or with other contexts and in temporal and historic dimensions. This valorisation of how the symptom fits within the individual and group context reintroduces the individual, neglected in the classical systemic models. The normal-dysfunctional relationship also undergoes transformation, given that it is understood that all systems have competences (self-curing solution). Simultaneously, they are self-organised, so it is through the activation of their competences that change may occur (self-solution). The practitioner (participant observer) has no control over or capacity to determine change, assuming the role of catalyser or facilitator of change. The intervention works without an *a priori* theory, the models here are (possible) *lenses* for reading and evaluation. It is the auto-reflexivity of the therapeutic system and the recursivity of client- therapist concerns which is sought. A solution (not *the* solution) presents itself because the families are competent (Ausloos, 1996), self-organised and contexts of change.

In this context, Doherty and Carroll (2002) introduce *family-centered community building* as an emerging arena which combines family perspectives with traditional community work. This confluence allows us to overcome three false dichotomies which have structured intervention paradigms: private *versus* public, the role of consumer/client *versus* practitioner; individual therapy *versus* community work.

The classic separation between private and public assumes that there are problems which are only private and others which are only public (including the cultural, economic and political spheres). By means of an example, the authors show the error of this distinction: people who have a serious and persistent mental illness are, as a rule, discriminated against and consequently abandoned by the community, which increases the frequency of their crises. By separating the roles of the consumer and the provider of a service, it is assumed that the professionals are specialists in the problems of the client, while these are only worried about getting the best service for themselves as individuals (without seeking anything good for the community). However, clients and practitioners are both citizens and this dichotomy excludes one alternative: a partnership between citizens. The barrier between individual therapy (clinical work with subjects, small groups or families) and community work (activities based on community groups) arises from the fact that the professionals of these areas are different (with different training and competences) and that the clients present disparate problematic circumstances. In fact, they are involved (however implicitly) in the work of community partnership.

3. THE SUCCESS /FAILURE OF INTERVENTION AND ASSOCIATED CONCEPTS

In the literature, the reference to success/failure of social and community intervention is associated to several meanings, which have been grouped in five areas (table 1): intervention process; client process; results; process/evolution; and satisfaction.

Table 1. Definitions of success/failure

Concept	Definition
1. Intervention process: planning and implementation of the intervention	
Fidelity of the intervention	Adherence to the intervention (whether the intervention went as planned) and differentiation (degree to which one intervention can be differentiated from another). It allows us to analyse whether one intervention is more successful than another.
1.2. Timing (time and duration of intervention)	In some cases the intervention should be immediate (for example, in the case of hunger), but in other situations more time is necessary (for example, in the case of substance abuse). Normally, the promptness and speed and the intervention is associated with success.
1.3. Process of negotiation or collaboration between professional and client	Adjustment of objectives and intervention strategies between professionals and clients has come to be considered an element of success.
2. Client process: way in which the clients accept and become involved in the intervention	
2.1.Retention and involvement	Clients who are involved in and remain in the process of intervention will have greater probability of obtaining better results.
2.2. Drop-out and refusal	An intervention is not successful if it is not acceptable to the clients.
2.3. Acceptance	An intervention which is accepted by the majority of potential clients is more successful, at least in retaining the target population.
2.4. Compliance	An intervention is more successful when the clients follow the instructions (prescriptions) of the professionals.
2.5. Involvement	When clients are involved in the planning of and decisions about the intervention, then it is more probable that the intervention will respond adequately to the needs of the clients.
2.6. Characteristics of the clients	The characteristics of clients determine the levels of success which can be reached (for example, a paraplegic person can enter the job market, but in the current state of scientific evolution they will not be able to walk again).

Table 1. (Continued)

Concept	Definition
3. Outcomes: effects of the intervention on the target public	
3.1. Meeting Objectives	This category is associated with: solving problems, modifying behaviours, reducing or eliminating symptoms. It is related to the objectives defined for the intervention after the diagnosis; a successful intervention reaches its objectives, normally associated with the attainment of more normative levels of functioning.
4. Change: related to the promotion of the functioning of the client, even if in a different direction from that initially defined for the intervention.	
4.1. Change (positive)	Centred on the process and the result. Success occurs when the client improves his/her well-being and quality of life.
4.2. Clinical Significance	This refers to the practical importance of the effect / process of intervention, or in other words if the intervention makes or not a real difference to the daily life of clients and those with whom they relate.
4.3. Adverse or undesired results	This refers to the undesired effects which lower the level of functioning of the client or increase the risk of diverse problems (health, soicla, phychological).
5. (Dis)Satisfaction: approval and disapproval of the intervention	
5.1. (Dis)Satisfaction of the clients	Clients reveal themselves to be satisfied or dissatisfied with the intervention.
5.2. (Dis)Satisfaction of the professionals	Professionals are satisfied with the intervention or feel frustrated and impotent.
5.3. (Dis)Satisfaction of the community	The community includes the client's informal network, diverse elements of the formal network not directly involved in the intervention, institutional directors, political decision-makers and the community in general. They may feel that the intervention is going well, since the clients no longer request support and display adequate social behaviours; or dissatisfied, since the clients remain in the support system.

Based on: Kazdin, 1986; Sorensen et al., 1988; Perkins, 1996; Hogue, Liddle and Rowe, 1996; Hampson and Beavers, 1996; Cunningham and Henggeler, 1999; Reppucci, Woolard and Fried, 1999; Tompson *et al.*, 2000; Lipsey and Cordray, 2000; Perkins, 2001; Chambless and Ollendick, 2001.

Intervention Process

Success/failure centred on the intervention process is translated into how the planning and implementation of the intervention contributes to the success/failure. In this context, three aspects stand out: the fidelity of the intervention, the time (timing and duration) and negotiation and/or collaboration between clients and professionals.

The fidelity of the intervention has been emphasized in recent years, involving two concepts: adherence (or integrity) and differentiation (e.g. Moncher and Prinz, 1991; Startup and Shapiro, 1993). Fidelity refers to the extent to which the intervention, as it is implemented, includes the stipulated (adequate) components and avoids those which are unpredicted (inadequate) (Yeaton and Sechrest, 1981). Adherence measures seek to answer the question (Hogue, Liddle and Rowe, 1996): did the intervention go as planned? Differentiation refers to the degree in which one intervention can be distinguished from another (Kazdin, 1986). The analysis of fidelity allows us to understand whether an intervention respects its presuppositions and is different from other interventions. Following this line of thought it can be understood whether one intervention is more successful than another and what factors interfere so that the intervention goes or not as planned.

Time has also emerged as a criterion of success/failure, associated to: timing, the intervention will be more successful if implemented at the right moment; duration, the intervention ought to be planned so that its duration is adequate for the problematic situation (e.g. Hazelrigg, Cooper and Borduin, 1987; Tubbs, Roy and Burtons, 2005).

Negotiation and/or collaboration between clients and professionals (or services) have also come to be increasingly pointed out as elements of success/failure, since it allows the intervention to be as adequate as possible for the clients. So, greater success can be expected when professionals and clients negotiate their objectives and strategies as equals (e.g. Hazelrigg, Cooper and Borduin, 1987; Madsen, 1999).

The Process of the Clients

Success/failure has also been conceptualised in terms of the client process, bearing in mind that: involving and retaining clients in the intervention is a determining factor; drop-outs and refusal/acceptance indicate whether an intervention is or not adequate; the fulfilment of the indications or the involvement of the client are elements which ought to be considered for the success/failure of the intervention; in addition the characteristics of the client condition the objectives and strategies of the intervention (for example, elderly clients tend to adhere less sell to interventional proposals).

The involvement and retention of clients constitute factors in the intervention process (Cunningham and Henggeler, 1999). It is often considered that the client has to be involved in and to accept the intervention; in other words, these are pre-conditions for intervention, and their absence will determine its failure. But more recent perspectives indicate that involvement and retention are crucial and relevant moments in the process of change. A successful intervention concentrates on involving and retaining the clients, but does not consider that failure is owed to the incapacity or lack of motivation of the client to commit to the intervention.

Drop-outs and refusal/acceptance rates should be taken into account in any reference to the success or failure of an intervention, since they are indicators of the degree of acceptance by the clients (Perkins, 2001). When success/failure is assessed, it is frequently the case that only subjects who accepted the intervention are included, despite the possible existence of a reasonable percentage of refusals and drop-outs. The literature suggests that for an intervention to be considered a success, it should be acceptable to the majority of clients to whom it is directed.

Traditionally, clients have been absent from the planning process and their participation limited to their account and demonstration of their symptoms and following the advice and/or guidelines of the practitioners. In this case, we are witnessing a dichotomy in the definition of success/failure: conceived as a process in which the clients comply or do not comply with the prescriptions of the professionals versus its definition as the degree to which the clients are or not involved in the decision-making process, development and implementation of the intervention (e.g. Sorensen *et al.*, 1998; Rojano, 2004).

The characteristics of the clients (be they individuals, families, groups or communities) have implications for the definition of success/failure, normally revealed in the expression (e.g. Hampson and Beavers, 1996; Summers, Templeton-McMann and Fuger, 1997; Tompson *et al.*, 2000): *every case is a case*. In fact, the success/failure that can be expected or is possible depends on the characteristics of the target group: for example: in the case of a paraplegic person, it is expected that they be as autonomous as possible and socially integrated; but, someone who has suffered an injury to a leg is expected to walk again. It is also found that professionals claim that failure is due, for example, to the clients' mental health problems when this was the reason for requesting the intervention (Sousa *et al.*, 2007).

Outcomes

Essentially, however, success/failure has been defined and measured at the level of the outcomes and of the process/evolution of the client.

When outcomes are the focus, we are assessing the degree to which an intervention reaches the desired outcomes and determining the impact of the programme (e.g. Gurman, Kniskern, and Pinsof, 1986; Perkins, 2001). The term outcome is habitually used to describe desirable effects and to describe "products" (visible at the end) of the intervention with the client (Lipsey and Cordray, 2000): such as, behaviours, knowledge, values, attitudes and competences. The intervention is focussed on reaching objectives defined at the outset, describing the logic which links the activities of the intervention to its outcomes (which has contributed greatly to the improvement of intervention). It is related to reaching the objectives defined for the intervention (associated with normative levels of functioning): reducing, eliminating or easing symptoms, solving problems and/or modifying risk behaviours. In this context, it is also relevant to look at the outcomes which occur during the intervention and the mediating variables, since they serve to identify the proximity/distance of the outcomes to what was expected.

Focus on the reduction, elimination or easing of symptoms has its roots in the field of mental health (Perkins, 2001). It is assumed that once this objective is reached, everything else will fall into place: the reduction of a symptom is a necessary and sufficient condition for the improvement of the quality of life of the person who experiences the symptom. Several authors have argued that this association is not linear or guaranteed (e.g. Mirin and Namerow, 1991), and so the occupational, family, social and cultural integration of the client must be looked at. In fact, reaching objectives which are associated with the solving of problems and/or the modification of behaviours has consequences for the prevention of other risk factors (Smith *et al.*, 1998). For example, knowing that problems with alcohol are associated with contingent factors, modifying the alcohol consumption behaviour can also alter the contingency.

Change (Process/Evolution)

Reference to the attainment of objectives is directly associated with the objectives defined for the intervention, which are, as a rule, concrete and measurable. When success/failure is defined as change, the autonomy of the systems in which the intervention takes place is taken for granted (in other words, the practitioner and the client enter into an interventional relationship), meaning that they can change/evolve in different directions. Thus, success/failure is a process and a result, which is co-constructed throughout the intervention (e.g. Sorensen *et al.*, 1998). Success means that, during the intervention, the client made positive (Mirin and Namerow, 1991) or clinically significant (Jacobson and Truax, 1991) changes, even if these do not coincide with the initial intentions of the interventions, but which improve the quality of life of the client. It is also relevant to mention adverse or undesired outcomes of the intervention (e.g. Mashal, Feldman and Sigal, 1989; Cunningham and Henggeler, 1999) which occur and demonstrate the importance of the evolving process. This reference reminds us of the need for the intervention to adjust and adapt and not be something which is defined at the outset and carried through to the end.

Positive change (Malarewicz, 1999) constitutes a process and an outcome, revealing credible evidence of progress towards a more funcional life and increased well-being for the client. Clinical significance (Kazdin, 1999) refers to the value or practical importance of the effects or changes resulting from the intervention; in other words, whether the intervention made a real (practical and genuine) difference to the life of the client and those with whom he/she interacts. It is related to the evaluation of practical and significant changes to the client which occur in the course of the intervention, including: improvement in interpersonal relationships and role taking, increase in self-esteem and self-confidence; improvement in the capacity to manage or to come to terms with a particular situation (crisis or problem); increase in social integration and reduced stigmatisation; increase in the sense of self-control and involvement in the activities. It is associated with the empowerment of the clients, defined as the promotion of autonomy of individuals, families, groups and/or communities.

Satisfaction

The emphasis on the satisfaction of those involved is also used as a measure of success/failure (Rogers *et al.*, 1997; Gingerich, 2000). The satisfaction of the practitioners tends to be associated with the sense of having done "a good job", with positive impact on the clients, which makes them feel motivated and competent. The dissatisfaction is, almost always, associated with the sensation that the effort given to the intervention did not have the desired results, leading to a sense of frustration, doubt in their competence and impotence (*they don't know how to do better*).

The clients experience satisfaction when they consider themselves well looked after by the services and the practitioners; in other words, they feel that the professionals tried to help them, solve their problems and/or that in some way they helped them create a more positive atmosphere in their lives. Dissatisfaction occurs when clients distance themselves from the formal services, when there are conflicts between clients and practitioners or the clients demonstrate apathy. These circumstances generate feelings of impotence and incapacity to improve the quality of their lives.

The same happens with the other members of the community, who are involved in the intervention process in some way. This perspective on success/failure reveals the possibility that there exist different expectations of success/failure, since not all those involved make the same evaluation of the intervention process.

4. RESEARCH ON SUCCESS/FAILURE OF INTERVENTION

Research on success/failure is very vast and has taken place in different domains of social intervention. A review of the literature indicates that it has centred on (e.g. Gurman, Kniskern, and Pinsof, 1986; Bell and Bell, 1989; Green and Herget, 1991; Newberry, Alexander, and Turner, 1991; Gingerich, 2000): comparing methods, programmes and schools of intervention; assessing intervention (experimental group); comparing groups not subject to intervention or subject to placebo intervention (control groups); there has been a tendency to group clients taking into account the diagnosis of the patient (for example, anorexia or depression); to study the effects of intervention taking into consideration the expected or desired effects; analyse variables which influence the process and outcomes (mediators and predictors); to analyse the satisfaction of clients and others involved.

The experimental design based on quantitative measures has been the most chosen method for this analysis, but it has been recognised that these methods of assessing the success/failure of intervention are problematic and a series of limitations have been recorded (e.g. Jacobson and Truax, 1991; Green and Herget, 1991; Gurman, Kniskern, and Pinsof, 1986; Lipsey and Cordray, 2000): i) the constitution and pairing of the experimental and control groups are problematic, for important sources of variability have been found after the recruitment of the sample; ii) they provide little information which explains why certain effects were or were not found; iii) the use of statistical significance tests is limited, principally because they don't provide information about the variability of answers in the experimental sample and statistical significance can have a limited connection with the clinical meaning of change; iv) as a rule, the samples are very reduced; v) normally the same type of measure is used (for example, scales, observation, the professional's report), although they may focus on diverse variables (for example, stress, satisfaction); vi) many studies fail to note who abandons the interventions and under what conditions.

Besides the limitations, these studies have provided fundamental contributions for the improvement of intervention at the most varied levels. But perhaps the main limitation is the focus on changes which occur as a result of the intervention, taking into account the objectives of the programme and the intervention plan. The majority of studies fail in their analysis of the process of change, of the positive and negative alterations which occur as a result of the intervention and of the influence of other factors (besides the intervention) in the results obtained. This is why evaluation is increasingly designed on the basis of theories which support the programmes and the extensive collection of data in order to include descriptive information about the implementation of the programme, the characteristics of the clients and patterns of change (Bernal, 2006).

Besides this, research has been very fruitful regarding the factors which determine the success/failure of interventions, but little attention has been given to the definition of success/failure. This seems to be a given *a priori*, as if it were obvious what success/failure are and that they are the same for everyone. The most common and deduced definitions of success/failure are based on the outcomes achieved, comparative to the objectives defined for the intervention (e.g. Perkins, 2001). This way of defining success/failure is based on a positivist perspective of intervention, enveloped in an aura of reparation. In any case, the success of a social intervention refers in general to the benefits, principally the impact of making a positive difference (which can be social, economic, family and/or personal) in the life of people (Jacobson and Truax, 1991).

The definitions of success/failure can be associated with two theoretical approaches: the medical model which conceptualises through results (more classical); and the collaborative model which defines through the process of change (more recent, 2nd cybernetics). These two approaches have two small, but relevant implications in the conceptualisation of the intervention: solving problems *versus* promoting change; the solution *versus* a solution; success *versus* some success.

5. SUCCESS/FAILURE IN SOCIAL INTERVENTION: MULTI-PROBLEM POOR FAMILIES

Intervention with multi-problem poor families has been characterised by a lack of success, principally because it is rare for these families to be removed from the multi-problem situation and from poverty. Dependency on the formal support services therefore continues (e.g. Summers, Templeton-McMann, and Fuger, 1997; Matos and Sousa, 2004). Intervention with these families has been based on a model of control, centred on normalisation, control and social regulation.

From this viewpoint, multi-problem poor families have been defined and understood through their problems, pathologies and fragilities (e.g. Kagan, 1986; Sousa and Eusébio, 2005). The control perspective obliges professionals to focus on aspects of deficit, and complicates the way in which families with problems are treated as the perception of their competences becomes more difficult. The idea of the professionals' expertise also means that these families are multi-assisted, because, living with multiple problems (individual and family) they need a range of specialists to solve each problem. (e.g. Imber-Black, 1998).

So success and failure tend to be defined as opposites: success is defined as the solution of the problems of the families and their members, expecting that they become self-sufficient families without problems. However, intervention on this basis of this model has not been successful, most of the reports indicating that the problems are perpetuated over generations, that these families remain attached to formal systems of support during many years and that frustration is experienced by professionals, who, in spite of feeling that they have been technically competent, see their efforts thwarted (e.g. Imber-Black, 1988; Sousa and Eusébio, 2005). Different aspects have been identified to justify this failure (e.g. Kagan and Schlosberg, 1989; Colapinto, 1995; Sharlin, Shamai and Sharlin, 2000; Sousa, Ribeiro and

Rodrigues, 2007): fragmentation and lack of coordination of the intervention; focus on problems and on individuals; absence of the family perspective in the intervention process.

Fragmentation and lack of coordination of the services derive from the fact that intervention is focussed on problems and individuals and on professional expertise to solve them. Multi-problem poor families receive intervention from diverse practitioners and institutions, since each problem has a specialist. In this way, the family process is also fragmented and the intention to unite and bond the family is not reached, since frontiers and family cohesion are weakened, leading to a growing dependency on formal services and the consequent incapacitation of families and their members (e.g. Elizur and Minuchin, 1989; Boyd-Franklin, 1989).

A focus on problems and individuals involves diagnosis (the basis of intervention in the medical model), centred on each problem of each subject; in other words, a process which attempts to transform a complex system of relationships and problems into a trivial and linear system composed of isolated problems so that the fulcral points of family relations are never reached and the problems continue to occur and to perpetuate (e.g. Kagan, 1986; Sousa, 2004). In these circumstances, the intervention does not have a clear direction and loses itself in the attempt to solve each problem, without reaching the functioning of the families, demanding huge commitment from professionals and the families without obtaining results which reflect this effort, since it was badly directed (Summers, Templeton-McMann, and Fuger, 1997). The perspective of the clients is neglected in the intervention process since it is the specialist who has the competence to determine what is wrong and to prescribe the solution which the client has to fulfil in order to reach the objectives.

A consequence of this model of intervention is the incapacitation of the families and their members (Sousa and Eusébio, 2005): i) if the intervention developed by professionals is successful, the subjects feel that the response to their problems is professional help and so they feel incompetent and incapable; ii) if the intervention is unsuccessful, the family feels that not even the professionals can manage to help them.

The findings and frustrations with failure have led to the rethinking of strategies and models of intervention. Essentially, it has been pointed out that the existing models are not adjusted to the characteristics of the families and, that success should be defined and constructed on the basis of these characteristics (e.g. Summers, Templeton-McMann and Fuger, 1997). In fact, the model underpinning social policies, institutional projects and even professional training is more directed towards families who face an isolated crisis and much less towards *chronically* dysfunctional families (Minuchin, Colapinto and Minuchin, 1998). The unique and special character of multi-problem poor families makes the usual interventions ineffective (e.g. Fleischer, 1975; Cerqueira *et al.*, 2003). In fact, the attempt is made to solve each of the identified problems, which is rarely successful (above all in the long-term) because *new* and *old* problems are constantly occurring. So the problem and the interventions are perpetuated as there is always a problem needing the intervention of a practitioner.

The choice of a collaborative model with multi-problem poor families demands the recognition that, as with all families, these have competences and problem-solving skills. Basically, studies with these families have focussed on the factors which determine the success/failure of intervention. The literature recommends that the intervention is associated with the characteristics of the families so that the success/failure of the intervention can be defined (e.g. Kagan and Schlosberg, 1989; Summers, Templeton-McMann, and Fuger, 1997; Krumer-Nevo, Slonim-Nevo and Hirshenzon-Segev, 2006).

The main characteristics of these families are (e.g. Kagan and Schlosberg, 1989; McMann and Summers, Templeton-McMann and Fuger, 1997; Sousa *et al.*, 2007): face multiple challenges; experience chronic crises; feel alienated; feel low self-esteem and incapacity; have fragile financial and emotional resources. Success is attained using strategies which respond to these characteristics and improve the quality of life of these families: establishing relations of trust, so that the family can feel accepted and is involved in the intervention; providing practical help and materials which allow the family to have a guarantee of economic subsistence and to be emotionally available for interventions which focus on individual and family functioning; recognising that for these families, intervention has to be extended in time, since the problems are vast and imprinted on their functioning, as a rule, over generations; organising a series of complementary interventions designed to respond to the diverse problems of the family; establishing a clear direction for the intervention, and sticking to it, even when a crisis has to be dealt with; indicating a case manager who has a relationship of trust with the family, keeps the intervention on track and articulates the contributions of other professionals and institutions; mobilising the families' competences to help them become more autonomous and self-confident. .

6. OBJECTIVES

This study intends to contribute to a better understanding of how professionals define success and failure in intervention with multi-problem poor families. The results will permit us to understand how these concepts may be influencing the success/failure of intervention and will have an impact on the definition of successful practices.

7. METHODOLOGY

Instrument

This study is based on an interview made up of four open questions:

1) Define the criteria which allow you to recognise the success/failure of an intervention.
2) Select a case which you consider successful and indicate the criteria which allow you to recognise the success of the intervention.
3) Select a case which you consider unsuccessful and indicate the criteria which allow you to recognise the lack of success of the intervention.
4) Imagining a scale of 0 to 20 (White and Epston, 1990), in which 0 indicates least success and 20 indicates most success, what score would you give to the case? How would you know that the family had risen a point or dropped a point?

All the interviews were carried out by the second author in the professionals' place of work. The interviews lasted between 27 minutes and 48 minutes.

Sample

The sample was collected in the district of Aveiro (Portugal) in the councils of Aveiro, Ílhavo and Albergaria-a-Velha. The sample was selected from the professionals of the Social Services and the Private Institutions of Social Solidarity (IPSSs), which develop intervention with multi-problem poor families. Authorisation was requested from the institutions to carry out the study, then the professionals were contacted and the objective of the research was explained to them. It was considered essential that each professional had to indicate a successful case and an unsuccessful case in order to: avoid positive utopias (everything always goes well) or negative scenarios (nothing is ever solved); be able to contrast the conceptualisation of the same professional regarding success and failure.

The criteria given to the professionals for the selection of the cases were: i) at the time of the interview, they should be in a finished or accompanying stage of intervention, but not in an active stage in order to be able to reflect better on the intervention's success or failure; ii) the most active stage of the intervention should have taken place about a year previously in order to avoid difficulties in remembering the process; iii) the professional should have been actively involved in the intervention. It is important to point out that all the professionals who were contacted found it easy to identify cases of failure and difficulty in finding cases of success.

After this contact with the professionals, 15 were selected for having accepted to be a part of the study and fulfilling the identification criteria of the cases. These professionals contacted the families and got their informed consent, in a context of research, anonymity and confidentiality, to answer questions about the intervention with the family. All the families agreed to cooperate.

The sample comprises 15 social service workers, all of the female gender, with an average professional experience with multi-problem poor families of 7.9 years (ranging from 2 years to 20 years). The average age of the interviewees is 32.9 years (ranging from 27 years to 42 years). Three interviewees work in the District Centre of Solidarity and Social Welfare and 12 in IPSSs in the councils of Aveiro (6), Ílhavo (2) and Albergaria-a-Velha (4) with agreements with Social Welfare.

Data Analysis

All the interviews were taped, transcribed and submitted to content analysis by the authors. In this process the literature and research in the area of success and failure of intervention and multi-problem poor families were taken into account, but we tried to be descriptive and to maintain, wherever possible, the discourse of the interviewed professionals (maintaining their words and/or expressions). There were two stages to the process: i) the characterisation of categories and subcategories of definition of success and failure, considering general definitions and those referring to cases; ii) the classification of responses into the identified (sub)categories. The first stage focussed on the creation and testing of a system of categorisation following a process of successive refinement. It involved two independent judges (the two authors). Each judge read the interviews and developed a list of categories and subcategories. Then the judges met to compare and discuss the proposals until agreement was reached. Then each judge randomly categorised two interviews in order to confirm the adequacy of the system of categorisation. Finally, a list of categories and sub-categories was made, including the definition and examples. (table 2). In a second stage, the two judges independently categorised each interview. They then met to analyse their (dis)agreements. The agreement between the judges (value calculated by the division of the number or agreements with the number of disagreements) was 94.2% for the general definitions and 95% for the definitions referring to the cases, which represents a good level of fidelity (Miles and Huberman, 1984). Finally, the situations in which there was disagreement were discussed and this process led to full agreement.

In the definition of the categories a difficulty emerged: the professionals defined the family as the nucleus of intervention, but in their discourse they referred to a family member (the user or client), as a rule, the one who has the problem, or symptom, the person who sought to get help or the member of the family who emerges as the link with the support services. For this reason the definition of the categories sometimes adopts the nomenclatura "the family", at other times "the client", reflecting the frequency with which professionals in their discourse associated one or other word to the (sub)category.

9. RESULTS

General Definition of Success and Failure

The interviewees indicated that it was very difficult to define the success and failure of an intervention without referring to a specific case: *"it depends, every case is a case!"*; *"it can't be pre-defined, it depends on the cases!"*

At the level of the global definition of success/failure (table 3), the two most salient categories for success and failure coincide, although in inverted positions: empowerment of the client (1st in success, 2nd in failure); client process (2nd in success, 1st in failure). The third most frequent category differs: negotiation process between professionals and clients (success) and process/change (failure).

When considering the subcategories of success and failure, the two most frequent are symmetrical: i) the client become autonomous *versus* the client remains dependent on formal services; ii) the client fulfils *versus* the client does not fulfil the objectives and/or plan of the intervention. The following subcategories differ: the objectives defined are suitable for the family and attainable and the involvement between the professional and the family is adequate (success); the client is not motivated for the intervention and/or change (failure).

Table 2. Categories and subcategories: definitions and examples

(Sub)Categories	Success	Failure
1. Planning of the intervention process: related to the suitability of the process of planning and implementation of the intervention		
1.1. Definition of objectives	1.1. Suitable for the family and attainable The objectives are suitable for the needs and skills of the family and/or user; they are attainable because there are resources. "The objectives were designed progressively in accordance with the goals met by the family!"	.1.1 Unsuitable for the family and /or unattainable The objectives are not suitable for the needs and/or skills of the families. Or do not exist formal resources for them to be reached. "We didn't get the desired effect because the mother's objectives were different from ours!"
2. Client process: refers to the involvement of the family/client and to the potentialities / difficulties which they reveal in order to involve themselves in the intervention process .		
2.1. (Non)fulfilment of the intervention plan by the client.	2.1. The client fulfils the objectives and the intervention plan. The client carries out the indications given by the practitioners, for example, going to the meetings or frequenting professional training courses. "The family did everything that was proposed!"	2.1. The client does not fulfil the objectives and the intervention plan The clients do not carry out the indications of the practitioners, for example, they miss the school meetings. The professionals think that the families do not carry out their instructions because: i) they don't want to (disinterested); ii) they have individual and/or cognitive limitations; iii) they are not capable of taking advantage of the resources at their disposal. "She didn't always comply. She accepted, but putting it into practice was difficult."
2.2. (De)Motivation of the client	2.2. The client is motivated for intervention and change The client is motivated and willing to change because he/she is aware of his/her needs and problems and so seeks help only when necessary. "The mother was a fighter; she did everything to improve her situation!"	2.2. The client is not motivated for intervention and/or change The client is unmotivated and/or unwilling to change, owing to: i) cognitive, social (e.g. lack of social support), personal (e.g. lack of self-esteem) and/or family (e.g. lack of support) limitations; ii) he/she has no expectation that life can improve: iii) he/she is not conscious (of the seriousness) of his/her problems and/or needs. "When people do not really know what is happening to them or do not want to know, it is very difficult to move forward!"
3. Process of negotiation between professionals and clients: related to the process of involvement relationship and communication between family and professionals.		
3.1. (Non)Cooperation of the family	3.1. The family cooperates The client accepts the intervention and is actively involved. "The husband accompanied the wife to the sessions in the Parenting School and discussed what he learnt with her!"	3.1 The family does not cooperate and/or refuses the intervention The client does not accept the intervention, or accepts but eventually gives up. "They agreed to participate, but then only turned up twice!"

(Sub)Categories	Success	Failure
3.2 (Non) Involvement between professional and family	3.2 The involvement between professional and family is adequate There is a relationship of proximity and good communication between the professional and the family; the professional always supports the family; family and professional negotiate and collaborate. "The practitioner was always supportive, he/she never gave up on the user; the practitioner really wanted to help!"	3.2. The involvement between professional and family is not adequate There is an absence of and/or difficulty in negotiation and/or collaboration between the professional and the client; little involvement on the part of the professional and/or the institution; absence of proximity and/or poor communication between professional and client. The professional loses *command* of the intervention, feels that s/he can not help; does not maintain a clear direction, does not manage to give support in a permanent way: does not know where to start or how to turn the situation round, does not pay attention and/or does not want to know. "We've spent too many years trying to get her to change! We no longer have the energy to keep trying!"
3.3. Interinstitutional articulation	3.3. Good interinstitutional articulation There exists systematic intervention on the part of the different professionals and good accompaniment. The professionals of the different institutions communicate with each other and articulate the intervention process. "The several professionals from diverse institutions always kept in contact with each other, exchanging information!"	3.3. Bad interinstitutional articulation The articulation between the diverse institutions/professionals is deficient, because: it is uncoordinated and fragmented; the strategies have not been defined together; or it is discrete and/or inadequate for the family. "We asked for collaboration from the institution X, they said yes, I think they did something, but they never met with us!"
4. Empowerment of the client: acquisition of competences which promote functional professional and/or cultural integration of the user and allow him/her to become autonomous		
4.1. Autonomy/dependency in relation to the formal services	4.1. The client becomes autonomous from the formal services After the intervention, the client does not need the support of the formal services, becoming autonomous and independent. "When people manage to walk and lead their lives by their own means and they don't need us (practitioners)!"	4.2. The client remains dependent on the formal services Accompaniment by the institutions has lasted for years (chronicity) and the formal supports are now part of the client's lifestyle and routine (dependency). "We have accompanied them for 10 years, and they are known to all the professionals. They are dependent on support!"
4.2. (Non)Acquisition of competences	4.2. The clients acquire new competences The clients acquire functional behaviours and competences: personal (greater self-esteem and confidence), professional and family; capacity to reflect on their needs; capacity to use their own resources. "She knew how to use what she had at her disposal! The mother acquired competences and then knew how to use them!"	4.2. The clients do not acquire new competences There is no acquisition of competences. "They repeat the same mistakes; they do not acquire new competences!"
4.3. (Non) Integration	4.3. The clients acquire social and professional integration The clients acquire integration: professional and consequently financial autonomy; at school, in the family; in the home. This allows them to break the cycle of poverty and reduce social stigma. "When he is completely integrated in society, there is a reduction in social discrimination!"	4.3. The clients do not acquire social and professional integration. The clients are not integrated: they do not get a job or they lose their job; they abandon their schooling; their family and/or social relationships get worse; their solitude increases; they lose formal support; they gain functional limitations. "Since he is always losing his job, he becomes more and more excluded!"

Table 2. (Continued)

(Sub)Categories	Success	Failure
5. Outcomes (attainment of objectives): related to the alteration of problems behaviours and/or symptoms		
5.1. (Non) attainment of objectives	5.1. (Some) of the objectives are reached. At the end of the intervention it is found that some or all of the set objectives have been reached. "At least one or two objectives were reached!"	5.2. The objectives are not reached. None of the expected objectives have been reached. "The objectives might not have been suitable, but the family did not reach any of them!
5.2. (Non) Elimination/ reduction of problems/symptoms	5.2. Some problems/symptoms are eliminated or attenuated. It is a matter of solving one problem (e.g. conflict between brothers) or eliminating a symptom (e.g. alcoholism), or attenuating (e.g. a chronic illness persists, but there are better coping strategies). "He gave up alcohol and the risk situation was eliminated!"	5.2. Problems/symptoms are not eliminated or attenuated. The problem persists; stagnation occurs. "He continued to consume, in spite of all our efforts!"
6. Process/Change: related to the reaching of more functional levels which translates into a better life for the families; they may or may not coincide with objectives laid down for the intervention. Related with the way in which the family evolves during the intervention process.		
6.1. Evolution	6.1. The client evolves in a positive way (progress). The objectives are or not being reached, but there is improvement or there is not a worsening of the living situation of the families. The evolution is a surprise, because it does not occur as expected. "She was limited by health problems, but from the emotional and relational point of view, she managed to make considerable progress!"	6.2. The client does not change or does not maintain the changes (relapses). Changes do not occur, or small changes occur which are not sufficient for the client to gain autonomy. The client does not manage to maintain the changes; there are advances and retreats that are successive relapses. "He was successful up to a certain point, and then he relapsed!"
6.2. Habits (life routines)	6.2. Harmful habits of life are modified. The clients modify some harmful life habits/routines (e.g. more care is taken with domestic hygiene), but the changes are not sufficient to improve life or to permit autonomy. These changes are important because they reduce the risk of other situations (e.g. the involvement of parents in their children's school reduces the probability of school failure). "The mother gives more attention to her daughter, but she should talk more with her!"	6.2 Harmful habits of life are not modified. Some negative habits are not altered and increase the risk situation and vulnerability (e.g. a family member who is not able to keep their job runs a greater risk of dependency on formal services). "He continues to drink and when this happens, he becomes more aggressive, only verbally, but this is bad for the whole family!"

From the analysis of the *commonalities* (subcategories which are referred to in common for the same case), in success it emerges that "the client becomes autonomous from the formal support services" is associated with: the objectives defined for the intervention are suitable for the family and attainable (7 times); the client fulfils the objectives and the intervention plan (7 times); some problems/symptoms are eliminated or attenuated (7 times); the involvement between professional and family is adequate (6 times); the clients acquire new competences (6 times). In addition, it is found that "the client fulfils the objectives and the intervention plan" is associated with: "the objectives defined for the intervention are suitable for the family and attainable (6 times); and the involvement between professional and family is adequate (6 times). The subcategories "the client fulfils the objectives and the intervention plan" and "the client becomes autonomous in relation to the formal support services" occur in common 7 times. Or, in other words, at the level of success, there are two subcategories which emerge as central in the interaction with other categories: autonomy from the formal services and compliance on the part of clients with the indications of the practitioners.

The analysis of commonalities in the general definitions of failure indicate that the subcategories "the client does not fulfil the objectives and/or the intervention plan" and "the client remains dependent on the formal services" occur in common 7 times; in addition, these two subcategories are associated with "the objectives defined are unsuitable for the family and/or unattainable" (5 times). Thus the non-compliance on the part of the clients with the indications of the professionals associated to the dependency on the services emerges as central elements of failure.

Definition of Success and Failure Centred on Cases

When questioned about success/failure with a focus on cases, the interviewees revealed less doubts and hesitations, in spite of revealing a sense that they were being evaluated which was disagreeable to them. Intervention in the cases of success lasted on average 2.1 years (between 1 and 5 years), while in the cases of failure they lasted on average 3 years (between 1 and 9 years).

The two most mentioned categories for success and failure are the same in inverted positions: empowerment of the client (1st in success and 2nd in failure) and client process (2nd in success and 1st in success). The third most mentioned category differs: attainment of outcomes/objectives (success) and process of negotiation between professionals and clients (failure).

As for the subcategories, two symmetrical subcategories emerge from amongst the most mentioned: the client is/is not motivated for the intervention and change; the client gains autonomy/remains dependent on the formal services. In the cases of success two more subcategories emerge: "the clients acquire new competences" and "the clients acquire social and professional integration". In the cases of failure, the other most noted categories are: "the client does not fulfil the objectives and/or the intervention plan" and "the client does not change or does not maintain the changes".

The most frequent *commonalities* in the cases of success are: "the client is motivated for intervention and change" and "the clients acquire new competences" (6 times); "(some) objectives are reached" and "the client evolves in a positive way" (5 times). In the cases of failure, the association is found between "the client is not motivated for intervention and/or change" and "the client does not change or does not maintain the changes" (8 times). The subcategory "the client is not motivated for intervention and/or change" is associated with "the client does not fulfil the objectives and / or the intervention plan" (6 times) and "the involvement between the professional and the family is not adequate" (5 times). In addition, it is found that "the client remains dependent on the formal services" and "the client does not fulfil the objectives and/or intervention plan" (6 times).

When questioned about the success and failure of intervention in relation to specific cases, the professionals highlighted: i) negative aspects, even when the intervention was successful (namely, late intervention, help is not always in tune with what the family was expecting and regression/relapses in success); ii) positive aspects, even then the intervention was unsuccessful (specifically, *she had some success while she was with us, then she got worse*; help was adequate; *it began as a case of success; he made some attempts to get better*). The interviewees also mentioned: incomplete or partial success, which is characterised by the need to intervene in other problematic areas or with other members of the family, contributing to their autonomisation; partial failure, or when success occurred in some areas, for example, *it worked for the children*.

During the interviews, the professionals indicated that, in cases of success, the clients are already competent in some areas (for example, they have habits of work, they value school) and/or they have minimally favourable living conditions (for example, they are healthy, they have their own home). Thus, the requested intervention was isolated and the result of some accidental crisis. Besides, the professionals referred to an empathetic relationship with successful families; they liked them and related well with them.

Definitions of Success and Failure: Generic Versus Case Analysis

Comparison between the generic definition of success and by reference to a case reveals that the main emerging categories are the same: empowerment and process of the client. However, comparison of the distributions by subcategory reveals significant differences between generic definitions of success and considering the cases of multi-problem poor families. It is found that the general definitions of success highlight clearly two categories: "the client becomes autonomous in relation to the formal services" (80%), "the client fulfils the objectives and intervention plan" (66.3%). In the definition of success by cases, no subcategory reaches such high percentages, the highest percentage being 53.3% in the subcategory "the clients acquire new competences". Amongst the most mentioned categories in the general and case definitions, only one coincides: "the client becomes autonomous in relation to the formal services" (80% in the general definitions and 46.7% in the case definitions). The remainder differ: in the generic definitions, the following subcategories stand out: "the client fulfils objectives and the intervention plan", "the objectives are suitable for the family and are attainable" and "the involvement between the professional and the family is adequate"; in the definitions by case, are highlighted: "the clients acquire new competences", "the client is motivated for intervention and change" and "the clients acquire social and professional insertion".

Table 3. Definitions of success and failure

Categories	Success						Failure					
	General			Cases			General			Cases		
	N	%	Rank order	N	%	Rank order	N	%	Rank order	N	%	Rank order
1. Planning of the intervention process												
1.1. Definition of objectives	8	53.3	3	1	6.7	10	7	46.7	4	1	6.7	8
2. Client process												
2.1. (Non)Fulfilment of the intervention plan	10	66.7	2	4	26.7	8	10	66.7	2	8	53.3	2
2.2. (De)Motivation of the client	6	40	6	7	46.7	2	8	53.3	3	12	80	1
3. Process of negotiation between professionals and clients												
3.1. (Non)Cooperation of the family	5	33.3	8	0	-		0	-		0	-	
3.2. (Non)Involvement professional/family	8	53.3	3	2	13.3	9	6	40	6	6	40	5
Interinstitutional articulation	1	6.7	12	1	6.7	10	1	6.7	7	2	13.3	7
4. Empowerment of the client												
4.1. Autonomy/ dependency	12	80	1	7	46.7	2	12	80	1	8	53.3	2
4.2. (Non)Acquisition of new competences	6	40	6	8	53.3	1	2	13.3	7	0	-	
4.3. (Non)Integration	2	13.3	10	7	46.7	2	0	-		6	40	5
5. Results (attainment of objectives)												
5.1. (Non)Attainment of objectives	2	13.3	10	6	40	6	2	13.3	7	1	6.7	8
5.2. (Non)Elimination problems/symptoms	7	46.7	5	5	33.3	7	0			0		
6. Process/Change												
6.1. Evolution	4	26.7	9	7	46.7	2	7	46.7	4	8	53.3	2
6.2. Habits	1	6.7	12	0	-		1	6.7	9	0	-	
Total	72			55			56			55		

Comparison between the distributions indicates that they are identical between: general definitions of success and failure (χ^2 (12) = 15.7016; $p \leq 1$); definitions of failure in general and by case (χ^2 (12) = 15.9292; $p \leq 0.20$); definitions by case of success and failure (χ^2 (10) = 15.9124; $p \leq 0.20$).

Comparison between the distributions indicates that they are different between: the definition of success in general and by case (χ^2 (12) = 23.3666; $p \leq 0.025$).

The same comparison, but focussed on the definition of failure indicates that the main emerging categories are the same: empowerment and process of the client. Significant differences between the distributions by subcategories do not emerge, given that the three most frequent categories coincide: "the client is not motivated for intervention and/or change", "the client does not fulfil the objectives and/or the intervention plan" an "the client remains dependent on the formal services".

It is also found that the definitions of success versus failure, in general and referring to cases, present identical distributions; in other words, they tend to be symmetric: success and failure tend to be defined as opposites.

Scaling

Scaling permits us to understand levels of success and failure and also how the practitioners plan/imagine the construction of success and the avoidance of failure. The interviewees were asked to score each one of the cases on a scale from 0 (total failure) to 20 (total success). The average for the successful cases was 14.2 (ranging from 12 to 19); for the cases of failure, the average was 5.1 (ranging from 1 to 9). Table 4 presents examples of the points attributed and their justification.

Table 4. Examples of scaling

Points	Example
Success	
12	"All the objectives have not yet been met!"
15	"The main victory in this situation was for the person themselves!" "Because the case is still accompanied by the services!"
16	"In spite of there having been collaboration and she having succeeded, there are still things to change … more responsibility!"
17	"It worked well because she had will-power!"
18	"I would give more but he hasn't managed to find a house with enough space for the family!"
19	"Because they managed to make all the changes they proposed; they always had an excellent performance in terms of competences and fulfilment!"
Failure	
1	"I would give zero, but I'm giving her the benefit of the doubt; I think there is some affection for the children!"
3	"They accomplished many things, but with a lot of insistence from the services: how to go to the appointments, school accompaniment, and hygiene care!"
4	"There were some conquests, something positive!" "Small changes which in the whole are not noticed!"
5	"The basic actions of the insertion programme were accomplished, but there was no change!" "They are still attached to the services ...but there has been no success in this stage!"

Points	Example
9	"It is a failure because she did not comply with the strategies and actions we defined, but she actually managed by herself to improve her economic conditions!" "Although this person has not recovered, she made many changes, became aware of her problems. She tried; the problem is that she moved forward and then backwards again straight away!"

Some aspects emerge in the justifications of the scaling which add some information about the perception of success and failure. For success, the professionals refer: to the user as the person most responsible for change, through her *will power*. In failure, two interesting aspects emerge: some scores are for failure in spite of the existence of positive changes, but which did not occur within the plans of the professional and which occurred without the fulfilment of the indications of the professional; the examples are always given in the positive, in other words the professionals highlighted the positive aspects of what was achieved (rather than justifying their scores by the negative).

Let us move to the analysis of the indications given by the professionals for raising or lowering the attributed score by one point.

For the cases of success, the professionals indicate the following reasons for decreasing the score given: the professional stops believing that the family can maintain the changes (*"I would lower a point if we had not continued to believe that it was possible for the family to change"*); problems of professional integration occur, like the loss of their job by a family member or failure in professional training (*"if she doesn't manage to finish the professional training course she is frequenting"*); problems of school integration occur (*"if the daughter started to have bad results at school again"*); reoccurrence or accentuation of health problems (*"if the mother went into depression again"*); family's lack of motivation for the intervention (*"if I began to feel some disinterest on the part of the family"*); reveal dependency on the services (*"if she began to come here and ask for help again"*); decrease in parental competences(*"not looking after her daughter's food"*).

For the cases of success the professionals indicate the following reasons for increasing the points attributed: the existence of more formal resources (for example, the existence of a psychologist to do therapy, the existence of social housing); luck (*"win the lottery"*); professional and/or school integration of a family member; resolution of family conflicts (*"talking to people again, re-establishing contacts"*); the family having projects for the future (*"if the daughter had a project for life, I'd like her to choose a profession she liked"*); autonomy in relation to the services (*"get the necessary autonomy, for example going alone to the services, but I am aware that this is owed to her difficulties, she's illiterate"*).

For the cases of failure, the professionals give the following reasons for lowering the points attributed: accentuation of problems of professional integration (*"not getting a job"*); and/or of school integration (*"the child begins to miss school a lot"*); reoccurrence of domestic violence (*"if there was another situation of ill-treatment I think she would fall into the same mistake of thinking that it is good to be with a companion even with the ill-treatment"*); not maintaining the changes achieved; not complying with the indications of the professionals; worsening of parental competences (*"being sloppy with her daughter's care"*; *"forgetting that the children exist"*).

For the cases of failure the professionals give the following reasons for increasing the points attributed: improvement of parental competences; better school integration (*"not skipping school"*); better domestic management (*"improve the son's room by buying a wardrobe"*); recovery from alcoholism; better financial management (*"if she took care of the electricity payments, so as to avoid expensive adjustments to the bill"*); revealing a will to change and to collaborate with the services by following the rules (*"if the couple comes to the sessions and show they are receptive to change in any of the areas tried"*). It seems to be less demanding in these cases than in the cases of success: in order to get a better score, only small changes are expected, the *"improvement of some aspects"*.

The grading exercise allows the professionals to be specific and to define small steps to be taken in the direction of success and to avoid failure. This methodology seems very relevant for use in supervision or as a technique for reflection when accompanying a case. In fact, the interviewees mentioned this: *"it seems that like this, I can see the intervention process more clearly"*. The practitioners noted that although the grading question was difficult (on account of its reflective nature), it was quite interesting and useful because they had never thought *"in that way"*: about what *"would be necessary to go up or down"*.

10. DISCUSSION

Definition of Success/Failure of Intervention with Multi-Problem Poor Families

The (sub)categories which emerged from the analysis of the interviews reveal a number of aspects which surround the work of professionals and which reveal their involvement in a moment between (Andolfi, 2000): i) control models (individualised and focussed on deficits) *versus* collaborative models (family and community, centred on competences); ii) passive *versus* active social policies; iii) a social context which places professionals in the role of support and/or control and social regulation, denoting tradition and professional training, institutional mandates which envelop the work of the professionals. So, the professionals experience dilemmas of theoretical, practical and political orientation, which may be difficult to conciliate: for example, they can try to be collaborative, while the community demands that they focus on social control.

The generic definitions of success/failure focus on: the autonomy *versus* dependency of the client in relation to the formal services; and the client follows or not the indications of the professional. The empowerment of the client (autonomy *versus* dependency on the formal services) reflects the current tendencies of social policies in Portugal, and, in general, in western countries. These policies, which emerged in Portugal in the 1990s, are characterised as active and participatory, stating as their goals the reduction of inequalities, solidarity and emancipation. These policies emerge out of criticism of the previous ones, which promoted the dependency of the beneficiaries, and privilege: social insertion and active participation of the beneficiaries in the design and application of the measures (rather than passive submission to the decisions of the professionals), personalisation of help (instead of massification) and co-responsibility of the giver and the beneficiary of services (Sousa, *et al.*, 2007).

But this dimension of success/failure emerges in contradiction to another one: the client follows or not the indications of the professional. Although in contradiction to the policies of active participation, this idea is in tune with traditional theoretical models characterised by control (Sousa, Ribeiro and Rodrigues, 2007). In these models, the professionals hold the solution to the problems of the clients, who simply have to adopt the *prescriptions* of the professionals in order for their problem to be resolved. These traditional approaches are still present when the interviewees refer to the definition of objectives (in)adequate to the needs and capacities of the families and (un)attainable taking into account the formal resources available. Thus, the intervention emerges as a responsibility of professionals and formal resources, forgetting the informal and family resources and the role of the family in the definition of its objectives (Sousa, 2005).

At the same time, some components emerge which are associated to more current (collaborative) models, namely the process of negotiation between professionals and clients, which highlights the involvement of professionals and family and inter-institutional articulation. But at the same time, it still coexists with the idea that "the family (does not) cooperate"; in other words, in which the emphasis is placed only on one side (the family), and the interaction between the family and practitioners is neglected.

The category "change" also reveals the coexistence of a traditional perspective and another more up-to-date one: positive evolution and improvement of life, which confounds expectations, showing that the family has competences and changes/evolves in accordance with its characteristics and self-organisation, *versus* a classic vision of change centred on the idea that after prescription, the adoption of the indications translates into immediate and permanent change. In fact, the processes of change are progressive, evolving through trial and error, advances and retreats and rarely occur just as expected, since families introduce and adapt information received from outside to their characteristics of functioning and organisation (autonomy) (Summers, Templeton-McMann and Fuger, 1997).

It is also possible to identify a more individualistic tradition of intervention as opposed to one centred on the family. The professionals' discourse is in fact contradictory: they tend to refer to the family as a unit of intervention, but associate the intervention to a client/user. At the same time the attainment of objectives reveals an individualistic tradition of intervention, less focussed on the family and more focussed on the subject. This tradition is also visible when the interviewees refer to incomplete or partial success (the necessity to intervene in other problems or with other members of the family) and partial failure, meaning that success occurred in some areas. In a family approach, it ought to be considered how these changes influenced the family's functioning, what new competences they encouraged and how they could be mobilised in order to promote the positive evolution of the family (e.g. Kagan and Schlosberg, 1989).

In addition, we can find the value or belief of normalisation, self reference, social control and social regulation, for example in the reference to the alteration of harmful habits. Obviously, some habits and life routines constitute risk factors in the family (for example, creating developmental problems for the children and impeding the social insertion of its members), but difference must also be accepted, for example at the level of domestic management, a perfection is often asked of these families which is not asked of other people.

The social support system often translated into professionals substituting the family in certain functions (for example, helping the daughters with family planning, without involving the parents). In the case of multi-problem poor families, this is often justified by the cognitive limitations of the family members or because, when faced with urgent problems, it is necessary to substitute the clients "in the rush" to help them. But paradoxically, the main goal of the intervention is to make the family autonomous in relation to the formal services.

In fact, the professionals who work directly with multi-problem poor families face multiple challenges: on the one hand, those inherent to the characteristics of the families; on the other hand, everything that is demanded of them or indicated in terms of theoretical models, social policies, institutional mandates and social expectations. The professionals are involved in demands and needs which may be contradictory. The greatest problem is failure with these families, especially when success is defined on the basis of autonomy in relation to services, a situation which is rarely achieved. Or, even if it comes to be achieved, it will not be in the short-term (for example, in interventions planned for one year, as is the case with the Social Insertion Fund).

In these (sub)categories found to define success and failure what seems to be missing are the dimensions which related the intervention to the specific characteristics of these families (cf. Summers, Templeton-McMann and Fuger, 1997): for example, the members of these families tend to have low self-esteem and learnt incapacity, and so motivating them is an element which is fundamental to the intervention; if motivation is an element for the client which is necessary *a priori* for success, it is most likely that failure will be the result. However, in the scaling data there is a closer connection to the specificities of the families: for example, the professional's belief that changes for the family are possible is a fundamental factor for families which are alienated and accustomed to living in a permanent situation of need and multiplicity of problems.

The definition of the success/failure of intervention with multi-problem poor families is a relevant topic principally because professionals believe that it is difficult to define in general, although pertinent when each case is analysed. In spite of this, the professionals' answers do not differ substantially when they are referring to success/failure in general or for specific cases. In any case, the question of whether standards should exist is raised, or whether success/failure should be defined for each case, or even whether it cannot be defined *a priori* or only after analysing the process and/or the outcomes.

Although the study we present here does not provide data which permit us to discuss this question in depth, we consider that standards or generic guidelines could exist, which define success/failure and then are moulded and shaped for each case. Taking into account the results obtained and the literature, standards should be related to the characteristics of the families and we consider a good option the one given by Rojano (2004). This author defines the fundamental objectives to be reached with multi-problem poor families, which would help them better their lives, and thus be part of a successful intervention: i) to locate the family income above the poverty line; ii) to promote availability of and access to new resources (families should know where to go for help and have the guarantee that their needs will be met); iii) to establish an individual plan of personal and professional development (for family members to be autonomous, they need to be independent and self-sufficient; for this they need a solid education and professional training); iv) to promote personal responsibility and self-sufficiency (helping the families to help themselves; for this, the clients should know what is expected of them); v) to develop leadership skills and civic involvement (so that the families regain self-esteem and self-confidence).

However, it should be pointed out that the professionals consider that success/failure should be defined on the basis of the cases, and more concretely, of the objectives for the case, but they adopt standardised, generalised procedures which are the same for almost all of the families (Sousa *et al.*, 2007).

Defining Success

Let us begin with the definition of success of intervention with multi-problematic poor families. The results show that the professionals define success in general and for specific cases in significantly different ways.

So the definition of success in general is perceived as the client becoming autonomous in relation to the formal services, which is almost always associated with fulfilling the objectives and/or the intervention plan, bringing together two of the main guidelines which frame the way of thinking and intervening of the practitioners: autonomy emerging from the directives of the social policies and compliance with prescriptions/indications of professionals as expressed in the medical model. However, these two dimensions are paradoxical: if a person obeys, they are not being autonomous; what's more, when we try to get a person to be obedient, we end up promoting their dependency. The intention of the professionals is that the users obey in order to become autonomous, but this is a utopia. This situation is reinforced by some other results: in the scaling of failure, some scores are negative in spite of the existence of positive changes, but which did not occur with the plans of the professional. In other words, when professionals have determined a path for that intervention/family, they end up neglecting or undervaluing positive processes of evolution only because they do not correspond to their intentions. But this is the situation in which the family really reveals autonomy.

Two other categories stand out: the defined objectives are suitable for the family and attainable and the involvement between professional and client is adequate. In this case elements of intervention emerge which are associated with the intervention process and the relationship between professionals and clients. When the definition refers to cases, the autonomy of the client in relation to the formal services also emerges, together with other dimensions: the client is motivated for intervention and change, acquires new competences and achieves social and professional integration. In this case all the subcategories are focussed on the client.

In this analysis we have to consider that the professionals have difficulty in finding successful cases, since these are less numerous than the unsuccessful cases. The professionals are used to dealing with failure and not with success in their interventions with multi-problem poor families. So it is probable that these definitions in general reflect theoretical positions which are still not very developed in their practical applications; the reference to cases reflects experience to a greater degree, even when this contradicts the theory: i) the autonomy of clients is important, although less so when referring to cases; ii) compliance with the indications of the professionals is in general very important, but in the analysis of the cases it assumes a lower profile; probably because the professionals have understood that there is positive evolution which is different from their indications; iii) the definition of objectives which are suitable for the family and attainable is important in general, but much less so in the cases, probably because in the cases there are generic goals, but the objectives are defined progressively with the family; iv) the involvement between professionals and clients is important in general, and much less so in the cases; this involvement is probably less valued in the cases on account of a question of definition, since in the scaling, elements emerge which underline the commitment of the professional, and belief in the family, but because this involvement seems non-technical, involving informality and proximity with the family, it is still difficult for professionals to believe in it. The quality of the relationship between professional and client is not the object of the interviewees' responses, but it is understood during the interviews; that is, the professionals do not clearly attribute success to the quality of the relationship, but rather to the intervention which they carried out. Nevertheless, in the cases of success, the more affectionate, empathetic tone in the discourse of the professionals is evident, revealing the existence of a strong involvement.

Defining Failure

Perhaps because of the familiarity with failure in intervention with multi-problematic poor families, the definitions in general and by case tend to coincide. Failure is perceived as: the client remaining dependent on formal services, non fulfilment of the proposals of intervention, not being motivated for intervention and/or change and not changing or not maintaining the changes. In other words, failure is located principally in the domain of the responsibility of the family and/or the client. Some fundamental aspects of the intervention process are probably neglected, such as: involving and motivating the client for intervention, fundamental for multi-problem poor families, characterised by low self-esteem and discredit in the services and amongst professionals; the involvement of professionals is fundamental for the establishment of a relationship of trust which allows the family to be motivated; the family has to feel that their immediate needs are being looked after; the non-maintenance of changes may not imply a lack of will to change, but difficulty in changing, being part of the advances and retreats which are typical in any process of change.

Defining Success Versus Failure

Comparison of the definitions of success *versus* failure indicates that they tend to be symmetrical: dependency *versus* autonomy in relation to the formal services; fulfilment *versus* non-fulfilment of the proposals of intervention; being *versus* not being motivated for intervention/change. Some specificity also occur: success appears associated with the acquisition of competences and better social integration; failure is associated to the absence of change or the inability to maintain changes. In addition the scaling revealed various levels of success/failure, underlining that it is a process or a path to be followed.

11. IMPLICATIONS

Influence of the Definitions of Success/Failure on Intervention

On the whole, little attention is given in the definitions to the specific characteristics of multi-problem poor families. For example, they live long-term and persistent problems, which for outsiders are dramatic, but for those who experience them, they are familiar. So it is natural that the families are not *aware of* and/or have no *perception* of the problem since it is an integral part of their lives (Sousa, 2004). For this reason, those who intervene will have to define the problems with the family, taking into consideration that those which the families do not perceive may be aggravated by the absence of this perception. At the same time, these families live long-term problems so change will be slow and autonomy will not occur in a short space of time (for example, in six months or a year). Besides, as these families are poor, the support in kind, goods and money (never mentioned in the interviews) are fundamental for them to feel confident in relation to aspects of subsistence and to recover emotionally in order to face other challenges in their lives. The improvement of the family's economic situation (Rojano, 2004) has been defined as one of the priorities of intervention and one of the central elements of success. As long as they remain poor, they are dependent on the services, at least in economic terms, although they may be *pushed* towards other types of support in order to keep the economic aid, but with little investment because their concern is with subsistence.

Failure is associated with the non-fulfilment by the families of the indications of the professionals, but probably, in spite of this non-fulfilment, the family process is in motion and the professionals will not be very attentive to other conquests (competences, social integration), which, even if they are minimal, can be expanded; if they are not valued for not corresponding to what is prescribed, they are not valued and the family will be demobilised.

It is equally relevant that the services and the professional reflect on how they may be contributing to failure, in spite of this not being their intention. In fact, failure is always attributed to the responsibility of the client, without questioning the intervention process and the practitioners. The professionals act as if they were doing well, without trying to understand what is not working. Reflecting on success is a way of understanding what works, underlining factors like: the acquisition of competences, motivation, integration, suitable and attainable objectives and the adequate involvement between professionals and clients.

Motivation and the involvement of the user are part of the intervention process. Multi-problem poor families and their members tend not to believe in the professionals and the support; they have no expectations of a different and better future, being only interested in financial help. In order to be involved, they need to see their most immediate (financial) needs looked after and to gain more emotional support (better self-esteem, more stability and hope). Only then can they be involved in other levels of intervention.

Relapses are a part of the process of change, so they should be accompanied; in other words, the family should be supported in the difficulties it has in maintaining change. Professionals seem to need training focused on the processes of change, in order to be able to accompany the family, to understand and to value small changes and also, not to be so intransigent in the face of some advances and retreats.

Fulfilling the indications of professionals is only partially an indicator of the family's involvement: in fact, those who comply do so because they are really committed to reaching an objective. But, in some cases, the families may have difficulty in putting into practice the indications of the professionals: for example, if they are told they have to establish more rules for their children, the family may try, but they may do so in a way which does not coincide with what the professionals thought, and are classified as not having complied; or families may have missed some meetings because they didn't have transport (or money for transport) and were ashamed to say so. It is relevant to bear in mind that whatever indication is supplied is always interpreted by the person who receives it in accordance with their values, beliefs and family's way of working, so it is necessary to negotiate and collaborate for there to be understanding and valuing of the family's efforts.

These diverse circumstances can have as consequences: i) the satisfaction of professionals for a client may be unrealistic, for example, a family stops seeking out the services, which is interpreted as being autonomous, but may continue to need support and not be doing it out of discredit, suspicion, conflict, apathy, fear or dissatisfaction with the support received; ii) success may be based on the resolution of isolated problems and so the families continue to seek help which only provide isolated answers /support and perpetuate the situation; iii) failure can be the result of an accelerated process in which objectives and strategies are defined, taking it for granted that if the families comply, they will become autonomous from the services; this attempt to reach rapid autonomy from the services and the underestimation of economic needs may contribute decisively to the failure of an intervention in spite of everything being correct from a *technical* point of view.

Practices of Success / Failure

Successful practices include the clarification of the objectives to be reached with the families taking into consideration their characteristics, for example, following Rojano (2004). Autonomy in relation to the formal services is important, but success defined in this way may be perverse; in other words, the family may abandon the services while still needing support. Besides, society today organises family life around support and cooperation with formal services (like school and day centres), so that contact with support services and practitioners can be good and necessary. Other practices which appear to be pertinent are: promoting the social, professional and school integration of clients; using grading as a form of planning, supervision and even dialogue/collaboration with the family, even in the absence of formal resources, being more creative, looking for alternative paths; understanding the processes of changes as being constituted by advances and retreats; investing in the family and in their parental competences, as a way to break the cycle of poverty.

Unsuccessful practices which emerge are: not attending to the specificities of the families; not including the family's motivation as an element of intervention; the professional not being involved and/or not focussing on the establishment of a relationship of trust and empathy with the clients; not including the family's changes as a success factor even when they do not follow the plan laid down for the intervention; lack of response to the family's financial and practical needs; considering compliance as the fundamental element of success. In addition, some problems, like health problems, debilitate families, may be chronic and remain; in this case, the family can only be helped to improve its *coping* strategies, and, probably, to maintain the support of the services.

CONCLUSION

Multi-problem poor families find themselves amongst the most vulnerable populational groups, at the same time as they are part of the most difficult groups to help. They don't stand out exactly because of a high incidence rate; it is calculated that they constitute around 6% of families who resort to the social protection services. However, they absorb around 50% of the services and of the time of the technicians, and the failure rate is high (around 75%) (Sousa *et al.*, 2007). Principally in developed societies, like those of the West, it is fundamental to create mechanisms of social support which enable all citizens to live with quality. Social and community intervention is one of the strongest instruments and demands a deep reflection on its theoretical and epistemological presuppositions and the validity of its most consolidated models.

Since success is a desired outcome in different experiences of our lives, it is fundamental to understand the meanings which are assumed when we focus on social intervention with multi-problem poor families. Research has focused on the determining factors of success / failure of the interventions, but little attention has been given to what failure is. This seems to be a given *a priori*, as if it were obvious what failure is, but in fact the definitions vary according to the perspectives of those involved, the objectives defined for the intervention, the field of intervention and the measures used to assess the results. Our study indicates that professionals who intervene with multi-problem poor families tend to define success/failure according to two orientations (the medical or control model and the collaborative model), which provides them with definitions and actions which are difficult to reconcile.

Success is defined principally through the empowerment of the client (autonomy form formal services), or through the client's compliance with the instructions of the professional. There is a contradiction here which is substantiated thus: those who are autonomous are able to take their own decisions; at the same time, families with economic difficulties are not able to become autonomous from the services without their needs being guaranteed. Thus, this definition will be able to contribute to failure, by paradoxically preventing the autonomy of the clients. Perhaps it is also necessary to redefine autonomy, without limiting it to the non-seeking of the formal services, but focussing on the capacity to take decisions and solve problems, even when it is necessary to ask for help/support (since everyone ends up by asking support from someone when they need to take some decisions).

Failure is perceived to be: when the client remains dependent on the formal services, not complying with the proposals of intervention, not being motivated for intervention and/or change and not changing or not maintaining the changes. The definition of failure places the responsibility with the client/family, assuming that the intervention and the professionals acted well, in spite of the intended results not being those which were intended. Successful practices should include definitions of success/failure which include the intervention, the practitioner, the client and the community context in which he/she is situated.

The concentration on results which characterise the definition of success/failure in multi-problem poor families seems to be blocking attention to the specificity of their characteristics and thus contributing to the failure of the intervention.

However, some elements emerge which demonstrate the reorientation of the practitioners towards more operational definitions which are more attentive to the needs and characteristics of these families, like, for example: promoting small changes; mobilising competences in different domains (parental, management, school and professional); supporting social integration.

The grading which was used as a research technique revealed itself to be a useful methodology for professionals to use in practice: both to reflect on their intervention practice and intervention; and for negotiating, with the clients/families, and defining the objectives and strategies to use.

In order to intervene with multi-problem poor families, it is necessary to understand what is meant by success and failure. In this study, the perspective of the professional was adopted, but future studies should be able to give the point of view of the families, of their social network and of the community.

REFERENCES

Andolfi, M. (2000). *El coloquio relacional*. Barcelona: Paidós.

Ausloos, G. (1996). *A competência das famílias*. Lisboa, Climepsi.

Bell, D. and Bell, L. (1989). Micro and macro measurement of family systems concepts. *Journal of Family Psychology*, 3 : 137-157.

Benoit, J. (1988). *Dictionnaire clinique des thérapies familiales systémiques*. Paris, ESF.

Bernal, G. (2006). Intervention Development and Cultural Adaptation Research With Diverse Families. *Family Process*, 45(2): 143–151.

Bowles, S. (2004). *Microeconomics: Behavior, Institutions, and Evolution*. United States: Russel Sage Foundation.

Boyd-Franklin, N. (1989). *Black families in therapy: a multisystems approach*. New York: Guilford Press.

Cerqueira, M.; Pires, S.; Figueiredo, D.; Matos, A. and Sousa, L. (2003). Os problemas das famílias multiproblemáticas. *Revista Serviço Social and Sociedade*, 76: 143-164.

Chambless, D. and Ollendick, T. (2001). Empirically supported psychological interventions: controversies and evidence. *Annual Review of Psychology*, 52 (Feb): 685-716.

Colapinto, J. (1995). Dilution of family process in social services. *Family Process*, 34: 59-74.

Cunningham, P. and Henggeler, S. (1999). Engaging multiproblem families in treatment: lessons learned throughout the development of multisystemic therapy. *Family Process*, 38: 265-281.

Doherty, W. and Carroll, J. (2002). The citizen therapist and family-centered community building: introduction to a new section of the journal. *Family Process*, 41: 561-568.

Doner, L. (1997). Charting the Course for Evaluation: How Do We Measure the Success of Nutrition Education and Promotion in Food Assistance Programs? *Summary of Proceedings*. USDA, Office of Analysis and Evaluation, Food and Consumer Service. http://findarticles.com/p/articles/mi_m0EUB/is_3_11/ai_53885194/print

Elizur, Y. and Minuchin, S. (1989). *Institutionalizing madness: families, therapy and society*. New York: Basic Books.

Fleischer, G. (1975). Producing effective change in impoverish, disorganized families: is family therapy enough? *Family Therapy*, 11(3): 277-289.

Gingerich, W. (2000). Solution-focused brief therapy: a review of the outcome research. *Family Process*, 39(4): 477-499.

Gondolf, E.W. (1987). Changing men who batter: A developmental model for integrated interventions. *Journal of Family Violence*, 2: 335-350.

Green, R.-J. and Herget, M. (1991). Outcomes of systemic/ strategic team consultation: III. The importance of therapist warmth and active structuring. *Family Process*, 30(3): 321-336.

Gurman, A.; Kniskern, D. and Pinsof, W. (1986). Research on the process and outcome of marital and family therapy. In S. Garfield and A. Bergin (Eds.), *Handbook of Psychotherapy and Behavior Change* (3rd ed., pp. 565-624). New York: Wiley.

Hampson, R. and Beavers, R. (1996). Measuring Family Therapy Outcome in a Clinical Setting: Families That Do Better or Do Worse in Therapy. *Family Process*, 35 (3): 347-361.

Hazelrigg, M.; Cooper, H. and Borduin, C. (1987). Evaluating the effectiveness of family therapies: an integrative review and analysis. *Psychological Bulletin*, 101: 428-442.

Hiebert, E. and Taylor, B. (1994). *Getting reading right from the start*. Boston: Allyn and Bacon.

Hogue, A.; Liddle, H. and Rowe, C. (1996). Treatment adherence process research in family therapy: A rationale and some practical guidelines. *Psychotherapy*, 33: 332-345.

Imber-Black, E. (1988) *Families and larger systems: a family therapist's guide through the labyrinth*. New York: The Guilford Press.

Jacobson, N. and Truax, P. (1991). Clinical significance: a statistical approach to defining meaningful change in psychotherapy research. *Journal of Consulting and Clinical Psychology*, 59(1): 12-19.

Kagan, R. and Schlosberg, S. (1989). *Families in perpetual crisis*. New York: W.W. Norton.

Kaplan, L. (1986). *Working with multi-problem families*. New York: Simon and Schuster.

Kazdin, A. (1986). Comparative outcome studies of psychotherapy: methodological issues and strategies. *Journal of Consulting and Clinical Psychology*, 54 (1): 95-105.

Kazdin, A. (1999). The meanings and measurement of clinical significance. *Journal of Consulting and Clinical Psychology*, 67(3): 332-339.

Krumer-Nevo, M.; Slonim-Nevo, V. and Hirshenzon-Segev, E. (2006). Social workers and their long-term clients: the never-ending struggle. *Journal of Social Service Research*, 33 (1): 27-38.

Lipsey, M. and Cordray, D. (2000). Evaluation methods for social intervention. *Annual Review of Psychology*, 51: 345-375.

Madsen, W. (1999). *Therapy with multi-stressed families*. London: Guilford.

Malarewicz, J-A. (1999). *Supervision en thérapie systémique: le thérapeute familial et son superviseur*. Paris : ESF.

Mashal, M.; Feldman, R. and Sigal, J. (1989). The unraveling of a treatment paradigm: a follow-up study of the Milan approach to family therapy. *Family Process*, 28(4): 457-470.

Matos, A. and Sousa, L. (2004). How multiproblem families try to find support in social services. *Journal of Social Work Practice*, 18(1): 65-80.

Maturana, H. and Varela, F. (1980). *Autopoïesis and cognition*. Boston: Reidel.

Summers, J., Templeton-McMann, O. and Fuger, K. (1997). Critical thinking: A method to identify best practices in serving families with multiple challenges. *Topics in Early Childhood Special Education*, 17: 27-52.

Miles, M., and Huberman, A. (1984). *Qualitative data analysis*. Beverly Hill: SAGE.

Minow, M. (1994). Learning from Experience: The Impact of Research about Family Support Programs on Public Policy. *University of Pennsylvania Law Review*, 143 (1): 221-252.

Minuchin, P, Colapinto, J., and Minuchin, S. (1998). *Working with families of the poor*. New York: The Guilford Press.

Mirin, S. and Namerow, S. (1991). Why study treatment outcome? *Hospital and Community Psychiatry*, 42: 1007-1013.

Moncher, F. and Prinz, R. (1991). Treatment fidelity in outcomes studies. *Clinical Psychology Review*, 11: 247-266.

Neher, J. (1988). The "slow code": a hidden conflict. *Journal of Family Practice*, 27: 429-430.

Neidig, P. (1986). The development and evaluation of a spouse abuse treatment. *Evaluation and Program Planning*, 9: 275-280.

Newberry, A.; Alexander, J. and Turner, C. (1991). Gender as a process. variable in family therapy. *Journal of Family Psychology*, 5(2): 158-175.

Perkins, R. (1996). Seen but not heard: can 'user involvement' become more than empty rhetoric. *The Mental Health Review*, 1: 16-19.

Perkins, R. (2001). What constitutes success? The relative priority of service users' and clinicians' views of mental health services. *The British Journal of Psychiatry*, 179: 9-10.

Prigogine, I. (1980). Ouvertures. *Cahiers Critiques de Thérapie Familiale et de Pratiques de Réseaux*, 3 : 7-18.

Relvas, A. (1999). Famílias, terapia e terapeutas. In A. Relvas (org), *Conversas com famílias*. Porto: Edições Afrontamento, 9-46.

Reppucci, N.; Woolard, J. and Fried, C. (1999). Social, community and preventive interventions. *Annual Review of Psychology*, 50: 387-418.

Rogers, E.; Chamberlin, J.; Ellison, M. and Crean, T. (1997). A consumer-constructed scale to measure empowerment among users of mental health services. *Psychiatric Services*, 48: 1042-1047

Rojano, R. (2004). The practice of Community Family Therapy. *Family Process*, 43(1): 59-77.

Rosnay, J. (1977). *O macroscópio – para uma visão global*. Lisboa: Arcádia.

Santisteban, D.; Suarez-morales, L. ; Robbins, M. and Szapocznick, J.(2006). Brief Strategic Family Therapy: Lessons Learned in Efficacy Research and Challenges to Blending Research and Practice. *Family Process* 45 (2): 259–271

Seybolt, T. (2007). *Humanitarian military intervention: the conditions for success and failure*. London: Oxford University Press.

Sharlin, S., Shamai, M. and Sharlin, S. (2000). *Therapeutic intervention with poor unorganized families: from distress to hope*. London: Haworth Press.

Smith, J.; Meyers, R. and Delaney, H (1998). The community reinforcement approach with homeless alcohol-dependent individuals. *Journal of Consultation and Clinical Psychology*. 66: 541– 48

Sorensen, G.; Emmons, K.; Hunt, M. and Johnston, D. (1988). Implications of the results of community intervention trials. *Annual Review of Public Health*, 19: 379-416.

Sousa, L. and Eusébio, C. (2005). When multi-problem poor individuals' values meet practitioners' values! *Journal of Community and Applied Social Psychology*, 15: 353-367.

Sousa, L.; Hespanha, P.; Rodrigues, S. and Grilo, P. (2007). *Famílias pobres: desafios à intervenção social*. Lisboa: Climepsi.

Sousa, L. (2004). Diagnósticos e problemas: uma perspectiva sistémica centrada nas famílias multiproblemáticas pobres. *Psychologica*, 37: 147-167.

Sousa, L. (2005). Building on personal networks when intervening with multi-problem poor families. *Journal of Social Work Practice,* 19(2): 163-179.

Sousa, L.; Ribeiro, C.; Rodrigues, S. (2007). Are practitioners able to think strengths-focused when working with multi-problem poor families? *Journal of Community and Applied Social Psychology*, 17: 53-66.

Startup, M. and Shapiro, D. (1993). Dimensions of cognitive therapy for depression: a confirmatory analysis of session ratings. *Cognitive Therapy and Research*, 17: 139-151.

Tompson, M.; Rea, M.; Goldstein, M.; Miklowitz, D. and Weisman, A. (2000). Difficulty in implementing a family intervention for bipolar disorder: the predictive role of patient and family attributes. *Family Process*, 39 (1): 105-120.

Tubbs, C.; Roy, K. and Burton, L. (2005). Family ties: Constructing family time in low-income families. *Family Process*, 44(1): 77-91.

White, M. and Epston, D. (1990). *Narrative means to therapeutic ends*. New York: W. W. Norton and Company.

Yeaton, W. and Sechrest, L. (1981). Critical dimensions in the choice and maintenance of successful treatments: Strength, integrity, and effectiveness. *Journal of Consulting and Clinical Psychology*, 49: 156-167.

In: Citizenship in the 21st Century   ISBN: 978-1-60456-401-3
Editors: L. T. Kane and M. R. Poweller, pp. 93-125   © 2008 Nova Science Publishers, Inc.

Chapter 3

HETEROGENEITY, DIVERSITY, CHANGE: NEW GOAL POSTS OR RETHINKING SCIENCE EDUCATION AND CITIZENSHIP IN THE 21ST CENTURY

Wolff-Michael Roth
University of Victoria, Victoria, BC, Canada

ABSTRACT

Current educational discourses about what school science students need to become citizens of the 21st century are focused on specific science content without any reference to what this science content will allow these future citizens to do. However, the "basics" that we are asked to return to by back-to-basics advocates, that is, many of the "scientific skills" students are subjected to today, may have been useful some 100 years ago, but are no longer found in modern research laboratories. More so, the skills students acquire in school science today have little use in coping with the demands of everyday life in a rapidly changing world—the massive prevalence of hand-held calculators makes it possible for students to get by without learning longhand division in the same way that the massive presence of high-level programming language allows computer scientists to get by without knowing machine code. If this is the case, we have to ask questions about the content of an education for this relatively new century. What form(s) of scientific literacy do the citizens of the 21st century need to master? What do student citizens need to be able to do not only for coping in a rapidly changing world but also to contribute to the way it continuously takes shape and reshapes itself? To begin a project of rethinking science education for the 21st century, I present a case study of one everyday situation where ordinary citizens have been involved in a struggle over access to the local water grid, which serves me as a context for articulating aspects of scientific literacy in and for a *democracy-to-come*. I then articulate a particular teaching experiment where seventh-grade students became involved in the environmental issues of the same municipality where the citizens simultaneously struggled for access to the local water grid.

INTRODUCTION

Not long after I changed universities and moved to my current home, I come across an issue of my local newspaper that draws my attention, likely because the headlines relate to our local water that had become of interest to my then emerging research project concerning water-related environmentalism and stewardship. The title of the feature carried on Pages 1 and 5 of the local newspaper reads, "How bad is the water anyway?" The picture, covering one-third of the spread, shows Larry Booth, a resident of Senanus Drive in the municipality of Central Saanich filling several 5-gallon plastic containers with water at a local gas station some five kilometers from his home. Like others who live on Senanus Drive, the article elaborates, Larry Booth makes frequent trips to the gas station, while others have drinking water shipped to their homes. For years, the residents on his street have said that they cannot drink the water in their homes, which they draw from wells because they are not connected to the water main that serves the other 15,000 inhabitants of this municipality. Although the residents of Senanus Drive have brought the issue to the attention of municipal officials for the past 25 to 30 years (with increasing pressure over the 1998–2003 period) the municipal council has not taken action. The newspaper story goes on, "So when the Capital Health Region began testing the area water last year residents thought they would finally gain scientific ammunition for their fight with Central Saanich Council. It still hasn't happened" (Woodley, 1998, p. A5).

When I first began reflecting more deeply on the situation about three years later, the dispute over access to safe water has not been settled and the access to the water main still has not come about—although more scientific, technological, and medical "experts" have been asked to investigate the issue and to file reports with the municipal government. Some of these experts agreed that there are biological and chemical problems with the well water, which (to this day) varies and even disappears as a function of the seasonally dependent groundwater levels. Other scientific experts suggest that there are only some "aesthetic objectives" that are not achieved, but that the water is safe for consumption, though boiling the water before consumption always is advised. The affected residents have suffered for years from lack of water during certain seasons (usually August to November) from high dissolved mineral concentrations (which destroy their appliances and plants that they irrigate) and from biologically contaminated water. Despite these problems and despite informing the community and local newspapers, the residents do not feel heard—the newspaper headlines at the time of my first reflections read, "Families desperate for water" (April 20, 2001), "Still can't drink the water" (November 28, 2001), and "Still can't drink the water, say residents" (January 16, 2002). The mayor and municipal council of Central Saanich have based their recommendations on a report that in turn has drawn on the expertise of scientists and engineers but has disregarded the local and historical knowledge and experiences of the residents of Senanus Drive who have been hurting the most. Together with a class of graduate students who also are residents of the larger district I analyze all the information available, including research reports that a PhD student in my laboratory has collected as a member of an environmental group. Our conclusions at the time is that, in this case, those who get hurt are not those who get heard and they are not those whose opinions are taken into account (Roth et al., 2004). At that time, I begin to ask, "What can we learn from this story for designing science curriculum that prepares students for their participation on one side or the other of such controversies?" and "What can be done to prepare school students to take their stand in controversial issues such as this?" Even more importantly, I begin to ask, "What abilities or competencies will a citizen of the new century need to adequately cope with an increasingly complex, diverse, diversified, and specialized world?"

Further research into the issues surrounding the Senanus Drive water problem reveals to me that the situation has been far more complex than simply gaining access to safe water. On the surface the problem has been one over health and safety issues (water for fire hydrants). Because of local fire regulations, the water main extension needs to be far greater than would have been if water supply were the only issue in need to be addressed. But as soon as a water main that responded to the fire regulation existed, the compulsory building lot sizes would be cut in half. For some stakeholders (including the mayor) the real issue therefore is one of increasing the development potential of the Senanus Drive area that is currently zoned as "rural estate." These stakeholders want to make development impossible by not extending the water main, though contradictorily, they actively have been developing other areas equally protected by their "rural estate" zoning. There also appear to be conflicts of interest, such as when one of those writing a report *against* a water main holds stocks in a company that offers individualized local water treatment solutions and mobilizes support against a water main (Lavin, 2001), which on top of it all, he too would have been required to pay for. One individual advocate, a professor of eco-law particularly shapes the debate, as he lives near Senanus Drive and wants to keep development away, and he is the person publicly charged with holding stocks in local water services companies. He also chairs the municipality's water task force; and he lectures internationally, for example, at UNESCO-sponsored events related to urban water issues, on the unreasonable nature of the Senanus Drive residents' demands and their irrationality (M'Gonigle, 2001). The scientific experts therefore are contributing (unwittingly perhaps) not only to the social construction of water quality and quantity but also to an eco-political debate over land development. For me, the issues surrounding this case of ordinary town folks requesting to be connected to the water grid that already serves all the other homes and farms in this valley of one of the major industrial nations has become one of social (distributive) justice. It has become a case for reflecting on what kind of scientific literacy I want for those affected by the decisions research scientists, scientific consultants, medical staff, and politicians make and for these decision makers themselves. How do we have to think and rethink scientific literacy so that it becomes appropriate for citizens of an industrialized nation in the 21st century? How do we go about changing education and educational systems that currently focus on schooling and, in this, do not do a good job in *educating* children to become active agents in designing the world in which they want to live?

Current educational discourses about what school science students need to become citizens of the 21st century are focused on specific science content without any reference to what this science content will allow these "future" citizens to do. (Because every human being is constitutive of society, I tend to think of children and students as citizens-to-come as well as adult citizens-to-come, that is, citizens always in the making, always undergoing change.) Thus, for example, middle and high school curricula require students to learn Newton's laws of motion which nobody in everyday life really needs, including myself, an individual with a MSc in physics and subsequent doctoral training in physical chemistry. Similarly, secondary students are required to learn about the structure of atoms and molecules, knowledge that I never have had to draw on after leaving my university science programs. The scientific skills (practices) students are to acquire have been useful in laboratories some 100 years ago—using a pipette or burette—but are no longer (or very seldom) found in any modern research laboratories where computers are much better in dispensing the required micro-quantities of liquids. To confirm this, all we have to do is watch the evening news about the latest medical (DNA) research, and we see arrays of computer-guided pipettes dispensing tiny amounts of liquid into arrays of test tubes. More so, our students can look around themselves on their street particularly and in society more generally and find that everyday people do very well without knowing the curriculum content of their science classes. In contrast, those competencies that citizens need to cope with life in the 21st century are not central parts in curriculum guidelines and lesson plans of teachers: successfully bringing about collective solutions to problems that are so complex that no individual can master the required knowledge of their own discipline, let alone the broad multi-disciplinary knowledges that have to be mustered even in the "simplest" of situations. Even today, necessary epistemic and material resources required for acting quickly change; and new resources for actions become available everyday thereby leading to the exponential explosion of cultural action possibilities, as seen for example with the arrival of the Internet or the mobile phone, which not only increased existing communicative capabilities but in fact have led to entirely *new forms* of relating to others and of producing culture. This potential of culture to change exponentially requires citizens of the 21st century to be flexible, adaptive, open to continual learning, problem focused, collaborative, and participating in the evolution of hybridized and heterogeneous specialized discourses that change with situations and problems (Roth, 2007b).

In this chapter, I suggest that science education has to be re-articulated in terms of requirements for being a citizen in the 21st century, which already is characterized by diversity, heterogeneity, and change and will be characterized in this manner even more so in the future of a democracy that is always in the making, which never fully arrives and therefore always constitutes a *democracy-to-come*.

> Here, the expression "democracy to come" does indeed translate or call for a militant and interminable political critique. A weapon aimed at the enemies of democracy, it protests against all naïveté and every political abuse, every rhetoric that would present as a present or existing democracy, as a de facto democracy, what remains inadequate to the democratic demand, whether nearby or far away, at home or somewhere else in the world, anywhere that a discourse on human rights and on democracy remains little more than an obscene alibi so long as it tolerates the terrible plight of so many millions of human beings suffering from malnutrition, disease, and humiliation, grossly deprived not only of bread and water but of equality or freedom, dispossessed of the rights of all, of everyone, of anyone. (Derrida, 2005, p. 86).

This 21st century will demand citizens to be more adaptive, ready and able to cope with continually changing (environmental, societal, technological) conditions; and this is particularly the case in a democracy-to-come, which asks all of us to engage in interminable militant critique when human beings are deprived not only of bread and, salient in this chapter, of water but also suffer in other ways, including from inequality, dispossessed of the rights of all, of distributed social justice. The currently identified problems facing humanity— environmental impact and global warming—will become even more extensive and complex, especially because any "'responsibility' or a 'decision' cannot be founded on or justified by any *knowledge as such*, that is, without a leap between two discontinuous and radically heterogeneous orders" (p. 145). It will demand citizens not only to understand themselves as cultural hybrids but also to hybridize to an increasingly extensive and faster extent.

In this chapter, I therefore suggest that we need to go differently about education generally and science education more specifically, especially if our goal is citizenship in the 21st century. I present my argument in two steps. First, I present the results of a ten-year ethnographic research effort in my municipality, where the inhabitants living along one street do not have access to the water grid that already supplies 98% of the residents, and where politicians refuse to provide this access even though the people on this and two other concerned streets are willing to pick up (some of) the costs. The politicians have based their decisions on the reports written by scientific and engineering consultants, but which, as one public meeting in particular shows, contain flaws of method and fact. I use this case to articulate some requirements for the types of competencies that citizens need for taking part in consciously shaping their world—*the* most fundamental competency that distinguishes humans from other animals—rather than submitting to being directed and governed as the citizens in an Orwellian state. In the second part of my argument, I present—based on three iterations and two years of ethnographic work in one school—a particular case of teaching science that has allowed middle school students to participate in shaping (changing) their local community and thereby already to take their part in ethico-moral aspects of citizenship. Even more so, I show how the participation in the environmental activities of their community engages students emotionally and ethico-morally, an aspect of human life virtually never addressed in the curriculum policy documents (e.g., *No Child Left Behind; Project 2061*) that shape what school districts, schools, and teachers do. These students are no longer merely prepared for life but they already participate actively in changing the life of their community and thereby enact citizenship in the 21st century and participate in a democracy-to-come rather than merely getting ready for it. As citizens-to-come, we always are involved in producing new forms of citizenship to the same extent as we reproduce existing possibilities for being citizens.

STRUGGLE OVER ACCESS TO WATER

Over a ten-year period (1997–2007), I have conducted an ethnographic research project concerning science and politics with respect to environmental issues in Central Saanich, a municipality in Western Canada where I am also a resident. In the course of this research project, I have come to document—together with several graduate student members of my research laboratory—the work of several non-governmental organizations focusing on the environment, school efforts to engage their students in science through environmental curricula, water stewardship, and the case of access to drinking water featured in my opening vignette. Here, I use the case of the struggle over access to the local water main that already supplies the residents of all other streets as a paradigm for rethinking (science) education and (scientific) literacy for the democracy-to-come in which political ideals about equity come to be realized more actively than they currently are. That is, I use this case to think about the role of education in preparing citizens to live in a democracy that always is to-come but never really arrives ("The 'to-come' not only points to the promise but suggests that democracy will never exist, in the sense of a present existence" [Derrida, 2005, p. 86]). In this democracy-to-come, not only science but also other areas of inquiry and knowledgeability will need to be brought to bear on salient issues. Rather than leaving decision-making in the hands of politicians and their scientific consultants and advisors, the citizens in the democracies-to-come of this century need the ability to expand continually their forms of civic participation, that is, they need heterogeneous knowledge-abilities including those that allow them to evolve and realize new, even more diverse knowledgeabilities to settle the issues at hand.

Figure 1. The municipality lies in a pristine valley with many farms heavily drawing on the groundwater level for irrigation purposes. The houses and farms in the area shown currently are not connected to the water main. (© 2005 Wolff-Michael Roth, permission granted).

Troubled Waters

The controversy over water at the core of this case study has been taking place in Central Saanich, a suburban municipality with rural character that is part of an urban district (Capital Regional District [Victoria], British Columbia) divided into 13 municipalities. The municipality of Central Saanich spreads across several watersheds, among which the one with Hagan Creek as its main water-bearing stream is the largest. The Hagan Creek valley is pristine, spotted with (hobby) farms (figure 1), vineyards, forests, and two main agglomerations with higher (but still relatively low) population densities. Despite its location in a geographical area of temperate rain forests, Central Saanich only receives about 850 millimeters of rain per year, most of it falling in the November to March period and very little during the remainder of the year. The local aquifers are insufficient to supply the municipality with water, which therefore has to be piped in from reservoirs in the Sooke Hills located about 40 kilometers to the west—which incidentally produce the rain shadow that keeps the precipitation low in the micro-climate of Central Saanich.

Recent developments have exacerbated the issues by altering the water flow over and through the ground. To drain the bogs that used to exist before the arrival of the European settlers, farmers had straightened the creek thereby turning it into a channel (figure 2). These changes allow the water to flow away faster—with the effect that in the summer months, the creek is but a trickle (10–20 liters/second) supplying insufficient water for resident farmers to water their fields (see figure 1), which, for some farms and in some years, yield 4 or 5 hay harvests. A considerable number of wells are used to draw water for irrigation for two reasons. First, the town water system does not reach into the lower reaches (approximately 4.5 kilometers) of the watershed. All the farms and private homes on the northern half of the valley (i.e., figure 1) draw their water from wells. Second, the costs of using water for irrigation from the water main even if one existed would be high. The combination of quick run-off and groundwater use for farming heavily tax the different aquifers running below the watershed. Other changes are related to urbanization and the increase in impervious surfaces (e.g., pavement, roofs, and concrete driveways) with concomitant use of storm sewers. Losses of forest cover throughout the watershed and along the stream banks, loss of wetlands and recharge areas, and the loss of natural stream conditions further increase the pressure on the aquifers. During an interview in the first year of my study, the leader of a local environmental group quickly points out that the Hagan Creek watershed is at the upper limit of total impervious surfaces that still allow for healthy watershed and streams.

Figure 2. Straightening of the creek and turning it into a ditch makes the water run off faster, which thereby is prevented from making it into the subsoil to replenish the groundwater levels. (© 2005 Wolff-Michael Roth, permission granted).

Senanus Drive, the area involved in the controversy, lies on a small wooded peninsula, about five kilometers away from the centers of both higher density areas (to the left of figure 1 in continuation of the forest and fields in the background). The residents, too, have individual wells that draw on the water in bedrock fissures. For years, the local and regional newspapers reported that in the summer months, some well water in the Senanus Drive area has been contaminated chemically and biologically, including the period reported in the opening vignette. Sometimes, Capital Health Region (i.e., the regional health board) repeatedly has advised residents not to use their water at all or to boil it for some time prior to consuming it. Many residents have opted for the same strategy as the Booth family in my introductory vignette to get their water from gas stations in one of the two high-density areas of the municipality. For more than 30 years, the residents of Senanus Drive demanded to be connected to the water main that supplies other residents of Central Saanich (McCullogh, 1999). During the period 1997 to 2003, they residents increased the frequency of their demands and sought exposure in the local media in support of their cause. They brought the issues forward to the Regional Water Commission, which decided that this was a municipal issue to be dealt with by the municipal council of Central Saanich (January 20, 1998, minutes of council meeting). However, the municipal council blocked all requests and demands in the attempt to prevent the extension of the water main to Senanus Drive. Lack of a water main directly impeded any effort to develop the area and thereby increase the population density.

Faced with an insufficient quantity of water that is of questionable quality, the residents have utilized a number of coping strategies. They have had water delivered, drilled multiple wells on their properties, spread out their water usage, stored water to be used against fires, chlorinated their water systems, regularly replaced corroded plumbing fixtures, and attempted to install individual treatment systems. There was the potential for business: delivery companies advertised their services along Senanus Drive (figure 3). During a public meeting, one resident described how his family has supplemented its water supply:

> We took measures to split the plumbing system in our house utilizing our well water for sanitary purposes and the outside irrigation in our garden and then contracting with a company called Stancel Water Services to fill our two water tanks on a regular basis. And this went on for a number of years until the Greater Victoria Water District revoked Stancel's water license on sanitary grounds and put into action, their own water delivery system which continued to supply our household for several years. Uh during this "truck period" I call it, the cost of delivery escalated nearly three hundred percent.

Other residents reported having had to drill more than one well in an attempt to locate suitable sources of water. An insufficient supply of water necessitates careful planning of water usage. The head of one family describes the situation: "Showers, bath, dishwashing, laundry, etcetera has to be spaced out, so that we don't run out of water. If we run the water for seven or eight minutes in the summer, we are dry for twenty minutes." Other residents agree, for example, by stating: "I don't water anything if I'm doing a washing so as not to use too much at one time. I keep my shower to a minimum and every other household use." Because the water in the Senanus Drive area tends to be corrosive, the residents constantly have to replace a variety of household fixtures: "During the past nine years, I have replaced one well pump, one reservoir pump, two pressure tank pumps, seven water heaters, four sets of swim-spa heating elements, a complete spa filter system, and numerous shut-off valves, taps, and shower heads." In an effort to improve the quality of their water, some residents have attempted to implement individual treatment systems.

Figure 3. On Senanus Drive, a sign advertises home delivery of water for a variety of home uses. (© 2002 Wolff-Michael Roth, permission granted).

To cope with their concerns about an inability to fight fires, some residents have built storage ponds in a make-do fashion. Some of these ponds have been integrated into the landscapes of the gardens, others residents have converted old swimming pools into holding ponds (figure 4).

The situation worsened sufficiently for the local newspaper to feature regular stories in which the various stakeholders express themselves about the issue of a water main for Senanus Drive. Over time, the situation becomes sufficiently serious for different political and health bodies to become involved, eventually leading to a public meeting in which all the relevant information was made available and different stakeholders came to speak to the issues, including the residents of Senanus Drive. This meeting, of which I obtained a fully audiotaped recording, has become for me a critical incident for rethinking what scientific literacy and science education for the 21st century ought to be and might look like. The following case materials not only exemplify the engagement of the residents but also the heterogeneous, diverse, and changing nature of knowledgeabilities required for relevantly articulating problems and anticipating and implementing solutions.

Public (Stand-off) Debate

In the spring and summer of 1999, a total of six reports addressing technical, scientific, and policy issues around the water crisis at Senanus Drive were produced. At a municipal council meeting in August, the mayor called for a public meeting to be held, where all the writers of the technical and scientific reports could gather in one place, present their work and respond to comments from the general public. It would also be a place and a time for the residents and other members of the municipality to present their ideas and arguments for a solution. The public meeting was held in the fall of 1999. Donavon Bishop, a member of the municipality's engineering staff, was in charge of moderating the meeting: First, the authors (or representatives) of the reports were asked to summarize the findings. The presenters included a representative of Capital Health Region, Dennis Lowen, a hydro-geologist hired as independent consultant in the case, the chair of the Water Advisory Committee [WAC] report), and an individual representing the dissenting report prepared by the members of the WAC in disagreement with the original document). Second, members of the community were provided with an opportunity to ask questions about the technical matters presented by the previous speakers. Third, time was allocated for community members to speak about their concerns more broadly.

Figure 4. A pool serves as a storage pond for irrigation and fire-fighting purposes. (© 2002 Wolff-Michael Roth, permission granted).

After the different scientists and representatives of the Water Advisory Task Force had presented summaries of their reports, the moderator of the public hearing encouraged members of the audience to ask questions and make comments pertaining to the technical issues of the reports. Whereas scientists are often portrayed as the guardians of scientific method—of which everyday folk are said to be ignorant (Shamos, 1995)—the community members in this meeting, here exemplified by Hayden, do not appear to be overly impressed by the scientists, their articulated degrees, or their expertise. In fact, an important dimension of all the questions is the appropriateness of the method used and the validity of the data collected to draw the conclusion that the independent consultant Lowen had presented.

Hayden: Yes uh, John Hayden. Six-o-one and six-o-five Senanus. Uh, you took water samples from our property. Now, uh, I was told that you let the water run, Doctor Lowen is it?

Lowen: Mister, Mister Lowen.

Hayden: Mister Lowen. Uh, the problem is first of all at any source you get is coming out of a cistern that is two or three thousand gallons. It's had a chance to settle out, number one. Number two, the water you've gotten has been mitigated through a water softener. Number three, it has been mitigated under a u-vee system to kill bacteria. How can you say we can mitigate our water? I mean much more mitigation can we do?

Bishop: Dennis, can you? Do you know about that particular well, whether you tested it right at the wellhead or whether it was through the system?

Lowen: I don't know of any well that we tested that had any kind of treatment. We went, we went to the cistern to get the water but we went, we went to where the water came into the cistern from the well. We didn't, uh I think there might have been one well that we tested from the cistern 'cause there was no other way to test it but all the others were uh before the cistern, and before any kind of treatment.

Hayden: Are you sure of that?

Lowen: Um, as sure as I can be. We went to the pump house and we asked the owners of the property if, "does this outside tap go through any treatment?" And we were assured that we were getting water from as close to the well as possible.

The first exchange opened with Hayden' questions about where the water samples had been taken. Hayden suggested that the sheer water quantity in his cistern would have implied that Lowen tested water that had been stagnant for a while, and therefore allowed any substances to settle. Stating the holding capacity of his cistern, 2,000 or 3,000 gallons of water contrasted the 15 minutes of letting the water run at the tap. Common sense tells any listener that a water tap running for 15 minutes does not empty 2,000 gallons of water necessary to have direct access to the water from the well. He thereby makes salient a potential problem in the sampling method, which implicitly raises questions about the validity of the findings "no wells were found unacceptable." Further, the water samples already would have been mitigated by their passage through a water softener and through an UV-irradiation–based bacteria-killing system.

In his response, we can understand Lowen as attempting to defend himself by saying, consistent with his initial presentation, that to his knowledge all water tested came from the wells rather than from cistern (with perhaps one exception). Hayden questions the veracity of Lowen's statements thereby portraying them as claims rather than as matters of fact as it comes across in Lowen's presentation and initial response. Hayden's subsequent question again puts the authority of Lowen's description of method into relief by stating that there had been no evidence on his property that Lowen had actually accessed the water at the only place where it could have been sampled in unmitigated form. This constitutes a legitimate critique of the hydro-geologic data, which would not be unbiased. Nevertheless, Lowen claims that even if he had not conducted *these* measurements appropriately his overall conclusion would not change.

Here, we see an ordinary citizen questioning the legitimacy of a scientific report. The transcript does not allow us to think of Hayden as an ignorant person. For example, although Hayden probably has had a conception of what a solution might be that is different from what Lowen proposes, he participates in the debate quite efficiently. In these circumstances, the transcript makes us acknowledge a person who, through his public participation in the hearing, continually produces knowledgeability about the operation of water softeners, UV filters and their action on bacteria (but not on other aspects of water quality), and the effect nearby septic fields have on drinking water. (In rural areas, many homes still use septic fields where wastewater is allowed to move through a special bed made of rocks, pebbles, and sand to enter the ground water.) This episode quite clearly illustrates how "lay expertise" and common knowledge can be mobilized for clarifying what is at stake in the context of a socio-scientific and socio-technical controversy. More so, I have been suggesting recently that we ought not think in terms of individual knowledgeabilities but in terms of what we collectively are able to do (Roth, 2003). That is, rather than seeing scientific method as the way of individuals to produce reliable knowledge, we might be better off to think it as the outcome of expansive learning (expansive because it increases the agential room to maneuver) of a collectivity (i.e., group, community, society), including engineers, scientists, doctors, and citizens, to bring science to bear on local issues.

The need to think in terms of scientific method and critique as a collective way of producing knowledge and decisions becomes clear throughout the meeting, where residents bring to bear their extensive local knowledge about the problems with the water supply, or in the evaluation of the appropriateness of the sampling methods used. In the following excerpt, another local resident, Tony Knott, asks the expert Lowen to evaluate his own results in the light of those apparently contradictory ones presented by another scientists in the service of the regional health authority. Here, the major issue is whether Lowen's data, collected at one time point during the year, represent an average value or whether they have to be interpreted as a short-term, best-case scenario. Knott not only asks the expert to make this evaluation but also, as his further questioning shows, brings out the pertinent issues that have led to the contradictions between the report Lowen authored, on the one hand, and that authored by the scientists from the Capital Health Region (based on two sampling episodes at different times of the year), on the other hand.

> Knott: Of course. And, and, and what we have umm, can you tell me the years that you have charted here, what years were those uh, the log years for?
>
> Lowen: Yeah. The, the observation well has been in service since nineteen ninety-seven but I can see here, and that's from October ninety-seven and we had data up to June of nineteen ninety-nine.
>
> Knott: Okay, so um, so, so uh, what is your understanding of what happened last fall and this spring with respect to uh, to uh, the water amounts of rainfall? Was this a heavy period or a normal period?
>
> Lowen: I know that it was a record period per rainfall but it's not reflected in water levels in the area because the peak water levels in the aquifer in nineteen eighty-eight were higher than in the winter levels in nineteen ninety-nine.
>
> Knott: Just a minute. You just said that it was a direct result of water and we've just had a record rainfall and it doesn't affect it? Well, there's something missing here.

Lowen: That means that only a certain amount of the rainfall can get into the aquifer being the heavy rains are running off. That's my interpretation.

Knott: Well, it could also–

Lowen: there's a limiting factor as to how much can get down into the–

Knott: well, well, it's, okay this is true but the thing is, is that what we've experienced is, rainfall in the order of five hundred twenty-two percent on average uh as far as monthly averages are concerned increase over the summer months. In other words what we've got through the winter period, through the five months previously preceding the, the your test results, there was uh, if you took that and compared that to an average summer month, a month through that period, it is, there's uh, there were five hundred twenty-two percent more. Now, it would seem to me that we're probably not dealing on an average result with your tests, we're probably dealing on the hydrostatic head feeding that aquifer up in the higher, very much higher ends, so that the readings that you're getting are very much diluted.

Lowen argues that his data—taken at a water level in the aquifer midway between its minimum and maximum values—represent an average and therefore constitute a representative value of the biological and chemical parameters of water quality. The scientists from Capital Health Region have suggested, on the other hand, that there are fluctuations in water levels such that during one half of the year, the quality values are in fact below the standards published by Health Canada. This is the same period when the residents are advised not to consume their water; this therefore deeply affects their quality of life. In this excerpt, Knott questions Lowen about the variations, the level of water in the aquifer at the time Lowen conducted his measurements. In this, this interaction constitutes a moment where the contradictory claims of acceptability of water quality become salient again in public.

Knott is but one of many residents of the Senanus Drive area. He asks Lowen to reflect on the results of his own readings after having access to another report, which has come to different conclusion. In particular, Knott asks Lowen to attend to and interpret the effect of the sampling episode to the amount of rainfall at and prior to the time of testing. In response to Lowen's description that all the water in the wells and in the aquifer comes from rainfall, Knott states that there should be a buffering effect included in the considerations. That is, changes in the aquifer do not directly correlate with the rainfall but are delayed by three to five months.

As Lowen makes another categorical statement that all water came from rain, Knott's interjection "but–" leads Lowen to retract or at least modify his earlier statement. He now admits that water would increase in dissolved minerals if it stayed for longer amounts of time in the ground. The subsequent question elicits from Lowen a statement about the groundwater levels: the hydro-geologist agrees that there have been record water levels prior to his measurements. But Lowen argues that these rainfalls did not affect the groundwater levels. However, Knott questions this claim by contrasting it with a previous, seemingly contradictory one. Lowen suggests that there are limits to absorption and that much of the rainwater would be carried away as run-off (cf. the ditches in figure 2). Knott exhibits dissatisfaction with this response suggesting that there was a 522% increase in rainfall from the summer to the winter months. The water levels could not have been "average" as the geological report states and that therefore, the chemical concentrations would generally be lower (more diluted) than under normal circumstances. Lowen, however, responds that the hydrograph shows an average reading.

In this episode again, we see a member of the general public question the content of a scientific report on water quality, the method for gathering the data, and for the inferences made on the basis of the data. Knott first casts doubt on Lowen's conclusion by evoking the possibility that an error could have been committed in using the average water level registered by the hydrograph in the months of April and May. More so, in a clever and astute rhetorical move, he squarely attributes the responsibility to the expert, "Could you be in error here?" Hayden and Knott, and all the other individuals who ask questions, do not appear to be intimidated by the social status usually attributed to scientific experts (here, several scientists were introduced by mentioning degree and rank in their respective institutional hierarchies). They pursue their lines of questioning which put into relief what otherwise are presented as authoritative statements about the quality of the water they are using. Indeed this constitutes an example of the "good use of experts," which constitutes one of the competencies individuals need to be prepared to produce and reproduce with others in debates over contentious issues and therefore also in the context of their science education (Fourez, 1997).

A Case of Distributive Social Justice

In these excerpts from the public meeting, we observe ordinary but concerned citizens engage scientists and science in exchanges over the nature of the water problem and the way in which the data documenting the levels of water quality had been established. The citizens ask a scientist to reflect on his own test results in the light of other results that have been made available during the public meeting or that the contributing individual made available. Additionally, citizens make salient forms of evidence that the scientists either omitted or labeled as unimportant. Thus, what appear to Lowen to be unimportant aesthetic indicators are in fact major problems in the lives of the residents—dying plants, corroding pipes and appliances, toxic levels of arsenic and lead—whose sole water supply, other than trucking this resource, lies in the wells. In contrast to the scientists, the residents are experts with respect to local and historically situated knowledge concerning the water in this area, its changing levels throughout the years, alternative supplies, increasing salination of the resource, difficulties of getting sufficient water by alternative means, and so forth. Yet scientists and politicians do not draw on residents' knowledgeabilities, though recent advances in the sciences have developed complex computer-aided tools to combine vastly different forms of knowledge, such as the ones scientists produce in their laboratories and the local knowledge of aboriginals and residents (e.g., Pauly, Pitcher, and Preikshot, 1998). Truly democratic decision-making processes take into account these local forms of expertise—which remain largely hidden resources for comprehending the ever-shifting connections between human behavior and environmental conditions. But we keep in mind that no form of knowledge can found rational decision and justify rational decision making because real situations always exceed the totality of collectively available knowledge, though they motivate the movement, history, and future-to-come of rationality and the knowledge-related resources it requires. Citizens are actively involved in the construction of the facts concerning the water, health, and environment in the area covered by Senanus Drive. Science in this case is not clean but tied up with the economics of the situation, the costs of the varying solutions (status quo, constructing water main, trucking, recycling wastewater) and the different ways of covering the costs (Senanus Drive residents, Central Saanich residents).

If democracy and equity are not to remain but obscene alibis, then the costs of stresses and damage to the environment have to be born by all. In the present instance, the sorry state of the local aquifers is due to the impact that the straightening of the nearby creek has had and the continuous pumping of water for irrigation purposes. The decreasing quantity and quality of the water, as attested to by the residents who have lived at Senanus Drive for up to 30 years, is an environmental issue. There appears to be inequity and injustice when environmental destruction consistently and negatively affect the lives, health, reproductive choices, and overall well-being of one group of people (here those who live in a "rural" area), while other groups (here those living in other parts of Central Saanich) consistently escape much of the burden of such destruction. The Senanus Drive issue therefore also is an issue of environmental justice, a term used in the context of changes of the environment the "benefits" of which are born by one group of people whereas the burden is born by another. Environmental justice is about the fair and equitable distribution of environmental goods, services, and "resources." Injustice is exacerbated when those who actually benefit from and enjoy the goods that resulted from environmentally destructive production processes, do not pay all the costs. Whatever the current law states, we need to act because justice always

> Exceeds law but at the same time motivates the movement, history, and becoming of juridical rationality, indeed the relationship between law and reason, as well as everything that, in modernity, will have linked the history of law to the history of critical reason. (Derrida, 2005, p. 150).

The context of this case study is a socio-political contest over access to safe drinking water. Water is a precious resource not only in countries with "terrible plight of so many millions of human being suffering from malnutrition" (p. 86). One might think that in an industrialized nation such as Canada, access to save drinking water would be a given, especially after (a) the much publicized disaster in another Canadian town, Walkerton, Ontario, which in May 2000 claimed the lives of seven people due to an *Escherichia coli-*contamination of the public water supply and (b) the recognition that more than 200 indigenous towns in Canada have to put up with water supplies that lack in quality or quantity. According to the Auditor General of British Columbia, the province in which Central Saanich is located, users of small water systems "should be able to expect some minimum level of source protection along with an appropriate level of information on the quality of their water source" (OAGBC, 1999, p. 121). My research over the years shows that even in Canada, one of the most industrialized nations in the world and member of the G-8, access to safe drinking water cannot be taken for granted. In the contest over access, politicians rally science and scientific expertise to deny the same resource that others in the same community—including themselves—freely have at their disposal. One might also think that in such a nation, distributive social justice concerning basic life necessities would be enacted and that all levels of government live up to their responsibility to ensure that citizens have access to services that meet basic needs. My study shows that even in a democratic country that is proud of its social programs (universal health care, general welfare), distributive social justice cannot be taken for granted inherently. Again, science and scientific expertise are rallied to deny some residents of one community the same services that others already receive. However, "reflections of an ethical, juridical, political, and, inseparably, technoscientific nature" do not simply add up "in a place where technicity, the great question of the technical and the logical of the prosthesis, would be not accessory but essential and intrinsic to the problematic of reason" (Derrida, 2005, p. 146). This is so because there are two different, discontinuous, and radically heterogeneous orders involved—that of the calculable, because fitting scientific and political law order, and that of the incalculable, because emergent, unreachable in a future that is always-to-come.

My case study is about the interaction between scientific experts, local residents, engineers, medical doctors, and municipal politicians in a contentious issue over access to safe water of sufficient quantity. My fine-grained analyses of the case exhibit much of the boundary work conducted within the community to distinguish between scientific and local knowledge, and the work done to delimit who speaks and who gets heard (Roth et al., 2004). This boundary work distinguishes those who have the right to access safe water and those who do not; and it distinguishes those who gain from changes to the environment on the part of farmers and local industries and those who have to carry the costs of this evolution. In this issue there existed efforts to delimit the role of local knowledge and to privilege scientific expertise as independent and therefore as superior to other pursuits. To me this means that scientific literacy in a democracy-to-come does not mean that citizens need to know more science but that scientists need to become knowledgeable about the usefulness of other forms of knowledge that may bear on attendant and contentious issues. As a citizen and as resident of the same municipality, I note my disaffection with the socio-political processes that exhibit unwillingness or inability to establish an *open* debate in which all sides attempt to articulate common interests and distributive social justice. In a democracy-to-come, we require citizens-to-come who do openly discuss all aspects of a contentious issue and attempt to find solutions in which gains and costs are distributed across all. Clearly, although the municipal council organized a public meeting, the residents have felt that they "had not been heard" and that their concerns have not entered the decision-making arena. Scientists' pronouncements have been elevated to truths and taken into consideration for making decisions, whereas residents' knowledgeabilities and contributions have been disregarded as mere opinion, unqualified to be taken into account to make a decision with regard to the water main extension. There remains much work to be done, including on the part of (science) educators, to make this democracy-to-come more equitable and socially just.

Once development guidelines have been put in place, the water problems will be able to be addressed as just that. It is clear that the community and its elected council need to address the issue of the quantity and quality of the water for the residents of Senanus Drive, but the present context of political wrangling is not going to lead to a solution that satisfies either of the groups. At the time of the public meeting, this community has not had realized the need for distributive environmental justice and the responsibility of all to resolve the access-to-water problem some of us faced. It seems that there indeed need to be resolutions to this issue that is satisfactory to all participants in the discussion. This might have involved the identification of a development plan that is seen to be strong enough to withstand pressure of councils-to-come to bow to the economic incentives and promises developers make to subdue policy makers and politicians. As seen in the case material presented, the members of this and other communities can be expected to scrutinize closely any scientific evidence. (There exist and have existed other contentious issues in this and neighboring municipalities, including the extension of the sewer system or the installation of a microwave tower; and in each case citizens rallied to voice their concerns and interrogate scientists, engineers, and politicians alike.) The case study presented here shows that any final decision must include data collected from all experts in the area—scientists, water management consultants, politicians, ethicists, engineers, and residents who live with the problem and residents who may have to share the cost of the solution—though, as I point out, the decision cannot be rationally founded or justified by any form of knowledge as such. That is, there is no formula into which all forms of knowledge can be entered to give a calculable solution. Rather, decision-making inherently means evolving solutions that draw on incommensurable data for their grounding: Decision-making requires making steps across an unbridgeable divide between what currently is and is available and the future-not-yet. Citizens of a democracy-to-come ought to be willing to participate in such decision-making at all levels of their individual and collective lives, whatever their varied and heterogeneous knowledgeabilities.

Clearly, the Senanus Drive controversy is crying out for distributive social justice. However, the questions "Who gets what?" and "On what grounds does s/he get it?" cannot be solved by banding together for the purpose of opposing partial interests. Common interests—that is, interests common to humanity generally and to those of all members of a specific society more particularly—are more important than partial interests. Common interests require a sense of solidarity. *Responsibility for the other* and *solidarity* with all other human beings exceed rational ethico-moral (e.g., Kantian) imperatives because they precede and are conditions of any Being. Here, solidarity is not the recognition of a core Self that is common to all human individuals, the core essence of humanity. Rather, it is the ability to see difference as such, that is, the ability to see difference and heterogeneity at the heart of Self (Roth, 2007a) in the face of similarities in the experiences of pain and suffering. Solidarity therefore involves a conversion from the use of "they" (as in "all *they* want is to develop the land") to the use of "we," a conversion from special, partial interests to universal, common interests. The human sense of solidarity is strongest when those with whom solidarity is expressed are thought of as peers, where the use of "us" in everyday talk generally means something smaller, more local, and more contingent than humanity as a whole. Out of this conversion contingently and unpredictably (because of a future that always recedes and therefore hides) develop new cultural forms of life and new vocabularies, both of which can be explained only retrospectively. Once we expand our knowledgeabilities to include new cultural forms and language, we can figure out how the good things that recently happened serve some more general good. In a truly democratic society—which always will be a democratic society-to-come—ideals are fulfilled by negotiation rather than force (in using force rather than persuasion, the US itself has acted like an undemocratic rogue state [Derrida, 2005]), by reform rather than revolution, by free and open encounters of current practices, and by suggestions of new practices. In such a society, all disciplines (rather than techno-science on its own) and feelings, desires, and values have their place within rational inquiry, though even taken together they cannot bridge the gap between the heterogeneous orders of justice and law, the unpredictable and predictable, the irrational and the rational. Pure science then becomes but a form of knowledge, treated like other forms of knowledge (esoteric pursuits of music, drama, or literature) in the more encompassing thread of collective human life.

This, then, constitutes the context in and for which (science) education ought to prepare its (present and future) citizens-to-come for participation in the democracy-to-come during the 21st century. Citizens need to be accepting not only of the differences with others but of the heterogeneities within themselves, prepared to contribute to public debates over contentious issues; and they need to be prepared to learn forever to cope with present circumstances and change the world in ever receding and unpredictable futures-to-come. We then might ask, "What can we (science) educators do to allow today's students to engage in the evolution of knowledgeabilities suitable for citizens-to-come in a democracy-to-come of the 21st century? In the following section, I report on a project designed to show the feasibility of doing (science) education differently, suitable for a critical participation in an every evolving society.

SCIENTIFIC LITERACY, KNOWLEDGEABILITY AND EXPANSIVE LEARNING

My larger study within the municipality of Central Saanich shows that there is a relationship between the well water and the aquifers that feed Hagan Creek. It is in the interests of the community as a whole to restore the creek, to find ways to manage water in the area, so that the aquifer is protected and a continual resource for future generations-to-come. In the Capital Regional District (sometimes denoted "Victoria), which comprises the municipality of Central Saanich, it is in the interest of the residents to minimize the use of water from the nearby reservoir that provides adequate safe water to all the residents only with some difficulty. The issue of the provision of water to some 30 homes at Senanus Drive has far reaching implications. It is one more in a recent series of events that points out our need to become much more aware of how we use the precious resource of water. Water- and watershed-focused environmentalism therefore is a legitimate form of activity that already existed in the municipality prior to my arrival and that constituted a context that I immediately considered suitable not only for introducing students to science but also to their roles as citizens of the 21st century. Already as a high school teacher, I had come to understand that students' control over the motive of activity is central to motivation and emotion; I had increasingly designed curricula where students learned science by designing their own projects and artifacts. As part of these initial studies during the early 1990s, I realized that there was a fundamental problem with school tasks in that they did not have their place in the larger scheme of society other than reproducing schooling through their own production of schooling. I began to argue that science educators needed to de-institutionalize science education so that students learn science or to interact with science by contributing to society at large (Roth and McGinn, 1997).

At the time, I had come to realize that (scientific) knowledge could not be thought of as something independent of its mobilization. Thus, what we teach and how we teach it always is based on particular values that science teachers, curriculum, and educators bring to their work. I believe that we continually learn as we engage in relevant, that is, meaningful, purposive, and responsible action. The problem is not one of understanding learning, which, as expansion of agential possibilities is desirable, enacted, and inevitable, but is one of understanding knowledge. Thus, we learn incidentally in the pursuit of worthy (as judged by the learner) goals. More so, science education designed for citizens of the 21st century needs to take into account that there is more to scientific literacy than understanding the world: the real point is to change it in and through knowledgeable participation. I also prefer action to unengaged understanding. My own predilection therefore lies with science education that not only *prepares* students *for* but also, and more importantly, immediately *engages* students *in* responsible action. In this way, students are citizens-to-come, always in the processes of becoming and never arriving at a static endpoint; through their participation, they reproduce and produce democracy-to-come, an equally open and unending process. To study the feasibility of a curriculum embedded in an everyday form of activity that is central part of Central Saanich, I planned and taught together with middle school teachers three iterations of an environmental curriculum as a context for students to engage in and with science.

To the middle school teachers in Central Saanich, I suggested that we teach primarily focusing on environmentalism both as everyday activity and as context for school science and that I would teach with them. Several doctoral students with backgrounds in biology and microbiology and other volunteers assisted me of over the two years. We organized the curriculum around ideas that students would learn science as they generated societally relevant knowledge, which they would contributed to the municipality through exhibits at an open-house event organized by environmentalists already operating within the village. Based on previous research (e.g., Roth and Bowen, 1995), I was convinced that students would learn much more than what the official curriculum for that grade level prescribed. In fact, by participating in community-based environmentalism (a societally motivated activity and practice), environmentalists, seventh-grade students, and volunteers helping to teach the unit knowledgeably participated in enacting science collectively by focusing on stream and watershed health and its sometimes-severe problems with quantity and quality of water that is threatening Central Saanich.

The Hagan Creek~□ennes Watershed Project was initiated by POLIS (Greek for city state), a university-based project on environmental governance. The Project arose from the concerns about water quality and was "fishing for community support" (figure 5). The actions initiated by the Project members included monitoring water quantity and quality or contributing the rewriting of community policies related to Hagan Creek, the watershed, and the quality and quantity of water available to the stakeholders (residents, farmers, industry). The Project brought about *concrete, lasting,* and *visible* changes to the community of Central Saanich by creating and actively promoting a stewardship program, building riffle structures in the stream to increase cutthroat trout habitat, building fences designed to protect the riparian areas (Figure 6), and monitoring the number of cutthroat trout in different parts of the creek. Other activities include replanting riparian areas for increased shading to result in a lowering of water temperature more suitable for fish. The environmentalists engaged in educational activities, including giving presentations throughout Central Saanich or assisting the seventh graders in their Hagan Creek-related investigations. Every now and then, a newspaper article featured the work of this group. It is with such newspaper articles that I have been beginning the science units at the middle school; the regular teachers and I used an article that called on citizens in the community to contribute to the currently available knowledge and direct actions to understand and change the health of the Hagan Creek watershed (figure 5, front center).

This description shows that there environmental concerns existed in the community and that they were publicly available, both through the newspaper articles and the participation of the environmentalists in a variety of activities including town hall meetings, signs that sprouted up in the watershed marking the creek and its fish habitat, fences they built (figure

6), through the public talks, and so on. This situation, therefore, constituted environmentalism as a legitimate *societal* activity. It existed in the community, continuously produced and reproduced in and through every action of the environmentalists and others who did something about the sorry state of the watershed. It is motivated activity, for it contributes to the long-term health of watershed and the people inhabiting it. Participating in such an activity, students not only contribute to the community but also produce and reproduce environmentalism as a legitimate form of societal activity, and thereby change their own forms of participation—i.e., students learn while being on a developmental trajectory of citizens-to-come. In this science unit, students therefore participated in a legitimate and authentic activity system. The people and groups that made up Central Saanich constituted their community rather than the teacher and other students. The division of labor goes far beyond traditional group work in that the students contribute knowledge to the activists' cause and thereby to Central Saanich at large. Many of the tools and rules for pursuing their goals are the very same ones that mediate the actions of other individuals and groups in the community. Thus, the students have moved beyond the school and learn science by participating in an activity system that is an integral part of their community. They do not solve fake problems but contribute their share to problems that are authentically those of their Central Saanich community.

Figure 5. The curriculum begins with articles from local newspapers and pamphlets from local environmental NGOs, explicitly inviting the community to become involved and thereby literally inviting the children to be and become environmentally concerned citizens.

Given the water-related problems in Central Saanich, it was not difficult to convince some of the teachers at the middle school to participate in a study where students would learn science by investigating issues concerning Hagan Creek and the watershed that it drains. I began teaching the unit in particular with one newspaper article (figure 5, center front) in which the coordinator of the Hagan Creek/Kennes Watershed Project encouraged community members to contribute to preserving the watershed by generating knowledge or contributing to its maintenance and improvement. Students, too, were excited about being able to do something that would be of value to their community generally and to their families in particular—some of them said during class discussion that their parents were fishing in the nearby inlet where fish and other aquatic life was affected negatively by the run off from Hagan Creek and other nearby creeks. The students' work, which legitimately contributed to an issue important to the community became purposeful and provided for a context in which they learned expansively whenever they needed a new skill or new knowledge for doing what they had set out to do. They also learned incidentally while pursuing worthwhile goals such as cleaning up sections of the creek or studying some aspects of it.

Figure 6. The Hagan Creek/Kennes Project concretely and lastingly changed the community in ways that were visible to many in their daily affairs, such as to students walking to school along this path. (© 2005 Wolff-Michael Roth, permission granted).

When the students first read about the sorry state of the water in their watershed and especially of Hagan Creek, they spontaneously wanted to do something about it. With a little scaffolding on my and other teachers' part (and in some instances by parents who had agreed to help out teaching), the seventh-grade students began to design and conduct their own research in and along Hagan Creek with the intent to report their findings at an open-house event organized each year by the members of the Hagan Creek/Kennes Watershed Project. This way of organizing the science lesson made it interesting for other members of the community to participate in various ways: (a) Parents drove students to the different sites along the creek or assisted students in learning or (b) environmentalists, scientists, elders, and politicians came to speak in the classroom or help out in conducting field work. That is, students produced knowledge in the context of a community that is much larger than "classroom community" characteristic of most educational practice and theory. School science and village life began to interpenetrate and, in the process, supported one another. Thus, members of the Hagan Creek/Kennes Watershed Project not only assisted in getting us started with the field work, but also came to the class to give talks, participate with students in measuring and recording such physical parameters as dissolved oxygen and turbidity or collected microorganism specimens. Among the participants was also a water technician working for a local farm interested in the revitalization of creek and watershed. She introduced the students to ways of collecting data, making available some of her instruments or using those that we had made available to the student in the school and brought to the field in plastic containers (figure 7).

Figure 7. Seventh-grade students and a water technician working for a local farm prepare a data collection at one of the regular sites in the creek. (© 1998 Wolff-Michael Roth, permission granted).

The water technician also introduced students to the idea of increasing the oxygenation of a creek by building riffles, that is, structures made from rock and fallen trees that serves to expose a lot of water to the air and thereby increase its oxygenation. Being introduced to a variety of monitoring techniques, the seventh-grade students then collected data in the main creek and its various tributaries (figure 8). The water technician and other individuals from the community thereby assisted students in expanding their knowledgeabilities for using instruments such as dissolved-oxygen meters or Serber samplers (a one-by-one foot square frame with a net mounted at 90° for trapping microorganisms that have been stirred up within the frame) and other nets.

On the days following the bi-weekly afternoons in the field, the adults came to the school to analyze data with students, to teach students about how to pick up organism with turkey basters, identify organisms under the microscope with the help of a field guide, separate the organisms into the different cubes of an ice-cube trays, and count them. Other adults worked with students to assist them in using field guides or in developing the knowledgeability required for using more advance forms of data analyses. In these instances, therefore, the students learned environmentalism by *engaging in the practice of environmentalism together with others who are already legitimate environmentalists.* But whatever the adults did, it always was on an as-needed and just-in-time basis, thereby making the students drivers of their expansive learning.

Figure 8. This video offprint features seventh-grade students collecting specimens and physical data (dissolved oxygen, turbidity) above and below a riffle, that is, a stone structure that helps the water turn over and increase its oxygenation rate. (© 1998 Wolff-Michael Roth, permission granted).

When I began my work of organizing science curricula in terms of activism, I still believed that all students should engage in their activities in ways that would foster scientific practices. I thought that "equity" meant every student had to be "treated the same," engage in the same tasks, and learn the same things. I did not realize yet the potential for growth (learning, change) that exists in heterogeneity and diversity both within and between individuals and communities. That is, I realized that pushing all students through the same square hole of the curriculum or sizing them to the same Procrustean bed constitutes the opposite of equity because it does injustice to their inherent differences. My former image of school science and of its future-to-come was based on the image of scientists' science, not as they practiced it but as represented in their scientific journals. Anything other was less than desirable. I soon realized that requiring all students to measure series of variables and to represent the creek using Cartesian graphs or histograms was experienced negatively by and therefore excluded especially female and aboriginal students; it met the interests and predilections of some but violated those of other students. While the latter students still participated in the collection of data, the subsequent data analyses and activities that focused on mathematical representations (e.g., graphs) generally turned them off. That is, not being in control of the means of production limited students to producing representations that were most appropriate to their current understanding.

Taking my lead from other activities in the community, where different representational forms were legitimately used to represent and talk about the woes of the watershed and creek (Lee and Roth, 2001), I began to encourage the seventh-grade students to define goals and investigate on their own terms, choosing their data collection and representational tools that best fit their interests and needs. Audio-recorded descriptions, videotaped records of the watershed and student activities, photographs, drawings, and other representations began to proliferate. This change provided forms of knowledgeabilities and expansive learning that led to an increasing participation of previously excluded students. It was a tremendous experience that made clear to me the need to abandon my traditional conception of what science and science education in the community might look like.

Ultimately, the seventh-grade students presented the results of their work at a yearly open-house event organized by the activists focusing on environmental health in the Hagan Creek watershed, for example, presenting posters that contained the results of their observations, photographs, measurements, or interviews with community members (figure 9). During these events, students exhibited their findings and productions among those of other community groups and environmentalists. Not privileging adult over student displays, the visitors engaged students in active exchanges in the course of which all participants expanded their possibilities further—adults learned about the creek and students learned to teach others. That is, students—including several who previously had been labeled "learning disabled" in their school—had developed such tremendous forms of knowledgeability that they became teachers of their more senior fellow citizens. It is in this that they actively contributed to the *production*, *exchange*, *distribution*, and *consumption* of knowledge in Central Saanich. In this way, the seventh graders not only prepared for but also actively and simultaneously produced and reproduced ordinary everyday citizenhood in very concrete and demonstrable ways.

Figure 9. This composite video offprint represents a moment during the open house event where the seventh-grade students exhibit the outcomes of their work alongside environmentalist and come to contribute to the expansive learning of their town. (© 2007 Wolff-Michael Roth, permission granted).

The students mounted posters that engaged other children and adults alike (figure 9, 10), who had come to the open-house events because of the exhibit generally rather than the students' work in particular. In this particular instance, figure 10 features one of four female students who had decided not to conduct measurements as other students and in the way many science educators might have asked their students to participate (e.g., the student to the left in figure 9 reports results using bar graphs and histograms). Rather, the four young women decided to shoot photographs of Hagan Creek in its various reaches to document its current (sorry) state, and to record their verbal descriptions on audiotape, which they subsequently transcribed. The young women also interviewed the mayor of the municipality and other adults in the municipality to find out more about their stances with respect to water and the environment. In their poster, the young women presented the result, focusing in particular on comparisons between reaches that had been cleaned up and appeared healthier than others (such as the one in figure 2). In addition, my students presented descriptions and photographs in the form of a website, which the visitors could peruse at the event because the children had brought a computer. After the open-house events, some of the results of the students' research also were published in the local newspaper and on the website of the environmental activists. Thus, both through their exhibits during the open-house event and the subsequent publication of their findings, the outcomes of the students' production re-entered the community in a process of knowledge distribution and consumption. The open-house event and the subsequent publications were key points in the unit because students' work became legitimated and legitimate as the community members accepted what they had done.

Figure 10. The students represent the outcomes of their work, which have been mediated by the collective object (concern for the environment), the chosen tools, and the ethico-moral commitments the students bring to their participation. Here one student presents photographs, transcript of descriptions, and interview material that she collected together with her peers. (© 1999 Wolff-Michael Roth, permission granted).

To the children, the science unit was successful not because they received high grades but because the unit was useful and contributed to community life. They began to notice the creek and its problems; they also remarked that the community (their parents and relatives) began to notice it as a result of their own actions. Students' actions had further impact in the community, as the environmental activists told me, because their presence in and contributions to the open house brought a greater proportion of community members (parents, family, neighbors) to the events.

The unit also points us to a path toward the future of education generally and science education more specifically. In their engagement, students literally responded to a call of an environmentalist to engage in an issue that is of central concern not only at the time of the interview but also, and even more so, in the future-to-come. In fact, these students did not merely participate in an environmental unit but rather, mediated by an anonymous call transcending the environmentalist, they oriented toward and enacted ethico-moral principles suitable for a democracy-to-come in which distributed social justice is the highest norm. And they did so with the positive emotional valence and associated satisfaction that comes with a "job well done," that is, when set goals have been achieved at or above the anticipated levels of quality. Thus, the unit not only spoke to the ethics of case that many students expressed at the beginning of the unit when they felt called to act on the request for community participation, but also allowed students to realize concretely their plans to do something *in* and *for* their community.

SCIENTIFIC LITERACY IN AND FOR A DEMOCRACY-TO-COME

In the past, science education, scientific literacy and science curriculum have been theorized from the perspective of an asocial and fictional view of the sciences. Given the substantial disaffection with the sciences among students and the problematic nature of scientists' contributions to the problems of the world, this approach to science education has to be questioned. It has to be questioned and critically interrogated in the light of the fact that the citizens-to-come of a democracy-to-come beyond the 21st century need to actively shape their political and material lives to prevent, mitigate, and turn around the negative impacts modernist humans of the industrial age have had on the environment that sustains them. I therefore propose to take the notions of citizenship and inclusive democracy as starting points for theorizing (science) education in and for the society-to-come. In other words, I want (science) education to contribute to citizenship and inclusive democracy rather than continuing to constitute a middle-class-favoring selection mechanism for the formation of a(n) (scientific) elite (e.g., Foucault, 1975) operating within the citadel that towers over and surveys and controls the (re-) public. I thereby mean that (science) education ought to contribute to expanding knowledgeabilities not only *about* constitutions, rules for elections, and the role of science in contentious issues but also means *ever becoming actively involved in* democratic processes.

Democratic ideals, particularly those consistent with inclusive democracy (Fotopoulos, 1999), imply a greater involvement of the public in policy-making issues that pertain to or involve science and technology. There are opportunities for new forms of solutions to emerge from the interaction of a greater variety of experts, including those with special traditional, local, and historical knowledge of the contentious issues at hand (Roth and Lee, 2002). However, aspirations to be more inclusive do not automatically eliminate the boundary work currently enacted to elevate scientists or engineers over others in society. As highly publicized jury trials show (as I am writing these lines, O. J. Simpson has been arraigned again, this time for break and entry), boundary work involves social and political judgments to decide who is competent with respect to a particular issue and what the level of this competence is. Rather than thinking such competencies in terms of unitary forms of knowledge, the individuals (identities) of the participants in such boundary work need to be thought in terms of heterogeneity, diversity, and identities that are forever to-come (Roth, in press-a). Knowledgeabilities are continually subject to the local and contingent bricolage of individual and collective agents that make do with the epistemic, technological, and discursive resources at hand. In the process, these resources come to be stitched together not in linear and cumulative forms, but through processes that continually batter, mix, and scramble the various cultural-historical resources for constituting and concretizing problems and their solutions (Roth, in press-b).

In the public meeting, the residents were engaged defending their real water-related needs, which politicians and the contracted scientists constructed differently to impede the citizens' legitimate access to a resource already available to all others in the municipality of Central Saanich. The citizens involved had immediate concerns—the outcome of the decisions to be taken would have direct bearing on their lives and that of the municipality, not the least being the decision about who pays how much for the solution to the water problem. Rather than passively accepting their fate, the residents of Senanus Drive actively interrogated scientists, science, and scientific method and thereby contributed to the collective enactment of science. They brought to bear their historical knowledgeabilities with respect to the water quantity and quality and the historical changes therein. It is in this debate that I propose to seek scientific literacy rather than in individuals. Scientific literacy therefore comes to be redefined as a process of change brought about in and through participation in inherently dialogic events over contentious and not so contentious issues relevant to all—i.e., relevant to *common* interests. Science educators might think that modeling such events by conducting mock discussions constitute suitable contexts for learning science. Yet in my view, this approach limits what students can learn, for there are no stakes and consequences in whatever decisions are made. By participating in concrete everyday activity the stakes and investments individual subjects make considerably shape the situation, both what is salient figure and what is contextualizing ground. Thus, the level of expertise in dealing with school-based case studies of socio-scientific and socio-technical problems will never predict accurately the level of expertise in real situations of which the cases are said to be models; these will never predict accurately in the same way that doing well on ethico-moral tests of reasoning does not predict the real decisions a person makes in and by acting in the world (Damasio, 1994/2000).

The public meeting provided an opportunity for scientific literacy to become a recognizable and analyzable, collective, and continually evolving phenomenon. A new form of collectively generated societal activity was made possible in the organization of the public meeting and in the provision of the questioning and comment periods. Already the knowledgeabilities of individual participants were heterogeneous, giving them more or less room to maneuver with respect to the scientific, engineering, technological, ethico-moral, historical, political, or environmental dimensions involved. These knowledgeabilities came to be hybridized to an even greater extent in the exchanges of the different participants, increasing heterogeneity and diversity, and therefore the potential to change. I understand scientific literacy to mean the ability to learn, to increase knowledge, and therefore, the process of expanding the action possibilities of individuals and collectives. In the public meeting about the water at Senanus Drive, scientific literacy of this form emerged because the citizens were involved in an issue where there was something at stake. The articulation of a problem with the "scientific" method employed, which had surfaced during the meeting, is not attributable to the engineer who had conducted water tests; and I resist in attributing the articulation to the residents who spoke up. Rather, the problem was an outcome of the collective conversation involving an engineer, a hydro-geologist, affected and concerned citizens, politicians, town engineers, doctors, and others. In the same way, the omission of important historical knowledge in previous decisions and deliberations was articulated in the public conversation at the meeting. Because it can teach us so much about participatory democracy, the case study of water for Senanus Drive became for me a crucial turning point in my thinking about science education, especially in rethinking science education as it might be designed for constitutive participants in a (Canadian) democracy-to-come of the 21st century. Here, the "to-come" also means that work remains; and rather than waiting until they reach maturity, we can involve middle and high school students actively as citizens-to-come in shaping the social and material environments that they inhabit now and will inhabit in the future—though they will never be able to anticipate what a democracy continually becoming will *be*, if there ever is anything as to be in the face of *to-come* and *becoming*.

Recent global and local developments in climates, the impact of technology and science on environment and people, show that the future-to-come will become more rather than less unpredictable. Events and conditions that can be anticipated—because they fall, "like a case, like the object of some knowledge, under the generality of a law, norm, determinative judgment, or technoscience, and thus of a power knowledge and a knowledge-power" [Derrida, 2005, p. 148])—do not in fact constitute real events. This is so because "[w]ithout the absolute singularity of the incalculable and the exceptional, no thing and no one, nothing *other* and thus *nothing*, arrives or happens" (p. 148). This raises serious challenges for any form of schooling that proclaims to be educating children and students for tomorrow. Does everyone participating in the public debate have to know the same facts, concepts, and theories? Does every student have to be competent on the same issues? What do we teach to ready students for the unpredictable future-to-come generally and for successfully coping with inherently un-anticipatable events?

We already know that the Renaissance has long passed, an era during which one individual could exhibit knowledgeabilities across many domains. Today there simply exist too many competing facts, concepts, and theories for any individual to know even in more constrained contexts and within the same paradigm. It will be increasingly important that we, as collectives, produce the substantive knowledges relevant to the problems at hand in and for a democracy-to-come. Yet few children and students are prepared to participate in public debates over real issues and concerns. Educators may be tempted to teach all the facts that were mentioned during the public meeting in Central Saanich. But then, we would spend much more time in school even if knowledge transfer from school to workplace and everyday life were less problematic then it already is. If it were possible to teach everybody the same, we also would end up producing future generations that all have the same set of blinders, think in the same way about GMOs, genetic manipulation, and designing new weapons. If we think of scientific literacy in different terms, as choreography of a particular kind in which we participate increasingly through learning expansively and by participating from the beginning, we take radically different approaches to teaching science in schools. For example, our children and students might already participate in activities that benefit their villages, towns, municipalities, and cities, and participate in the ongoing discourses and concerns that are relevant to their parents and the community at large.

Greater involvement of the public in public affairs, however, poses new questions: "How do ordinary citizens participate in critically reflecting on science and technology—i.e., technicity—that the concept of *democracy-to-come* implies?" and "What level of scientific and technological literacy do citizens have to bring to be legitimate participants in the public debate?" More so, it poses questions about the nature of a scientific literacy that scientists, engineers, and experts from other socio-scientific and socio-technical fields to be able to participate in democratic decision-making processes without expecting all other participants to bow to a scientific view. There are examples in the literature that show how certain groups of citizens shift existing unequal relations between themselves, with particular types and levels of expertise and more traditional experts. Public participation can contribute to create effective dialogical (rhetorical) spaces that legitimate rather than discredit the stories of ordinary people as co-producers of environmentally sound knowledge and behavior. In such processes, expertise pertaining to local particulars (such as knowing the history of the wells, their fluctuations, and seasonal contaminations) shifts traditional boundaries of what is considered to be legitimate expertise. Local expertise gains ground and even becomes central to, and can be used for calling into question, evidence presented under the guise of decontextualized, scientific expertise. That is, public participation potentially contributes to produce a more inclusive and better science.

If we abandon the idea (really, the ideology) that all students should demonstrate scientific competencies and accept that scientific literacy means the collective production of certain competencies and free access to all the mediating resources collectives require to make sense and act, then what might we do? We might begin by providing opportunities for the *collective* production of scientific literacy to be brought forth. Some readers might be tempted to say that this is a dream because literacy for all does not emerge unless we make everyone learn the right stuff. Not only is it possible but also has been done already. For example, Bernard Collot (2002), the former elementary school teacher in Moussac, France did not "teach." He did not tell students what to study ("they do well without me"). He did not follow a prescribed curriculum. But he provided the opportunities for the collective (children and villagers) to engage in activities together. It was in the context of this larger community that all children came to know, but not necessarily the same things. And yet, on standardized examinations the children scored above the national norm. It was in the context of collective activity that each child found its place and became literate. Children, when they came to school (they decided themselves at what time) wrote on the board what they would be doing that day, including writing a letter to a pen pal, inventing a piece of music, building something in the shop, or writing poetry while sitting near the pond behind the school. Throughout the day, children interacted with each other and the adults who came as resource persons for playing chess or tending the garden. In the course of pursuing activities of their interest, all children learn to read, write, and do arithmetic; and, by doing them, they expanded their agential possibilities concerning everyday mundane things, like how to post a letter, how to garden, how to write poetry, how to compose music, and how to dream. Collot did not have to "teach" these things. Responding to a visiting journalist, he said "I learned that when the children are part of a group that really exists as a community, when there is a real setting, when the interactions with this setting, with other children and adults, when this context really exists, at that point, all children without exception learn to read" (Roth, 1998, p. xiv). It was out of the existence of this community that literacy emerged. In my own case study, we saw that the seventh-grade students contributed to producing scientific literacy in and with their community, and they did so despite and because of all the heterogeneity and diversity observable in them and their productions.

This issue also is of interest to the larger community because it demonstrates how the conflict between urban and rural development can find itself played out over the issue of a limited resource on the island: fresh water. The Senanus Drive residents have the same rights to safe and plentiful water that all other citizens of Central Saanich have. The most efficient and cost effective way for this to happen is to have a water main extended to their street. The community members who opposed the water main extension have claimed that there are alternatives to the water main extension that had not been fully examined. This group is against urban encroachment in the area, so they see any water main extension as an invitation for some residents to subdivide their large properties, thereby increasing the population density of the area. The solution to this problem therefore must involve a decision-making process in the community that is perceived as being fair, and the clear identification of the development goals of the area.

To sum up, "scientific literacy for the 21st century" does not mean to me knowing a bunch of facts, concepts, and theories. There simply are too many in any subfield of science let alone in all those scientific fields that produce knowledge relevant to life in society. Scientific literacy means being knowledgeable, that is, being able to engage, *with* and *for others,* in expansive learning that leads to ever further knowledgeability. Knowledge-ability means ability to continuously transform and be transformed by knowledge-in-the-making, always a knowledge-to-come however unpredictable any future knowledge inherently is. Because of the progressive division of labor that functions in society and the associated exponential increase and deepening of factual knowledge, few if any individuals will be able to know relevant facts, concepts, and theories in the different disciplines relevant to a problem or to have anything like a cursory understanding. It will be more important for any democracy-to-come to be constituted by citizens-to-come that have developed abilities for expanding their knowledge mobilization (knowledge-abilities) in collective contexts with others that are on very different trajectories of knowledgeabilities-to-come. And precisely the enactment of knowledgeabilities-to-come will constitute the democracies-to-come that is, one in which distributive social justice is the uppermost ethico-moral principle.

AN ENDING WITH A HAPPY ENDING?

Many stories in our lives do not have a happy ending. For a long time I was unable to see any change that would have granted the Senanus Drive residents the same access to water that characterizes others in the community. But the active engagement in seeking assistance from the municipality and the provincial government paid off for the Senanus Drive residents, even if it did not directly "cause" a recent turn of events. Just one week prior to my writing this chapter, I happened to glance at the local newspaper when I found my gaze drawn to the headline: "Feds fund Senanus Water Line: Wait for drinking water over" (George, 2007, p. A1). The article begins, "Irene Booth has been waiting for clean water at her home on Senanus Drive for 47 years now" (p. A1). Although I had researched the issue for nearly 10 years, I had not followed whether there was any change concerning the water situation at Senanus Drive. I instantly remembered the photograph of a certain Larry Booth, who bent over three 5-gallon jugs that he is in the process of filling them with water at the gas station. Here Senanus was back in the news, interestingly enough featuring one of the same individuals (Irene Booth) that had been central to the story that first caught my attention.

A little further on, the article reads: "Booth's home, along with 63 others on Senanus and in the Mount Newton X Road area as far east as Thompson Road, will be connected to two water mains thanks to $1.1 million in funding from the Canada-British Columbia Municipal Rural Infrastructure Fund" (p. A1). What has happened that made this sudden funding possible after the often-acrimonious exchanges between the residents and the town administration? In part, the political situation and changes therein both at the provincial and national level created a context that made possible funding the costs, which in the meantime had increased dramatically from the original $300,000 that the project had been costed for 10 years earlier (1998). The local member of parliament Gary Lunn is Minister of Environment and Natural Resources of the current minority government—both the national party generally and Gary Lunn in his riding specifically were elected with only 37% of the popular vote—attempting to secure gains in the constantly looming ("snap") election. The provincial government, too, is preparing for the next election so that it comes as little surprise if the local member of the legislative assembly and ruling party and the provincial minister of community services joined the federal minister in the announcement. In part, the long struggle and the accompanying media coverage may have contributed to keeping the light on the injustices and inequities incurred by the residents. Thus, the provincial minister of community services "congratulated the home owners and the municipality for their perseverance in bringing forward their request for infrastructure funding. . . . 'These projects, one by one, are contributing to a greener healthier BC [British Columbia]'" (p. A2).

My proposal for a different way of thinking about and planning scientific literacy is designed to scaffold the evolution of knowledgeabilities—i.e., the learning potential—of all citizens independent of their age to actively and agentially change their material, physical, environmental, and societal life conditions toward a democracy-to-come where the achievement of *common* interests rather than *partial* interests (enriching oneself at the expense of the poor and working class) are the main orienting principles. The "aim of 'good life' *with* and *for* others in just institutions" (Ricœur, 1990, p. 202, my translation and emphasis) may then be realized as the highest ethico-moral principle. One of these institutions that I have in mind is a democracy-to-come, that is, a democracy that is always open to the future and to the input of all its citizens that themselves are projects of continual development, that is, they never *are* but always *become* citizens. But this also means that democracy-to-come inherently is subject to bringing about its own fall—there are many examples attesting to this strength and frailty of the democracy-to-come, beginning with the Weimar Republic that gave rise to Adolf Hitler, the Chile of Salvadore Alliende that General Augusto Pinochet took hostage, or the democratic Pakistan that gave rise to the coup d'etat that swept General Pervez Mousharraf to power. Citizens of the democracies-to-come in and of the 21st century ought to (knowledge-) ably participate in the public discourses in ways that always leave open negotiation and subvert attempts to overturn and abolish them.

REFERENCES

Collot, B. (2002). Une école du 3ième type ou *"La pédagogie de la mouche."* Paris: L'Harmattan.

Damasio, A. R. (2000). *Descartes' error: Emotion, reason, and the human brain.* New York: HarperCollins. (First published in 1994).

Derrida, J. (2005). *Rogues: Two essays on reason.* Stanford: Stanford University Press.

Fotopoulos, T. (1999). Social ecology, eco-communitarianism and inclusive democracy. *Democracy and Nature,* 5, 561–576.

Foucault, M. (1975). Surveiller et punir: Naissance de la prison. Paris: Gallimard.

Fourez, G. (1997). Scientific and technological literacy as a social practice. *Social Studies of Science,* 27, 903–936.

George, C. (2007, September 5). Feds fund Senanus water line: Wait for drinking water over. Peninsula News Review, pp. A1, A2.

Lavin, L. (2001, November 28). Still can't drink the water. *Peninsula News Review,* p. A3.

Lee, S., and Roth, W.-M. (2001). How ditch and drain become a healthy creek: Representations, translations and agency during the re/design of a watershed. *Social Studies of Science,* 31, 315–356.

McCullogh, S. (1999, March 17). Anger overflows at water. *Times Colonist,* p. C2.

M'Gonigle, R. M. (2001). Macro/micro gridlock: The implications of a local territorial conflict for central regulatory reform. In J. A. Tejada-Guibert and Č. Maksimović (Eds.), *Frontiers in urban water management: Deadlock or hope?* (pp. 292–300). Paris: UNESCO.

Office of the Auditor General of British Columbia (OAGBC). (1998/1999). Report 5: Protecting drinking-water sources. Available at http://oag.bc.ca/PUBS/1998-99/Other/AReport1998.pdf. (Accessed September 16, 2007).

Pauly, D., Pitcher, T. J., and Preikshot, D. (1998). Back to the future: Reconstructing the Strait of Georgia ecosystem. Vancouver, Canada: University of British Columbia.

Ricœur, P. (1990). Soi-même comme un autre. Paris: Seuil.

Roth, W.-M. (1998). Designing communities. Dordrecht, The Netherlands: Kluwer Academic Publishing.

Roth, W.-M. (2003). Scientific literacy as an emergent feature of human practice. *Journal of Curriculum Studies,* 35, 9-24.

Roth, W.-M. (2007a). Grounding solidarity and responsibility, ontologically (categorically). *Cultural Studies in Science Education,* 2 (4).

Roth, W.-M. (2007b). Toward a dialectical notion and praxis of scientific literacy. *Journal of Curriculum Studies,* 39, 377–398.

Roth, W.-M. (in press-a). Bricolage, métissage, hybridity, heterogeneity, diaspora: Concepts for thinking science education in the 21st century. *Cultural Studies in Science Education,* 3, .

Roth, W.-M. (in press-b). Éloge de la mêlée: vers une conception philosophique de l'alphabétisation scientifique. In A. Hasni (Ed.), Nouveaux enjeux de l'éducation scientifique et technologique: visées, contenus, compétences et pratiques (pp. -).

Roth, W.-M., and Bowen, G. M. (1995). Knowing and interacting: A study of culture, practices, and resources in a grade 8 open-inquiry science classroom guided by a cognitive apprenticeship metaphor. *Cognition and Instruction,* 13, 73–128.

Roth, W.-M., and Lee, S. (2002). Scientific literacy as collective praxis. Public Understanding of Science, 11, 33–56.

Roth, W.-M., and McGinn, M. K. (1997). Deinstitutionalizing school science: Implications of a strong view of situated cognition. *Research in Science Education,* 27, 497–513.

Roth, W.-M., Riecken, J., Pozzer, L. L., McMillan, R., Storr, B., Tait, D., Bradshaw, G. and Pauluth Penner, T. (2004). Those who get hurt aren't always being heard: Scientist-resident interactions over community water. *Science, Technology, and Human Values,* 29, 153–183.

Shamos, M. H. (1995). The myth of scientific literacy. New Brunswick, NJ: Rutgers University Press.

Woodley, K. (1998, December 16). *Senanus residents still wait for water.* Peninsula News Review, pp. A1, A5.

In: Citizenship in the 21st Century
Editors: L. T. Kane and M. R. Poweller, pp. 127-153   © 2008 Nova Science Publishers, Inc.
ISBN: 978-1-60456-401-3

Chapter 4

SHOULD I DO IT OR NOT?
AN INITIAL MODEL OF COGNITIVE PROCESSES PREDICTING VOICE BEHAVIORS

Dan S. Chiaburu,[1]* Sophia V. Marinova[2]# and Linn Van Dyne[3]†

[1] Pennsylvania State University; Smeal College of Business;
Business Building 403A; University Park, PA, 16802.
[2] University of Illinois- Chicago; Department of Managerial Studies (MC 243);
College of Business Administration; Suite 2210, University Hall;
601 South Morgan Street; Chicago, Illinois 60607.
[3] The Eli Broad Graduate School of Management; Michigan State University;
N424 North Business Complex; East Lansing, MI 48824-1122.

ABSTRACT

In this chapter, we advance the idea that organizational citizenship behaviors (OCBs) are discretionary and, as a result, employees engage in decisional processes before acting. Emphasizing conceptual differences in affiliative OCBs, such as helping, compared to challenging OCBs, such as voice, we propose that voice is a function of more elaborate cognitive processes than helping. Extending this idea, our primary objective is to develop a conceptual model that explicates cognitive processes as antecedents to employee voice behavior. We draw on work in social psychology with an emphasis on dual process decision-making theories (e.g., systematic vs. heuristic processing: see Smith and DeCoster, 2000, for a review) to guide our model. We aim to stimulate research on voice and other comparatively neglected forms of challenging OCB (e.g., personal initiative, taking charge) as well as research on decision processes that should enhance our ability to predict and encourage these important citizenship behaviors.

---

* Phone: (814) 865-1263; E-mail: dchiaburu@psu.edu.
# Email: smarinov@uic.edu.
† Tel: (517) 432-3512; Email: vandyne@msu.edu.

INTRODUCTION

The Organizational Citizenship Behavior Domain

Interest in discretionary employee behaviors started as early as the 1940's with Barnard's (1938) discussion of the important functions of the business executive and later continued with Katz's (1964) discussion of prosocial employee behaviors. One of the key issues that Katz discussed was the importance of engendering cooperation to enhance organizational adaptability and consequently, organizational effectiveness. Since then, organizational researchers have witnessed a proliferation of research articles examining antecedents and outcomes of beneficial employee behaviors beyond the call of duty, which came to be labeled by Organ (1988) as organizational citizenship behaviors (OCBs). The growing momentum of OCB research has also generated great interest in defining the domain. Academics have started asking questions such as: What types of behaviors comprise OCBs? Is there a comprehensive framework for defining and assessing all discretionary behaviors that contribute to organizational effectiveness? Do the different types of behaviors warrant attention as separate and unique behavioral phenomena, contributing uniquely to individual, group and organizational effectiveness?

There are several notable answers with respect to these questions. Recently, Podsakoff, MacKenzie, Paine and Bachrach (2000) identified at least seven common behavioral themes including helping behavior, sportsmanship, organizational loyalty and compliance, individual initiative, civic virtue, and self-development. One way to organize them is based on the framework proposed by Van Dyne, Cummings and McLean Parks (1995). One critical distinction lies in the nature of the behavior as affiliative versus challenging. They also reasoned that behaviors can be promotive or protective, a dimension that intersects with affiliative and challenging to produce four types of behaviors: (1) affiliative-promotive (e.g., helping coworkers), (2) affiliative-protective (e.g., stewardship), (3) challenging-promotive (e.g., voice), and (4) challenging-protective (whistle blowing). In this chapter, we focus on promotive behaviors in general, and on one specific type of challenging-promotive behavior in particular, that is voice. In general, *affiliative-promotive* behaviors such as helping tend to be cooperative and interpersonal (Van Dyne and LePine, 1998), while *challenging-promotive* behaviors such as voicing one's opinions to bring about positive change or taking personal initiative are often intended to challenge the status-quo (Chiaburu and Baker, 2006; Fuller, Marler, and Hester, 2006; Morrison and Phelps, 1999; Van Dyne, Ang, and Botero, 2003).

Consistent with understanding affiliative-promotive behaviors such as helping and cooperation, extensive research has been conducted on the premises of a social exchange perspective (Blau, 1964), according to which employees may develop high quality relationships and engage in beneficial behaviors to reciprocate favorable treatment by the organization or by agents of the organization such as leaders (Podsakoff et al., 2000; Zellars and Tepper, 2003) or work group peers (Kamdar and Van Dyne, 2007). Antecedents such as perceived organizational support (Eisenberger, Armeli, Rexwinkel, Lynch, and Rhoades, 2001; Rhoades and Eisenberger, 2002), fairness (Ball, Treviño, and Sims, 1994; Konovsky and Pugh, 1994; Masterson, Lewis, Goldman, and Taylor, 2000), and leader-member exchange (Settoon, Bennett, and Liden, 1996) have been explored using a social exchange framework.

We recognize the importance of a social exchange relational perspective to enhancing our understanding of organizational processes underlying *affiliative-promotive behaviors,* but our focus is consistent with recognition of the growing role that *challenging-promotive behaviors* are likely to play in an increasingly dynamic business environment (e.g., Crant, 2000; Grant and Ashford, 2007). For example, Moon, Van Dyne and Wrobel's (2005) review of the citizenship behavior literature suggested that we know more about the affiliative aspects of OCBs whereas the more challenging aspects have been comparatively less studied. We aim to redress the balance and, as a result, we explore the antecedents of voice behavior through a cognitive lens. Specifically, given the more challenging "rocking-the-boat" nature of voice behaviors, they may have both positive consequences as well as negative repercussions for the employees who engage in behaviors that may challenge the status-quo (Morrison and Phelps, 1999). This foreshadows the theoretical relevance of a more calculative perspective, in which cognitive and decision-making perspective processes are prominent, to attempt to map the dynamic decision of "should I do it or not?" that employees are likely to make with respect to challenging-promotive behaviors.

Given the growing importance of challenging-promotive and various types of proactive behaviors (Grant and Ashford, 2007), we turn our attention to the unique processes likely to underlie these behaviors. Specifically, we begin by comparing them to a more traditional type of affiliative-promotive behavior such as helping (Organ, 1988; Van Dyne and LePine, 1998). Then, we examine the relevance of dual-process decision-making to explicate the cognitive processes likely to trigger systematic and heuristic voice processing (Petty and Wegener, 1999). Our overall objective is to open the black box of decision-making with respect to voice behaviors and to integrate it with extant literatures on predictors of voice behaviors as well as to propose new directions. We start out by reviewing some of the existing literature on challenging-promotive behaviors to outline what the main findings have been. ThenFinally, we propose an integrative model of cognitive decision-making and challenging-promotive behavior (with a focus on voice) to extend the current literature.

What We Know and What We Don't Know About Challenging-Promotive OCBs

We have witnessed a growing number of studies examining the domain of challenging-promotive behavior in the past decade. For instance, LePine and Van Dyne (1998) examined group characteristics (e.g. group size) as well as individual characteristics (e.g. self-esteem, satisfaction) as predictors of voice. Other research has looked into job and supervisory characteristics (Frese, Teng, and Wijnen, 1999; Morrison and Phelps, 1999) as predictors of making suggestions. Another line of research has examined the role of felt responsibility and the development of role-based self-efficacy as predictors of engaging in change-oriented behaviors (Fuller et al., 2006; Morrison and Phelps, 1999; Parker, 1998). Our understanding of challenging-promotive behavior antecedents has, thus, been enriched. However, we still lack an overarching cognitive perspective that would capture more precisely the decision-making process that employees engage in. Such a perspective is important because it can uncover important mechanisms that would explain and refine current models of voice. Below we provide an overview of dual process models of decision-making and then we apply them to the prediction of challenging-promotive behaviors (with an emphasis on voice) in the workplace.

Even though interest in the challenging-promotive area has greatly increased over the past decade (for reviews and propositions, see Crant, 2000 and Grant and Ashford, 2007), the cognitive decision-making processes underlying engaging in these behaviors has remained relatively unexplored. For example, although it is recognized that "the decision to take charge will be affected by two judgments" (i.e., likely success and likely consequences), Morrison and Phelps (1999) recognize that "we did not assess the two proposed judgments in this study," despite the fact that, as the authors recognized, they were used as a theoretical justification (p. 405-406). This shows the need to unpack how employees make decisions when taking charge or when engaging in voicing their suggestions for change.

Dual Process Decision-Making Models

Dual process decision-making models describe the distinction between "heuristic" and "systematic" processing in information processing and persuasion contexts (Chaiken, Liberman, and Eagly, 1989; Petty and Wegener, 1999). Although a variety of dual process models exist (for reviews and critiques, see Kruglanski and Orehek, 2007, and Smith and DeCoster, 2000), we build our framework on the elaboration likelihood model (ELM; Petty and Wegener, 1999) for several reasons. First, it covers the full continuum of cognition from heuristic to systematic, a range necessary for capturing the way decisions are made about engagement in behaviors that one has discretion on. Second, our framework is selected based on demonstrated applications of ELM to various decision-making situations in organizations, such as job seekers' decision processes (Jones, Shultz, and Chapman, 2006) and ethical decision making (Street, Douglas, Geiger and Martinko, 2001).

Concretely, the elaboration likelihood model (ELM) posits that in making a decision about a communicated message, individuals engage in the two distinct modes of decision-making processing — heuristic or systematic (as outlined above). In this way, individuals may engage in more heuristic processing (using a peripheral information processing route) that does not require as much time and effort and might, therefore, involve more surface than deep-level processes. On the other hand, under certain circumstances such as increased personal relevance, individuals tend to engage in more systematic processing (using a central information processing route), which increases the extent to which the alternatives of a decision are carefully scrutinized.

Further, the model specifies that individuals differ in the amount of *cognitive elaboration* (the extent to which individuals rely on information processing to decide on target objects or potential actions (Petty, Haugtvedt, and Smith, 1995). This forms the core of the model, for which we use terms consistent with various applications of ELM, such as elaboration likelihood (Petty and Cacioppo, 1986), cognitive expenditure (Street et al., 2001), and depth of processing (Zalesny and Ford, 1990). Consistent with the original model and its applications, we emphasize that elaboration likelihood is a *continuum* ranging from low elaboration (heuristic mode or peripheral information processing route) to high elaboration (systematic mode or central route processing route; Petty and Cacioppo, 1986; Street et al., 2001). For simplicity purposes, we formulate propositions around the central concept (cognitive elaboration and its synonyms), with arguments based on extreme values (low vs.

high; heuristic vs. systematic; peripheral processing vs. central processing) to clarify our points.

DUAL PROCESS DECISION-MAKING MODELS AND CHALLENGING-PROMOTIVE OCBS

As discussed earlier, challenging-promotive citizenship behaviors, and especially voice, entail potential threats to the status-quo. A prerequisite to behavioral action will require more than minimal cognitive elaboration: employees will have to figure out which issues to voice, when, and to whom (Ashford, Rothbard, Piderit, and Dutton, 1998; Dutton, Ashford, Wierba, O'Neill, and Hayes, 1997). Based on dual-process models, cognitive elaboration or likelihood to elaborate mentally may be subject to both situational and individual opportunities and constraints. It is our objective to enrich the current literature on voice by examining situational and personal factors within an ELM framework to predict voice in the workplace. Figure 1 presents our model, organized using facilitating and impeding factors predicting cognitive elaboration that further leads to voice behaviors. These relationships are modified by contingent elements (i.e., scripts, schemas, modes of self-regulation) that help to complete our overarching framework and refine our main propositions, due to their consistency with our cognitive anchoring of the model. The influence of cognitive elaboration on behaviors is a function of individuals' repertoires of organized structures (or schemas; Fiske, 1995), and we capture these aspects using cognitive-based boundary conditions.

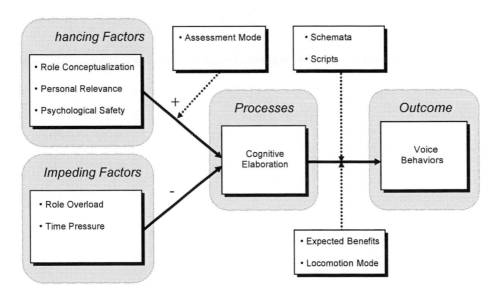

Figure 1. Model of proposed relationships.

The Road Ahead: Predictors, Processes and Voice Behaviors

Consistent with our intention to predict cognitive elaboration pertaining to voice and voice behaviors, we present a number of factors that can enhance and inhibit these mental processes. Our mode of presentation maps closely with the logic of elaboration likelihood models, where various components (e.g., personal relevance, quality of cues) can enhance or impede elaboration likelihood (Petty and Cacioppo, 1986). We also maintain congruence with the ELM principles and postulates (e.g., individuals do not intend to be intentionally biased, they vary on the amount of cognitive elaboration, etc.; Petty and Wegener, 1999).

Our propositions are organized in the following way. First, we provide theoretical arguments for the relationship between cognitive elaboration and the two promotive discretionary behaviors described above (affiliative and challenging; Van Dyne et al., 1995; Proposition 1). We further present two categories of predictors of cognitive elaboration as distal antecedents, one facilitating and one impeding elaboration. To present a more focused framework beyond this point, our model is limited to predicting *voice*, defined as a "constructive challenge intended to improve rather than to merely criticize" (Van Dyne and LePine, 1998, p. 109) as one particular type of challenging-promotive behavior.

Following Figure 1, we propose that broad role conceptualizations, personal relevance, and psychological safety (a set of predictors typically examined in relationship to discretionary behaviors such as OCBs and voice) stimulate cognitive elaboration (Propositions 2 to 4). If mental processes are to be accounted for, time becomes an essential component, and our framework captures it by focusing on role overload and time pressure (Propositions 5 and 6) which will act as constraining factors. The main relationships are modified by other components congruent with our cognitive approach to predicting voice behaviors. Specifically, we theorize that two types of schemas (self-construal, Proposition 7) and event schemas (or scripts, Proposition 8), cost-benefit analyses (Proposition 9) and two types of self-regulation (assessment, Proposition 10 and locomotion, Proposition 11) enhance or attenuate the main relationships.

Cognitive Elaboration, Affiliative- and Challenging-Promotive Behaviors

In addition to task performance behaviors, which allow less procedural or outcome-related latitude, employees have discretion to engage in or refrain from a variety of work behaviors, such as helping colleagues with their workload or suggesting ways to improve procedures. According to Van Dyne and colleagues (1995), extra-role behaviors aimed at supporting the organization (promotive behaviors) can be classified as either affiliative or challenging. Although our focus in this chapter is on one particular challenging-promotive behavior (i.e., voice), future integration of our propositions across the entire discretionary behavior spectrum can be facilitated if, before delving deeper in our area of interest, we explore the extent to which cognitive elaboration is present across these two behavioral domains and why.

Affiliative and challenging behavior are similar along a number of dimensions (e.g., both are based on an overall affective state of satisfaction), and they also present important differences. For affiliative behaviors, employees exhibit primary allegiance to proximal relationships, are present oriented, and view the current situation in the organization as acceptable. Challenging behaviors are based on being committed to high standards of performance, future orientation, and a belief in the possibility to improve the current organizational or work situation (Van Dyne et al., 1995). Logically, based on these conceptual differences, employees should use more cognitive processing when deciding to engage in challenging-promotive behaviors. An orientation toward the future requires information processing, as does the need to uphold a high standard of performance and the desire to improve the current state of things. In addition, voicing ideas for improvement has the likelihood to challenge and even upset the status quo (Detert and Burris, 2007), is associated with perceptions of risk (Milliken and Morrison, 2000), and brings additional uncertainties related to how the behavior will be perceived by supervisors or peers (Van Dyne, Kamdar, & Joireman (in pressVan Dyne et al., 2003).

In contrast to affiliative behaviors (such as helping or supporting the company through prosocial behaviors) that require significantly less cognitive effort and mental elaboration, we suggest that employees will engage in more cognitive elaboration before deciding to voice issues. First, the definitions and terminology for affiliative behaviors argue for and are indicative of less elaboration. Although behaviors such as *organizational spontaneity* (protecting the organization, developing oneself, spreading goodwill; George and Brief, 1992) are not impulse- but volition-based (George and Jones, 1997), they may require only a fraction of the cognitive elaboration, analyses, and ruminations related to challenging behaviors (Edmondson, 1999; Morrison and Milliken, 2000; Withey and Cooper, 1989). Second, voice behaviors are sometimes described as "speaking up," to capture the directionality of voice: subordinates typically voice their concerns, ideas, and suggestions to managers who are situated at a higher hierarchical level, and who might be responsible for creating or implementing the procedures challenged by the employees. Higher-ups also control formal reward and punishment systems and manage less formal resource allocation (opportunities for training and development, rotations to other positions in the organization). As a result, employees are more likely to pause and mentally elaborate before speaking up, taking charge, or otherwise prior to engaging in any type of challenging behavior. Current research also shows that due to such pronounced asymmetries between voice and helping, employees may also prefer to remain silent in a defensive or prosocial stance (Van Dyne et al., 2003), in addition to thinking longer and harder before irreversibly committing to positions that have potentially negative personal consequences.

Proposition 1: Employees will rely more on cognitive elaboration before engaging in challenging-promotive (e.g., voice) behaviors than before engaging in affiliative-promotive (e.g., helping) citizenship behaviors.

Factors Enhancing Cognitive Elaboration

Role Conceptualization
Role conceptualization is the degree to which employees view specific behaviors as an expected part of their role (Kamdar, McAllister, and Turban, 2006; McAllister, Kamdar, Morrison, and Turban, 2007). In general, we propose that when employees view their roles broadly (Coyle-Shapiro, Kessler, and Purcell, 2004; Morrison, 1994) and conceptualize OCB as an expected part of the job (Kamdar et al., 2006), this should enhance cognitive elaboration

relative to voice. There is growing recognition that even though OCBs may go beyond the formally-prescribed job description, employees differ in the extent to which they view these behaviors as IRB (in-role) or ERB (extra-role) (Morrison, 1994; Van Dyne et al., 1995). In addition, an increasing amount of empirical research demonstrates that role conceptualizations influence attitudes and behavior at work (Chiaburu, 2007; Kamdar et al., 2006; Morrison, 1994; Tepper, Lockhart, and Hoobler, 2001; Tepper and Taylor, 2003).

In this work, broader role definitions have, in part, been attributed to justice perceptions leading to a role enlargement effect and, in part, to individual differences such as empathy and perspective-taking. Moreover, research examining specifically the more "active" components of employee behavior, consistent with our focus, has found that *flexible role orientation*, a construct similar to a broad role definition was positively related to proactive work behavior (Parker, Williams, and Turner, 2006). As Parker and colleagues (2006) reasoned, broader role definitions enable employees to engage in behaviors beyond their strictly in-role *task performance:* "Individuals with flexible role orientation define their roles broadly and, as such, feel ownership of goals and problems beyond their immediate set of technical tasks, seeing them as "my job" rather than as "not my job" (Parker et al., 2006, p. 639).

How does role definition impact the decision-making process regarding engaging in challenging-promotive behaviors? If employees perceive that providing suggestions for improvement is part of their role, they would likely increase the systematic processing with respect to this type of voice engagement. Given that systematic processing is more effortful than heuristic processing and that it often requires a state of heightened motivation and personal involvement (Chaiken et al., 1989), employees can be expected to engage in more careful cognitive and effortful processing of voice engagement only to the extent to which they view it as part of required by their role.

Proposition 2: Employees with broad role conceptualizations will engage in more cognitive elaboration with respect to voice behavior (compared to those with more narrow role conceptualizations).

Personal Relevance

The focus of voice behavior can vary from something that directly concerns the focal employee to changes that have less direct personal relevance. The definition of voice in the organizational behavior literature incorporates the idea that employees speak up on existing issues with suggestions for improvement (i.e. they "constructively challenge the status quo": Van Dyne and LePine, 1998, p. 109). As pointed out in proposition 1, voice behaviors due to their challenging nature are likely to require more deliberation and more cognitive processing than other promotive behaviors such as helping. Directly related to personal relevance is the concept of "felt responsibility", which has already received some attention in the literature (Fuller et al., 2006; Morrison and Phelps, 1999), and results show it predicts change-oriented behavior. Extending past research, we suggest that incorporating personal relevance will further add to our understanding of motivational factors that cause employees to deliberate and engage in voice.

According to elaboration likelihood research, personal relevance is a motivational factor that increases the likelihood of systematic processing to reach the best decision (Petty and Wegener, 1999; Tesser and Shaffer, 1990). For instance, a persuasion study by Petty and

Cacioppo (1984) demonstrated that personal relevance (involvement) led to greater consideration of the quality rather than mere quantity of persuasion arguments – providing a more cognitively-engaged and systematic path of processing. Further, a meta-analysis by Johnson and Eagly (1989) confirmed the importance of considering personal involvement or relevance by showing that outcomes depend on type of involvement: value-relevant, outcome-relevant, and impression-relevant. Value-relevant involvement is a psychological state "created by the activation of attitudes that are linked to important values" (Johnson and Eagly, 1989). Outcome-relevant involvement is prompted by increasing the relevance by linking a decision to a valued outcome. Lastly, impression-relevant involvement has to do with the psychological state induced by the social context and expectations of others. As suggested by the persuasion literature, personal relevance increases involvement and the use of the more engaged systematic processing route. Applying this to work contexts, we argue that personal relevance will have a motivational effect by energizing employees to engage in more cognitive processing with respect to challenging-promotive behavior such as voice. Employees who feel that an issue of importance to them is at stake are more likely to deliberate and engage in voice.

Proposition 3: The higher the personal relevance of the issue, the more the cognitive elaboration with respect to voice.

Psychological Safety

Psychological safety captures the extent to which individuals feel free and safe to express thoughts and ideas at work (Kahn, 1990; May, Gilson and Harter, 2004). Psychological safety has been linked to engagement at work (May et al., 2004) as well as to team learning (Edmondson, 1999), and employee voice (Detert and Burris, 2007). Systematic processing from an ELM perspective requires a careful examination of the issues at hand (Petty and Wegener, 1999). Since voice behavior may challenge the status-quo, employees must experience a sense of psychological safety in order to engage in careful consideration of voice alternatives. For instance, Detert and Burris (2007) argued that "In in keeping with the argument that employees estimate perceived costs prior to speaking up, psychological safety (the belief that engaging in risky behaviors like voice will not lead to personal harm) has been described as a key *affect-laden cognition* influencing voice" (p. 871, italics ours).

In the absence of psychological safety in the workplace, employees may deliberately choose to withhold voice behaviors, thus, engaging in what has been referred to as defensive or acquiescent silence (Van Dyne, Ang, and Botero, 2003). If psychological safety is present, on the other hand, employees should feel empowered to consider voice behaviors, which would increase their cognitive engagement and the extent of systematic processing with respect to challenging-promotive behaviors such as voice.

Proposition 4: The higher the psychological safety, the more the cognitive elaboration with respect to voice.

Factors Impeding Cognitive Elaboration

Role Overload

Employees might feel that excessive activities are expected from them, given the existing amount of time, their abilities, and other organizational constraints; in other words, they experience role overload (Rizzo, House, and Lirtzman, 1970) which will likely decrease cognitive elaboration. For instance, role overload has been linked to a range of negative consequences such as decreased perceptions of safety climate and safety consciousness on jobs that require attention to safety (Barling, Loughlin, and Kelloway, 2002), decreased spontaneous helping behavior due to the increased emphasis placed on task performance (Wright, George, Farnsworth, and McMahan, 1993), decreased positive influence of organizational resources on self-efficacy, which makes the relationships for self-efficacy and goal level with performance insignificant (Brown, Jones and Leigh, 2005).

Further, Deckop, Mangel and Cirka (1999) hypothesized that strong pay-for-performance linkages (i.e. link between incentives for task performance) decrease OCB in the presence of low employee commitment. This is based on the idea that setting high expectations in the job performance domain by emphasizing pay-for-performance decreases the willingness of employees to engage in non-task behaviors, especially if they are not highly committed to the company. Further, research on goal-setting by Schweitzer and colleagues has suggested that unmet goals can have negative effects by prompting individuals to engage in unethical behavior (Schweitzer, Ordóñez, and Douma, 2004). Thus, the desire to fulfill job requirements in the presence of job overload may focus cognitive resources on job task performance. Applied to voice behaviors, feelings of role overload should detract from cognitive elaboration and enhance heuristic processing with respect to voice behavior.

> *Proposition 5*: The higher the role overload, the less the cognitive elaboration with respect to voice.

Time Pressure

Using similar arguments, we also propose that when employees experience a sense of time pressure – pressure to accomplish more in shorter periods of time - they will engage in less cognitive elaboration relative to voice. For instance, the literature on negotiation has shown that time pressure tends to lead to quicker negotiations often leading to sub-optimal outcomes (Carnevale and Lawler, 1986; Ross and Wieland, 1996). Carnevale and Lawler (1986) demonstrated that time pressure combined with an individualistic orientation decreased the extent of information exchange between negotiating parties. Further, under high time pressure, negotiators sent more pressing and less inaction messages (at later rounds in the negotiation), providing an indication of their desire to settle the negotiations quickly regardless of the extent to which outcomes are optimal (Ross and Wieland, 1996). In addition, time pressure may cause more mismatching in negotiation (Smith, Pruitt, and Carnevale, 1982).

On the basis of the negotiation studies, we can infer that time pressure reduces the ability to process information systematically, thus, leading to more heuristic processing. Moreover, the literature on creativity also suggests that time pressure may have a role in the process of generating creative ideas. For instance, Amabile, Conti, Coon, Lazenby, and Herron (1996) argued that workload pressures (including time pressure) would serve as impediments to a creative environment. Even though they did not find direct empirical evidence for the negative effect of workload pressures, their theory suggested that indeed, in some cases time pressure may be detrimental to creativity. Baer and Oldham (1996) found a negative linear relationship between time pressure and creative performance. They further hypothesized and found a more complex relationship such that when support for creativity was high, the relationship between intermediate time pressure and creativity was positive whereas under high time pressure, the relationship became negative. Under time pressure, employees need to focus on speedy processing. To meet goals, they are likely to take short cuts and use heuristics. Thus, an emphasis on speed and rapid processing as indicated by time pressure should enhance heuristic processing with respect to voice. This is because time pressure reduces the time for cognitive elaboration.

Proposition 6: The higher the time pressure, the less the cognitive elaboration with respect to voice.

Boundary Conditions: Modifying the Relationship between Cognitive Elaboration and Voice Behaviors

Schemas: Building Blocks for Thinking

While cognitive elaboration captures the extent to which employees engage in thinking, the concept is silent about the presence or absence of knowledge structures that might impede or facilitate the process. Knowledge structures, such as schemata, can illuminate the connection between cognitive elaboration and behavior. As noted by philosophers (Kant, 1957) and later by social psychologists (Bartlett, 1938; Bruner, 1957), schemata are fundamental cognitive structures. Concretely, "schemata … lie at the foundation of our perceptions. The schema of a triangle can exist nowhere else than in thought and it indicates a rule of the synthesis of the imagination in regard to figures in space" (Kant, 1957). Closer to the organizational world, and in more general terms, schemas are preconceptions of theories applied to the social world (Fiske, 1995). These knowledge structures include self, person, role, and event schemas (Fiske and Taylor, 1984; Taylor and Crocker, 1981) and should enhance our understanding of the connection between cognitive elaboration and voice. Extending this, we focus below on the role of self-construal.

From the possible ways of self-construal (e.g., schematics vs. aschematics; Markus, 1977; Markus and Wurf, 1987; ideal and pragmatic, Kivetz and Tyler, 2007) the independent – interdependent continuum of self-perception has the most relevance from a decision making perspective. In general, individuals can engage in individual, relational, or collective types of self-construal (Brewer and Gardner, 1996), and each of these has unique correlates. Individual self-construal relies on comparisons with others, leading to a sense of uniqueness derived from comparisons and a focus on self-interest. Relational construal focuses on the individual in dyadic relationships, while collective self-construal involves identification with the group (see Brewer and Gardner, 1996; also, for a more detailed discussion of how self-construal relates to frames of references, goals and motives, see Flynn, 2005).

As for empirical studies, self-construal has been studied in relationship to organizational outcomes such as fairness, commitment, and discretionary behaviors (e.g., Johnson and Chang, 2006; Johnson, Selenta, and Lord, 2006). Individuals with collective self-concepts tend to have high levels of affective organizational commitment whereas those who construe themselves in individual terms tend to focus on inter-individual comparisons that emphasize uniqueness and distinctiveness in these relationships (Johnson and Chang, 2006). Extending these conceptual arguments and findings, we suggest that employees with collective self-construal will adopt a frame of reference involving the group and will engage in exchanges that involve less immediate reciprocation.

Given that voice can be viewed, especially in the short run, as risky since others may not appreciate suggestions for change (Nemeth and Staw, 1989), we propose that collective self-construal schemas will strengthen the relationship between cognitive elaboration and voice. In other words, those who define themselves in terms of their group affiliations and identity will be more willing to act upon their ideas and take the risk of speaking up. Thus, collective self-construal should enhance the elaboration – voice link (compared to individual or relational self-construal).

Proposition 7: Employee self-construal schemas will moderate the relationship between cognitive elaboration and voice behavior, such that having a strong collective self-construal schema will strengthen the positive relationship between elaboration and voice.

Scripts: Building Blocks for Doing

Scripts (or event schemas) depict appropriate sequences of events in social situations (Fiske, 1995; Schank and Abelson, 1977). For example, an employee may have ideas for ways to improve existing procedures but may not have a cognitive script for understanding how to express these ideas for change appropriately and effectively in a particular context. Scripts help employees make sense of potential ways micro-sequences of actions can unfold. They also help employees anticipate specific consequences that are likely to occur as a function of specific behaviors. Thus, cognitive elaboration is a precursor of action (Fiske, 1995) in the presence of scripts, such that employees will be more likely to speak up and engage in voice when they have scripts that allow them to engage efficiently and productively in the behavior (e.g., voice). Two types of scripts have relevance to voice: weak versus strong and low versus high situational specificity. Weak scripts organize expectations about events or behaviors without clarity of specifying more detailed aspects such as sequences or substitutability of behaviors. In contrast, strong scripts stipulate both event expectations and more detailed aspects, including sequences, variations of scripts or tracks (Abelson, 1981). Likewise, situational scripts can vary from low to high in specificity to a particular context such as sequences of events for specific situations or planning scripts consisting of particular plans for action (Schank and Abelson, 1977).

Applying these ideas to our focus on factors predicting voice, we suggest that the existence of strong scripts (outlining sequences of events) and of scripts with high situational specificity (Lord and Kernan, 1987) will strengthen the positive relationship between cognitive elaboration and voice. In other words, having knowledge of behavior sequences viewed as appropriate in a particular situation will make it more likely that employees will go beyond elaboration and speak up by voicing their ideas and suggestions for change. In contrast, in the absence of strong scripts detailing successful voice behaviors or in the presence of scripts wherein sequences are uncertain or the components of the terms for the required "performance" are unclear (Gioia and Poole, 1984), employees will be less likely to express their ideas, concerns, and suggestions even if they have engaged in cognitive elaboration.

Proposition 8: Strong scripts and situation-specific scripts will moderate the relationship between cognitive elaboration and voice such that strong scripts (from past behavioral episodes) and situation-specific scripts (from prior experience and/or observation in the situation) will strengthen the positive relationship.

Expected Benefits Based on Cost-Benefit Analysi Analyses

From a decision-making standpoint, rational decision-makers tend to engage in behaviors which they think will increase positive outcomes and minimize negative ones (Connolly, Arkes, and Hammond, 2000; Tesser and Shaffer, 1990). Since voice at work involves taking risks and is not always viewed favorably (Milliken, Morrison, and Hewlin, 2003), the link between elaboration and voice should also be influenced by assessment of expected costs and benefits. In decision-making, rational decision-makers estimate probabilities for desired and undesired outcomes based on their behaviors and tend to select the decision or behavior with the highest utility. Similarly, in the motivation literature, the valence-instrumentality-expectancy framework (Parker et al., 2006; Morrison and Phelps, 1999; Vroom, 1964) identifies three elements to motivation: valence is expected desirability of an outcome, instrumentality is extent to which a behavior is expected to produce a desired outcome, and expectancy is the personal belief that one can engage in the behavior.

We suggest that cost-benefit analysis captures judgments of valence and instrumentality, which have not been extensively tested with respect to voice behaviors. Higher expected benefits and lower expected costs should increase judgments of valence and instrumentality. Parker and colleagues (2006), for instance described taking charge (Morrison and Phelps, 1999) as involving "a *calculated* decision process in which individuals assess the likelihood that they will be successful as well as the likely consequences of their action, such as whether the risks outweigh the benefits" (p. 638, italics ours). Applied to our model, we suggest that cognitive elaboration will be more strongly related to voice when expected benefits are high (and relative costs low). Thus, based on rational decision-making analysis and cognitive evaluation of costs and benefits of voice, we propose an interaction wherein expected benefits will enhance the cognitive elaboration – voice relationship.

Proposition 9: Expected benefits based on cost-benefit analysis will moderate the relationship between cognitive elaboration and voice, such that high expected benefits will strengthen the positive relationship.

Self-Regulatory Modes: Preference for Assessment Versus Locomotion

Voice behavior can also be considered from a goal pursuit and self-regulatory perspectives. Based on self-regulation theories (e.g., Carver and Scheier, 1990; Higgins, 1989), Kruglanski, Thompson, Higgins, Atash, Pierro, Shah and Spiegel (2000) conceptualized goal pursuit as a function of two self-regulatory modes: assessment and locomotion. Employees with a proclivity for *assessment* ("do the right thing") focus on evaluating goals and the means to reach end states (Higgins, Kruglanski, and Pierro, 2003). They emphasize comparison of alternatives and searching for new options before engaging in action. For example, Avnet and Higgins (2003) demonstrated that individuals with preferences for assessment compare all the options on all existing attribute dimensions when choosing among a set of alternatives. In contrast, employees with a preference for *locomotion* ("just do it") focus on goal attainment (i.e., the movement from the current to the desired end state). They are proactive and tend to take action, with less concern about carefully considering options. For example, Avnet and Higgins (2003) showed that those with a preference for locomotion eliminated the worst option at each step and made decisions faster. They were quicker to act. Applying these individual difference tendencies to our model of cognitive elaboration and voice, we suggest that self-regulatory modes, conceptualized as preference for assessment versus preference for locomotion, will function as moderators in our model.

Specifically, we propose that the self regulatory preference for assessment will strengthen the relationships between facilitating factors (role conceptualization, personal relevance, and psychological safety; presented in propositions 2 to 4) and cognitive elaboration. For example, the positive relationship between role conceptualization (viewing voice as a role expectation by employees) and cognitive elaboration will be especially strong for those with a preference for assessment. Likewise, personal relevance will be more strongly related to cognitive elaboration for those high in preference for assessment. Similarly, the psychological safety – cognitive elaboration link will be strengthened for those with this self-regulation tendency. In each of these instance of moderation, the factors that enhance cognitive elaboration will be further strengthened because a preference for assessment inclines employees to be thorough in their analysis and consideration of alternatives in an effort to "do the right thing" (Higgins et al., 2003; Kruglanski, Pierro, Higgins, and Capozza, 2007), and thus should further enhance the underlying positive relationship.

Proposition 10: Preference for assessment will moderate (strengthen) the relationships between enhancing factors such as (a) role conceptualization, (b) personal relevance, and (c) psychological safety and cognitive elaboration with respect to voice.

In contrast, and consistent with the action orientation of employees with a preference for locomotion, we propose that this second self-regulatory mode is more relevant to the connection between cognitive elaboration and voice - that it will positively moderate this relationship. Assessment and locomotion are theoretically (and empirically) independent (e.g., correlations of -.14 to .13 across four samples; Kruglanski et al., 2007), and individuals can be "high on both assessment and locomotion" (Kruglanski et al., 2000, p. 794). As used in our framework, assessment operates primarily in pre-decision stages (more cognitive) and locomotion in post-decision stages (implementation-related). This positioning is consistent with the complex patterns presented by Kruglanski and colleagues (2000, p. 804-805), demonstrating that assessment is negatively and locomotion is positively related to action initiation. In other words, individuals in assessment modes prefer to dwell (and even ruminate) on decisions, engage in evaluations, social comparisons, and look for validation. Less concerned about these issues, their locomotion-based counterparts are more likely to focus on getting to action. Importantly, locomotion modes are also associated with a high need for cognitive closure. Once cognitive elaboration ends, those who are proactive and prefer to "just to do it" versus "doing the right thing" (Higgins et al., 2003) will emphasize movement toward goals, and this will strengthen the cognitive elaboration to voice relationship.

Proposition 11: Preference for locomotion will moderate (strengthen) the positive relationship between cognitive elaboration and voice.

DISCUSSION

In this chapter, we focus on cognitive processes that influence voice behavior as a unique type of OCB. Since voice is discretionary, it is surprising that prior research has not considered more elaborate models that explicate these cognitive processes. We set out by delineating how challenging-promotive behaviors are distinct from affiliative-promotive behaviors. Our research is driven by the assumption that the distinctly change-oriented nature of voice sets it apart as a unique behavior, which is likely to require more cognitive attention than other forms of citizenship behavior. For example, although Konovsky and Organ (1996) contrasted affective and cognitive components as antecedents of OCB, little research has expanded upon their initial ideas. Given the rich literature on elaboration and decision making, this gap is unfortunate. This chapter is a first step toward expanding our understanding of antecedents of voice by going beyond social exchange, personality, individual differences, and situational predictors (LePine and Van Dyne, 2001; Detert and Burris 2007) to focus more specifically on cognitive decision making predictors of voice.

Thus, we aimed to redress the balance and propose that voice can stream from cognitive elaboration. Our emphasis on cognition is consistent with studies on voice or issue-selling, which include general aspects of decision making such as context evaluation (Dutton and Ashford, 1993), sensemaking (Dutton et al., 1997), and calculations (Morrison and Milliken, 2000). At the same time, we advance beyond broad concepts included in prior studies by providing a more detailed model based on specific cognitive processes that should have special relevance to voice.

Because its versatility in capturing a continuum of decision making and cognitive elaboration, the ELM model has inspired theoretical and empirical applications to organizational issues including marketing segmentation decisions (Eckert and Goldsby, 1997), interviewer's' and job seeker's' decision processes (Forret and Turban, 1996; Jones et al., 2006), and ethical decision-making (Street et al., 2001), among others. In this chapter, we integrated elaboration likelihood principles with the existing literature on voice to build a framework focused on predicting voice behavior at work. We focused on both sides of the predictor space, by presenting factors that can enhance (e.g., role conceptualization) or detract from (e.g., role overload) cognitive elaboration, and by proposing ways these relationships are strengthened or attenuated by moderators. One key contribution of this chapter is that it complements existing frameworks explaining citizenship behaviors in general and voice in particular, which use as predictors individual differences (e.g., LePine and Van Dyne, 2001), social exchange (Masterson et al., 2000; Settoon et al., 1996), leadership influences (e.g., Detert and Burris, 2007), and contextual factors (e.g., Ashford et al., 1998) with a focus of underlying cognitive processes.

Another contribution of the current research is in directing researchers' attention to a variety of intervening factors that modify how cognitive processing influences behavior. In addition to their position as moderators in our model, the mechanisms we present (i.e., schemas, scripts, self-regulation modes) are important but neglected correlates or precursors of voice. For example, the existence of appropriate schemas to determine voice originators (e.g., which employees, based on their self and role schemas), targets (based on person schemas), and favorable media for the action (based on situational schemas) remain scarcely theorized upon in current models and, as a result, under-investigated. Our propositions can provide impetus to more theoretical development in this direction. Similarly, we have suggested that self-regulation modes, including preferences for assessment and locomotion are additional factors that influence elaboration (assessment) and voice (locomotion). (e.g., Benjamin and Flynn, 2006; Kruglanski et al., 2007).

Theoretical Implications

The model and the propositions provide several theoretical contributions. First, our focus on cognitive factors leading to challenging behaviors in the form of voice opens a new area of inquiry, which is different from existing models of voice. Cognitive elaboration is central to the framework, and provides information in terms of processes (elaboration extent) consistent with elaboration likelihood principles and postulates (Petty and Wegener, 1999). In addition, in an effort to illuminate the dynamics of the decision process, we introduce content-related cognitive aspects, in the forms of schemas and scripts. These predictors are not only typically unexamined in the current voice literature, but they can also inform research designs and should have practical implications for managers and employees.

As a second contribution, our model recognizes a continuum from low elaboration (heuristic processing) to high elaboration, with low elaboration (heuristic mode) requiring relatively less effort while high elaboration (systematic mode) entailing the expenditure of more cognitive resources. Since organizations are arenas where specific goals have to be accomplished, they provide limited resources, as well as time and resource constraints (Amabile et al., 1996; Baer and Oldham, 2006). Thus, factors in the organization as they pertain to the individual motivation can lead to routinization and/or mindlessness (Ashforth and Fried, 1988) as well as intentional change and alertness (Morrison and Milliken, 2000). Therefore, both the constraints and enhancing factors in the context and in the motivational orientations of employees should be recognized as central to cognitive elaboration. We incorporate both aspects in our model, in an effort to encompass a broader spectrum of cognitive processes. A similar integrative trend has emerged, for example, in the organizational justice literature, where researchers proposed that fairness-related judgments can incorporate both systematic and heuristic aspects with equity theory (Adams, 1965) representing more systematic processing, and fairness heuristic theory (Lind, Kray, and Thompson, 2001) representing more heuristic processing (see the review by Cropanzano, Byrne, Bobocel, and Rupp, 2001).

Our development of the nomological network around this basic cognitive structure, accounts for both positive (enhancing) and negative (constraining) cognitive elaboration preconditions. Although research on voice has attempted to incorporate these polarities in more specific forms (e.g., the influence of leaders' supportive and abusive behaviors on voice; Burris, Detert, and Chiaburu, 2007in press), simultaneous consideration of both positive and negative antecedents is promising, especially when cognitive aspects are involved. We suggest that discretionary behaviors, especially those that are challenging and change-oriented such as voice, can benefit from models that acknowledge both enhancing and constraining influences, rather than in isolation. In addition, since positive and negative influences are not necessarily balanced or symmetrical (e.g., Baumeister, Bratslavsky, Finkenauer, and Vohs , 2001), including both in the same model can enhance predictive power, provide insights, and spur new directions of investigation.

Finally, we hope that our propositions will stimulate further research, including additional conceptual development as well as empirical testing related to the cognitive nature of voice. One of the strengths of the model is its testability. To date, most voice behavior research has used field designs and questionnaires. In contrast, our propositions are amenable to laboratory experiments which can address causality. For example, schemas and scripts can be embedded in conditions (scenarios, task framing) and tested in experimental settings where researchers vary role conceptualizations, personal relevance, psychological safety, role overload, and time pressure. In addition, locomotion and assessment modes of self-regulation have been successfully manipulated with subjects in laboratory conditions (Avnet and Higgins, 2003) and could also be included in an experimental study.

Implications for Practice

If, as surmised above, voice is a function of cognitive elaboration, which can be influenced in various ways (e.g., by direct leaders or by features of the organizational context, such as role overload), there are implications for those who want to encourage and those who want to engage in voice. From a vertical and hierarchical perspective, leaders can facilitate employee voice by influencing role conceptualizations, emphasizing personal relevance, and creating psychologically safe work environments. They also can reduce role overload and time pressure. This is consistent with research that demonstrates the importance of leaders and leadership for voice and issue selling (e.g., Ashford et al., 1998; Burris et al., , Detert, and Chiaburu, 2007in press; Detert and Burris, 2007; Parker et al., 2006). Focusing on more concrete applications, leaders can influence the distal predictors of our framework in ways that should enhance cognitive elaboration and increase voice. Leaders in organizations can also institute practices such as formally setting aside time for employees to engage in contemplation of voice behaviors, a practice which has precedent in the high-tech world at companies such as Google (Warner, 2002).

For employees, our model highlights factors that should facilitate or constrain cognitive elaboration and actual voice. Knowing that role overload is likely to reduce cognitive elaboration can provide helpful insights for employees who value voice. For example, they may want to set aside blocks of time devoted to thinking about suggestions for changes to work processes – when they ignore other role demands in an attempt to reduce feelings of role overload or time pressure.

In our propositions above, we proposed that schemas, scripts, and self-regulatory modes of assessment and locomotion change the basic relationships in our model. From a practical perspective, these relationships offer important possibilities for creating opportunities for voice. According to situated cognition theories, scripts are not exclusively internal to an individual and can be influenced by the organizational context (e.g., Elsbach, Barr, and Hargadon, 2005; Lant, 2002). In contexts where this is possible, managers can purposefully design and reinforce schemas consistent with speaking up. They can also highlight particular scripts so subordinates can set aside time for elaboration and understand how to express voice effectively in that context. These practical suggestions hinge on several preconditions, including empirical research that supports our model and predictions as well as generalizability of the findings to practitioner settings.

Future Research

Some notable limitations, determined by the boundaries of the model have to be mentioned before presenting ideas for future research. Our focus on cognitive processes based on application of the elaboration likelihood model (Petty and Cacioppo, 1986) can be enriched with other aspects of dual process models. For example, viewing issues through the lens of heuristic and systematic models (HSM; Chaiken, 1980; see Chen and Chaiken, 1999 for a recent review) should facilitate understanding voice decisions based on a multiple-motive framework. Individuals may consider whether or not to speak up based on motives such as accuracy, defense, and/or impression management (Chen and Chaiken, 1999) since research links motivational orientations with proactive behaviors (e.g., Chiaburu, Marinova, and Lim, 2007). In more general terms, the framework can also be enriched by incorporating emotion and affect (e.g., George and Brief, 1992) at various stages of the model. For example, in parallel to the low cognitive elaboration predicted as a consequence of impeding factors, employees can experience a variety of negative emotions (from frustration to anger), resulting from a context-constrained inability to speak up. Thus, cognitive elaboration colored by negative emotions (e.g., anger, fear, frustration) can affect the types of voice employees engage in and the resulting organizational actions, in the light of studies showing that only appropriate expression is accepted in organizations (depending on gender, status, or form of expression; Geddes and Callister, 2007; Tiedens, 2000).

Second, some of the issues presented in this chapter in their simplest form (e.g., such as the emphasis on "inside-the-head schemas and scripts" and dispositional modes of self-regulation (locomotion and assessment) can be further expanded. As a first step, we contrasted collective with individual and relational schemas, but further distinctions are possible. Indeed, individuals with both relational and individual schemas can speak up, although their motivational bases, venues for voicing issues, and expected outcomes could be different. For instance, a person with an individual self-construal may be prompted to speak up when voice would benefit their individual standing in the group whereas a person with a collective self-construal may experience enhanced motivation to engage in voice when voice would benefit the collective. Further, schemas and scripts can be specific to the individual and measured as such (e.g., independent and interdependent self-construals: Singelis, 1994), or activated externally, as explored in various models of situated cognition (e.g., Lant, 2002). Thus, a more detailed elaboration can be offered on how schemas and scripts are created and maintained (Ashforth and Fried, 1988), become available and accessible at a specific point in time or in an event sequence, as well as what their unique impact may be on decisions and behaviors. Similarly, assessment and locomotion, the two self-regulation modes presented above can be measured as dispositions (Benjamin and Flynn, 2006) and also activated by specific contexts. We did not explore the activation potential of available knowledge structures (termed accessibility; Higgins, 1996) in this chapter. This is, however, a fruitful area of investigation. Similar to energy cells, knowledge units such as schemas exist in long-term memory and become accessible and are subsequently used for judgment and decision making when charged with energy (e.g., Higgins, Bargh, and Lombardi, 1985).

Looking at specifics of the model, we did not discuss at length the interplay between elaboration and other types of individual differences – which are central to the elaboration likelihood model because of the postulate that elaboration is a function of the individuals' motivation and ability (Petty and Wegener, 1999) – and how this might modify relationships in our model. For example, individuals differ in the extent to which they prefer simple, structured, and predictable actions; they also vary in the extent to which they like to think, handle arguments and make decisions; finally, while some people need firm answers to questions, others are more tolerant of uncertainties and ambiguities. These cognitive factors, termed need for structure (Neuberg and Newsom, 1993), need for cognition (Cacioppo and Petty, 1982; Cacioppo, Petty, Feinstein, and Jarvis, 1996), and need for closure (Kruglanski, 1989) are central to cognitive models and can be incorporated (both as direct influences and intervening mechanisms) in future models of voice . Overall, researchers can refine and extend the proposed relationships to extend and build upon the preliminary model we have presented in this chapter.

One of our main objectives was to provide a testable model and, as a result, we recommend that future research should test the relationships we have proposed. For some of the constructs (e.g., psychological safety, role overload, role definitions), measurement instruments are readily available (e.g., Edmondson, 1999; Tepper et al., 2001; Thiagarajan, Chakrabarty, and Taylor, 2006). Others, including our central construct, cognitive elaboration and its two extremes (heuristic and systematic processing), need thoughtful design to capture the extent to which employees think about engaging in voice and how this situates them on a continuum from low to high elaboration (for examples of designs, see Petty and Cacioppo, 1986; Petty, Cacioppo, and Schumann, 1983).

In a field study, for example, researchers could measure distal and intermediate constructs at two different times, with voice measured later. Alternatively, laboratory experiments could capture, with higher precision, the modes of cognitive processing such as collecting information on the extent of elaboration, both in terms of degree of elaboration (heuristic or systematic) and content (existing schemas and scripts). Researchers could also examine the extent to which assignment to high versus low role overload influences cognitive elaboration and voice. Ideally, combinations of r studies executed in both field and laboratory settings can increase the validity of the inferences.

An additional avenue for future research could consider quality of voice behaviors following cognitive elaboration. For instance, we do not explicitly address more distal consequences of voice in light of more or less cognitive elaboration prior to voice. Specifically, does more cognitive elaboration lead to higher quality of voice behaviors? Are there situations in which triggering a more heuristic process of voice behavior may be beneficial? Are voice behaviors based on more cognitive elaboration viewed more positively by leaders or peers in the organization? All of these questions go beyond our current model, which takes a first step at recognizing the importance of cognitive decision-making processes involved in voice behavior.

Finally, future research can also address boundaries of our model. To maintain parsimony, we focused on one particular type of challenging-promotive behavior, voice. It is reasonable, however, to ask whether the model has to be substantially modified for other behaviors from the challenging-promotive (Van Dyne et al., 1995) or proactive (Grant and

Ashford, 2007) behavioral sets. Based on similarities between voice and taking charge as well as personal initiative such as an emphasis on changing the existing order of things and challenging the status-quo, some parts of the model may operate similarly for other promotive challenging behaviors. . For instance, taking charge involves changing how one's job is executed (Morrison and Phelps, 1999) and personal initiative is based on proactive behavior (Fay and Frese, 2001). At the same time, other parts of the model may not apply to other promotive-challenging behaviors. For example, taking charge and personal initiative assume that employees have the latitude to engage in changes, possibly because some of these behaviors are required by their roles (Grant and Ashford, 2007). Conversely, voice behaviors are more risky, and involve the intermediate step of speaking up (often to one's supervisor) before engaging in changes. Thus, cognitive elaboration and the content of the thoughts likely differ s for voice ("should I do it or not?") versus initiative or proactivity ("how can I do this better?"). Consequently, it is possible that psychological safety is less important for cognitive decisions related to taking charge or initiative compared to voice.

CONCLUSION

We started this chapter with several objectives. Namely, we wanted to emphasize the unique nature of voice behavior as a form of challenging-promotive behaviors that is distinct from affiliative-promotive behaviors such as helping. Specifically, we built upon the idea that promotive-challenging behaviors such as voice entail constructively *challenging* the status-quo and therefore, are likely to require a higher level of cognitive engagement on the part of employees. Building on the ELM model of persuasion as well as extending existing research on different forms of proactive behaviors with an emphasis on voice in particular, we advanced a model of factors that influence cognitive engagement of employees with respect to voice behaviors and their subsequent voice behavior. Further, we refined our model by proposing that schemas, scripts, locomotion/assessment mode, and cost-benefit analysis moderate relationships in the model. We hope this chapter stimulates additional theory and empirical research on employee voice.

ACKNOWLEDGEMENTS

We are grateful to Jennifer Kish Gephart, who provided constructive suggestions on an earlier draft of this chapter.

REFERENCES

Abelson, R. P. (1981). The psychological status of the script concept. *American Psychologist*, *36*, 715-729.

Adams, J. S. (1965). Injustice in social exchange. In L. Berkowitz (Ed.) *Advances in experimental social psychology*. (Vol. 2) New York, NY: Academic Press.

Amabile, T. M., Conti, R., Coon, H., Lazenby, J. and Heron, M. (1996). Assessing the work environment for creativity. *Academy of Management Journal, 39*(5), 1154-1184.

Ashforth, B. E., and Fried, Y. (1988). The mindlessness of organizational behaviors. *Human Relations, 41*, 305-329.

Ashford, S. J., Rothbard, N. P., Piderit, S. K., and Dutton, J. E. (1998). Out on a limb: The role of context and impression management in selling gender-equity issues. *Administrative Science Quarterly, 43*, 23–57.

Avnet, T., and Higgins, E. T. (2003). Locomotion, assessment, and regulatory fit: Value transfer from "how" to "what". *Journal of Experimental Social Psychology, 39*(5), 525-530.

Baer, M. and Oldham, G.R. (2006). The curvilinear relation between experienced creative time pressure and creativity: Moderating effects of openness to experience and support for creativity. *Journal of Applied Psychology, 91*(4), 963-970.

Ball, G.A., Treviño, L.K., and Sims, H.P. (1994). Just and unjust punishment: Influences on subordinate performance and citizenship. *Academy of Management Journal, 37*, 299-322.

Barling, J., Loughlin, C., and Kelloway, E. K. (2002). Development and test of a model linking safety-specific transformational leadership and occupational safety. *Journal of Applied Psychology, 87*(3), 488-496.

Barnard, C. I. (1938). *The Functions of the Executive.* Cambridge, MA.: Harvard University Press.

Bartlett, F. C. (1932). *Remembering.* Cambridge: Cambridge University Press.

Baumeister, R. F., Bratslavsky, E., Finkenauer, C., and Vohs, K. D. (2001). Bad is stronger than good. *Review of General Psychology, 5*, 323-370.

Benjamin, L., and Flynn, F. J. (2006). Leadership style and regulatory mode: Value from fit? *Organizational Behavior and Human Decision Processes, 100* (2), 216-230.

Blau, P. (1964). *Exchange and power in social life.* New York: Wiley.

Brewer, M. B., and Gardner, W. (1996). Who is this "We"? Levels of collective identity and self representations. *Journal of Personality and Social Psychology, 71*, 83-93.

Brown, S. P., Jones, E., and Leigh, T. W. (2005). The attenuating effect of role overload in relationships linking self-efficacy and goal level to work performance. *Journal of Applied Psychology, 90*, 972–979.

Bruner, J. S. (1957). On perceptual readiness. *Psychological Review, 64*(2), 123-152.

Burris, E., R., Detert, J. R., and Chiaburu, D. S. (2007in press). Quitting before leaving: The mediating effects of psychological attachment and detachment on voice. *Paper under journal reviewJournal of Applied Psychology.*

Cacioppo, J. T., and Petty, R. E. (1982). The need for cognition. *Journal of Personality and Social Psychology, 42*, 116-131.

Cacioppo, J. T., Petty, R. E., Feinstein, J. A., and Jarvis, W. B. G. (1996). Dispositional differences in cognitive motivation : The life and times of individuals varying in need for cognition. *Psychological Bulletin, 119*(22), 197-253.

Carnevale, P. J. D. and Lawler, E. J. (1986). Time pressure and the development of integrative agreements in bilateral negotiations. *Journal of Conflict Resolution, 30(4)*, 639-659.

Carver, C. S., and Scheier, M. F. (1990). Origins and functions of positive and negative affect: A control-process view. *Psychological Review, 97*, 19-35.

Chaiken, S. (1980). Heuristic versus systematic information-processing and the use of source versus message cues in persuasion. *Journal of Personality and Social Psychology, 39*(5), 752-766.

Chaiken, S., Liberman, A., and Eagly, A. H. (1989). Heuristic and systematic information processing within and beyond the persuasion context. In J.S. Uleman and J.A. Bargh (Eds.), *Unintended Thought* (pp. 212-252). New York : Guilford Press.

Chen, S., and Chaiken, S. (1999). The heuristic-systematic model in its broader context. In S. Chaiken and Y. Trope (Eds.), *Dual-process theories in social psychology* (pp. 73–96). New York: Guilford Press.

Chiaburu, D. S., and Baker, V. L. (2006). Extra-role behaviors challenging the status-quo: Validity and antecedents of taking charge behaviors. *Journal of Managerial Psychology, 21*, 620-637.

Chiaburu, D. S. (2007). From interactional justice to citizenship behaviors: Role enlargement or role discretion? *Social Justice Research, 20*,(1) 207-227.

Chiaburu, D. S., Marinova, S. V., and Lim, A. S. (2007). Proactive and helping extra-role behaviors: The influence of motives, goal orientation, and social context. *Personality and Individual Differences, 43*, 2282–2293.

Connolly, T., Arkes, H. R., and Hammond, K. R. (2000). General introduction. In T. Connolly, H.R. Arkes K.R. Hammond (Eds.), *Judgment and decision-making: An interdisciplinary reader* (2nd edition). New York: Cambridge University Press.

Coyle-Shapiro, J. A.-M., Kessler, I., and Purcell, J. (2004). Exploring organizationally directed citizenship behavior: Reciprocity or It's my job? *Journal of Management Studies, 41*, 85-106.

Crant, J.M. (2000). Proactive behavior in organizations. *Journal of Management, 26*(3), 435-462.

Cropanzano, R., Byrne, Z. S., Bobocel, D. R., and Rupp, D. E. (2001). Moral virtues, fairness heuristics, social entities, and other denizens of organizational justice. *Journal of Vocational Behavior, 58*, 164-209.

Deckop, J.R., Mangel, R., and Cirka, C.C. (1999). Getting more than you pay for: Organizational citizenship behavior and pay-for-performance plans. *Academy of Management Journal, 42*(4), 420-428.

Detert, J. R., and Burris, E. R. (2007). Leadership behavior and employee voice: Is the door really open? *Academy of Management Journal, 50*(4), 869-884.

Dutton, J. E., and Ashford, S. J. (1993). Selling issues to top management. *Academy of Management Review, 18* (3), 397-429.

Dutton, J. E., Ashford, S. J., Wierba, E. E., O'Neill R. M., and Hayes, E. (1997). Reading the wind: How middle managers assess the context for selling issues to top managers. *Strategic Management Journal, 18*, 407-425.

Eckert, J. A., and Goldsby, M. G.(1997) Using the elaboration likelihood model to guide customer service-based segmentation. *International Journal of Physical Distribution and Logistics, 27*, 600-615.

Edmondson, A. (1999). Psychological safety and learning behavior in work teams. *Administrative Science Quarterly, 44*, 350-383.

Eisenberger, R., Armeli, S., Rexwinkel, B., Lynch, P.D., and Rhoades, L. (2001). Reciprocation of perceived organizational support. *Journal of Applied Psychology, 86*, 42-51.

Elsbach, K. D., Barr, P. S., and Hargadon, A. B. (2005). Identifying situated cognition in organizations. *Organization Science, 16*(4), 422-433.

Fay, D., and Frese, M. (2001). The concept of personal initiative: An overview of validity studies. *Human Performance, 14*, 97-124.

Fiske, S. T. (1995). Social Cognition. In A. Tesser (Ed.), *Advances in social psychology* (pp.148-193). New York. McGraw-Hill.

Fiske, S. T., and Taylor, S. E. (1984). *Social cognition.* New York: Random House.

Flynn, F. J. (2005). Identity orientations and forms of social exchange in organizations. *Academy of Management Review, 30*, 737-750.

Forret, M., and Turban, D. (1996). Implications of the elaboration Elaboration Likelihood Model for interviewer decision processes. *Journal of Business and Psychology, 10*(4), 415-428.

Frese, M., Teng, E. and Wijnen, C.J.D. (1999). Helping to improve suggestion systems: predictors of making suggestions in companies. *Journal of Organizational Behavior, 20*, 1139-1155.

Fuller, J. B., Marler, L.E., and Hester K. (2006). Promoting felt responsibility for constructive change and proactive behavior: Exploring aspects of an elaborated model of work design. *Journal of Organizational Behavior, 27*, 1089-1120.

Geddes, D., and Callister, R. R. (2007). Crossing the line(s): A dual threshold model of anger in organizations. *Academy of Management Review, 32*(3), 721-746.

George, J. M., and Brief, A. P. (1992). Feeling good-doing good: A conceptual analysis of the mood at work-organizational spontaneity relationship. *Psychological Bulletin, 112*(2), 310-329.

George, J. M., and Jones, G. R. (1997). Organizational spontaneity in context. *Human Performance, 10*(2), 153.

Gioia, D. A., and Poole, P. P. (1984). Scripts in organizational behavior. *Academy of Management Review, 9*, 449–459.

Grant, A. M., and Ashford, S. J. (2007). The dynamics of proactivity at work. *Research in Organizational Behavior.* In Print.

Higgins, E. T. (1989). Self-discrepancy theory: What patterns of self- beliefs cause people to suffer? *Advances in Experimental Social Psychology, 22*, 93-136.

Higgins, E. T. (1996). Knowledge activation: Accessibility, applicability, and salience, in E. T. Higgins and A. W. Kruglanski (Eds.), *Social psychology: Handbook of basic principles* (pp. 136-168). New York: Guildford Press.

Higgins, E. T., Bargh, J. A., and Lombardi, W. (1985). Nature of priming effects on categorization, *Journal of Experimental Psychology: Learning, Memory and Cognition, 11*(1), 59-69.

Higgins, E. T., Kruglanski, A. W., and Pierro, A. (2003). Regulatory mode: Locomotion and assessment as distinct orientations. *Advances in Experimental Social Psychology, 35*, 293-344.

Johnson, R. E., and Chang, C.-H. (2006). 'I' is to continuance as 'We' is to affective: the relevance of the self-concept for organizational commitment. *Journal of Organizational Behavior, 27*(5), 549-570.

Johnson, B.T., and Eagly, A. H. (1989). Effects of involvement on persuasion: A meta-analysis. *Psychological Bulletin, 106*(2), 290-314.

Johnson, R. E., Selenta, C., and Lord, R. G. (2006). When organizational justice and the self-concept meet: Consequences for the organization and its members. *Organizational Behavior and Human Decision Processes*, *99*(2), 175-201.

Jones, D. A., Shultz, J. W., and Chapman, D.S. (2006). Recruiting through advertisements: The effects of cognitive elaboration on decision making. *International Journal of Selection and Assessment*, *14*(2), 167-179.

Kahn, W.A. (1990). Psychological conditions of personal engagement and disengagement at work. *Academy of Management Journal*, *33*, 692-724.

Kamdar, D., McAllister, D. J., and Turban, D.B. (2006). « All in a day's work » : How follower individual differences and justice perceptions predict OCB role definitions and behavior. *Journal of Applied Psychology*, *91*(4), 841-855.

Kamdar, D. and Van Dyne, L. (2007). The joint effects of personality and workplace social exchange in predicting OCB and task performance. *Journal of Applied Psychology, 92,* 1286-1298.

Kant, I. (1958). *Critique of pure reason*, trans. by Smith, N. K. New York: Modern Library. Originally published in 1781.

Katz, D. (1964). The motivational basis of organizational behavior. *Behavioral Science, 9,* 131-146.

Kivetz, Y., and Tyler, T. R. (2006). Tomorrow I'll be me: The effect of time perspective on the activation of idealistic versus pragmatic selves. *Organizational Behavior and Human Decision Processes, 102*(2), 193-211.

Konovsky, M. A., and Organ, D. W. (1996). Dispositional and contextual determinants of organizational citizenship behavior., *Journal of Organizational Behavior* (Vol. 17, pp. 253-266): Jossey-Bass, A Registered Trademark of Wiley Periodicals, Inc., A Wiley Company.

Konovsky, M.A. and Pugh, S.D. (1994). Citizenship behavior and social exchange. *Academy of Management Journal, 37,* 656-669.

Kruglanski, A. W. (1989). *Lay epistemics and human knowledge: Cognitive and motivational bases*. New York: Plenum.

Kruglanski, A. W., Thompson, E. P., Higgins, E. T., Atash, M. N., Pierro, A., Shah, J. Y., and Spiegel, S. (2000). To "do the right thing" or to "just do it": Locomotion and assessment as distinct self-regulatory imperatives. *Journal of Personality and Social Psychology, 79*(5), 793-815.

Kruglanski, A. W., and Orehek, E. (2007). Partitioning the domain of social inference: Dual mode and systems models and their alternatives. *Annual Review of Psychology, 58,* 291-316.

Kruglanski, A. W., Pierro, A., Higgins, E. T., and Capozza, D. (2007). "On the Move" or "Staying Put": Locomotion, need for closure, and reactions to organizational change. *Journal of Applied Social Psychology, 37*(6), 1305-1340.

Lant. T. K. (2002). *Organizational cognition and interpretation. The Blackwell Companion to Organization*. Oxford: Blackwell.

LePine, J.A. and Van Dyne, L. (1998). Predicting voice behavior in work groups. *Journal of Applied Psychology, 83*(6), 853-868.

LePine, J. A., and Van Dyne, L. (2001). Peer responses to low performers: An attributional model of helping in the context of groups. *Academy of Management Review, 26,* 67–84

Lind, E. A., Kray, L., and Thompson, L. (2001). Primacy effects in justice judgments: Testing predictions for fairness heuristic theory. *Organizational Behavior and Human Decision Processes, 85*, 189-210.

Lord, R. G., and Kernan, M. C. (1987). Scripts as determinants of purposeful behavior in organizations. *Academy of Management Review, 12,* 265–277.

Markus, H (1977). Self-schemata and processing information about the self. *Journal of Personality and Social Psychology, 35*, 63-78.

Markus, H., and Wurf, E. (1987). The dynamic self concept. *Annual Review of Sociology, 38*, 299-337.

Masterson, S.S., Lewis, K., Goldman, B.M., and Taylor, M.S. (2000). Integrating justice and social exchange: The differing effects of fair procedures and treatment on work relationships. *Academy of Management Journal, 43*, 738-748.

May, D. R., Gilson, R. L., and Harter, L. M. (2004). The psychological conditions of meaningfulness, safety and availability and the engagement of the human spirit at work *Journal of Occupational and Organizational Psychology*, 77(1) 11-37.

McAllister, D. J., Kamdar, D., Morrison, E. W., and Turban, D. B. (2007). Disentangling role perceptions: How perceived role breadth, discretion, instrumentality and efficacy relate to helping and taking charge. *Journal of Applied Psychology, 92*, 1200-1211.

Milliken, F. J., Morrison, E. W., and Hewlin, P. F. (2003). An exploratory study of employee silence: Issues that employees don't communicate upward and why. *Journal of Management Studies, 40*, 1453–1476.

Moon, H., Van Dyne, L., and Wrobel, K. (2005). The circumplex model and the future of organizational citizenship behavior research. In D. L. Turnipseed (Ed.), *Handbook of Organizational Citizenship Behavior* (pp. 3-23). New York: Nova Science Publishers.

Morrison, E. (1994). Role definitions and organizational citizenship behavior: The importance of the employee's perspective. *Academy of Management Journal, 37*, 1543-1557.

Morrison, E. W. and Milliken, F. J. (2000). Organizational silence: A barrier to change and development in a pluralistic world. *Academy of Management Review, 25*, 706-725.

Morrison, E. W., and Phelps, C. C. (1999). Taking charge at work: Extrarole efforts to initiate workplace change. *Academy of Management Journal, 42*, 403-419.

Nemeth, C. J., and Staw, B. M. (1989). The tradeoffs of social control and innovation in groups and organizations. In L. Berkowitz (Ed.), *Advances in Experimental Social Psychology*, (Vol. 22, pp.175-210). New York: Academic Press.

Neuberg, S., and Newsom, J. T. (1993). Personal need for structure: Individual differences in the desire for simple structure. *Journal of Personality and Social Psychology, 65*, 113-131.

Organ, D. W. (1988). *Organizational Citizenship Behavior: The good soldier syndrome.* Lexington, MA: Lexington Books.

Parker, S. K. (1998). Enhancing role-breadth self-efficacy: The roles of job enrichment and other organizational interventions. *Journal of Applied Psychology, 83*(6), 835-852.

Parker, S.K., Williams, H.M., and Turner, N. (2006). Modeling the antecedents of proactive behavior at work. *Journal of Applied Psychology, 91*(3), 636-652.

Petty, R.E. and Cacioppo, J.T. (1984). The effects of involvement on responses to argument quantity and quality: Central and peripheral routes to persuasion. *Journal of Personality and Social Psychology, 46*(1), 69-81.

Petty, R. E. and Cacioppo, J. T. (1986). The elaboration likelihood model of persuasion.(In L. Berkowitz (Ed.), *Advances in Experimental Social Psychology* (Vol. 19, pp. 123—203). New York: Academic Press.).

Petty, R. E., Cacioppo, J. T., and Schumann, D. (1983). Central and peripheral routes to advertising effectiveness: The moderating role of involvement. *Journal of Consumer Research, 10,* 135-146.

Petty, R. E., Haugtvedt, C. P., and Smith, S. M. (1995). Elaboration as a determinant of attitude strength: Creating attitudes that are persistent, resistant, and predictive of behavior. In Petty, R. E., and J. A. Krosnick (Eds.), *Attitude strength: Antecedents and consequences* (pp. 93–130). Mahwah, NJ: Erlbaum.

Petty, R.E. and Wegener, D.T. (1999). The elaboration likelihood model: Current status and controversies. In S. Chaiken and Y. Trope (Eds.), *Dual process theories in social psychology* (pp. 41-72). New York: Guilford Press.

Podsakoff, P.M., MacKenzie, S.B., Paine, J.B., and Bachrach, D.G. (2000). Organizational citizenship behaviors: A critical review of the literature and suggestions for future research. *Journal of Management, 3,* 513-563.

Rhoades, L., and Eisenberger, R. (2002). Perceived organizational support: A review of the literature. *Journal of Applied Psychology, 87,* 698-714.

Rizzo, J. R., House, R. J., and Lirtzman, S. I. (1970). Role conflict and ambiguity in complex organizations. *Administrative Science Quarterly, 15,* 150-63.

Ross, W.H. and Wieland, C. (1996). Effects of interpersonal trust and time pressure on managerial mediation strategy in a simulated organizational dispute. *Journal of Applied Psychology,* 81(3), 228-248.

Schank, R. C., and Abelson, R. P. (1977). *Scripts, plans, goals, and understanding.* Hillsdale, NJ: Erlbaum.

Schweitzer, M.E.., Ordóñez, L. and Douma, B. (2004). Goal setting as a motivator of unethical behavior. *Academy of Management Journal, 47*(3), 422-432.

Settoon, R. P., Bennett, N., and Liden, R. C. (1996). Social exchange in organizations. *Journal of Applied Psychology,* 81, 219-227.

Singelis, T. M. (1994). The measurement of independent and interdependent self-construals. *Personality and Social Psychology Bulletin, 20*(5), 580-591.

Smith, E. R., and De Coster, J. (2000). Dual-process models in social and cognitive psychology. *Personality and Social Psychology Review, 4*(2), 108-131.

Smith, D.L., Pruitt, D.G. and Carnevale, P.J.D. (1982). Matching and mismatching: The effect of own limit, other's toughness, and time pressure on concession rate in negotiation. *Journal of Personality and Social Psychology, 42*(5), 876-883.

Street, M. D., Douglas, S. C., Geiger, S. W., and Martinko, M. J. (2001). The impact of cognitive expenditure on the ethical decision-making process: the cognitive elaboration model. *Organizational Behavior and Human Decision Processes, 86*(2), 256-277.

Taylor, S. E., and Crocker, J. (1981). Schematic bases of social information processing. In E. T. Higgins, C. P. Herman, and M. P. Zanna (Eds.), *Social cognition: The Ontario symposium on personality and social psychology* (pp. 89-134). Hillsdale, NJ: Erlbaum.

Tepper, B.J., Lockhart, D. and Hoobler, J. (2001). Justice, citizenship, and role definition effects. *Journal of Applied Psychology,* 86(4), 789-796.

Tepper, B. J., and Taylor, E. C. (2003). Relationships among supervisor's and subordinates' procedural justice perceptions and organizational citizenship behaviors. *Academy of Management Journal, 46*(1), 97-105.

Tesser, A. and Shaffer, D.R. (1990). Attitudes and attitude change. *Annual Review of Psychology, 41*, 479-523.

Thiagarajan, P., Chakrabarty, S., and Taylor, R. D. (2006). A confirmatory factor analysis of Reilly's Role Overload Scale. *Educational and Psychological Measurement, 66*(4), 657-666.

Tiedens, L. Z. (2000). Powerful emotions: The vicious cycle of social status positions and emotions. In N. Ashkanasy, W. Zerbe, and C. Hartel (Eds.). *Emotions in the workplace: Research, theory, and practice.* (pp. 71-81). Westport, CT: Quorum Books.

Van Dyne, L., Ang, S. and Botero, I.C. (2003). Conceptualizing employee silence and employee voice as multidimensional constructs. *Journal of Management Studies, 40*, 1359-1392.

Van Dyne, L., Cummings, L. L., and McLean Parks, J. (1995). Extra-role behaviors: In pursuit of constructs and definitional clarity (a bridge over muddied waters). In L. L. Cummings and B. M. Staw (Eds.), *Research in organizational behavior* (Vol. 17, pp. 215-285). Greenwich, CT: JAI Press.

Van Dyne, L and LePine, J. (1998). Helping and extra-role behaviors: Evidence of construct and predictive validity. *Academy of Management Journal, 41*, 108-119.

Van Dyne, L., Kamdar, D. A. and Joireman, J. (in press). In-role perceptions buffer the negative impact of low LMX on helping and enhance the positive impact of high LMX on voice. *Journal of Applied Psychology.*

Vroom, V.H. (1964). *Work and motivation.* New York: Wiley.

Warner, F. (2002). How Google searches itself. *Fast Company*, July, 50-52.

Withey, M. J. and Cooper, W. H. (1989). Predicting exit, voice, loyalty, and neglect. *Administrative Science Quarterly, 34*, 521-539.

Wright, P.M., George, J.M., Farnsworth, S.R. and McMahan, G.C. (1993). Productivity and extra-role behavior: The effects of goals and incentives on spontaneous helping. *Journal of Applied Psychology, 78*(3), 374-381.

Zalesny, M. D., and Ford, J. K. (1990). Extending the social information processing perspective: New links to attitudes, behaviors. *Organizational Behavior and Human Decision Processes, 47*(2), 205-246.

Zellars, K. J. and Tepper, B. J. (2003). Beyond social exchange: New directions for organizational citizenship behavior theory and research. *Research in Personnel and Human Resources Management, 22*, 395-424.

In: Citizenship in the 21ˢᵗ Century   ISBN: 978-1-60456-401-3
Editors: L. T. Kane and M. R. Poweller, pp. 155-183   © 2008 Nova Science Publishers, Inc.

Chapter 5

21ˢᵀ CENTURY BRITISH YOUTH: POLITICALLY ALIENATED OR AN ENGAGED CRITICAL CITIZENRY?

Janine Dermody and *Stuart Hanmer-Lloyd*
University of Gloucestershire, UK

INTRODUCTION

In this chapter we set out to explore what may be described as part of a global paradox. On the one hand, democracy is triumphant throughout the world with new waves of democracy occurring in Eastern Europe, Latin America and Asia (Huntingdon 1991; Vanhanen 1997). But on the other hand, fewer citizens are willing to turn out and vote in many of these democracies, when electoral participation is essential for the operation of democratic politics (Dalton and Wattenberg 2000; Norris 2002). We see this decline in voting very clearly in Britain where the 59% turnout in the 2001 general election was the lowest recorded in modern British history (Pattie et al 2004). This trend continued in 2005 with 61% turnout.

Against this background, there are increasing concerns about changes in society that are undermining the effectiveness of democratic institutions and weakening traditional conceptions of citizenship. These changes include a growing public cynicism about politics and a widespread disaffection with political institutions, (Knight and Stokes 1996; Nye et al 1997); a decline in the institutions that underpin civic society and democracy such as political parties (Whitely and Seyd 2002); and the long-term decline in electoral turnout in the majority of democratic countries (Dalton and Wattenberg 2000). This reduction in electoral engagement is most starkly represented among young first-time voters, with 63% of 18-24 year olds not voting in the 2005 British general election. Thus, this group, who can be said to constitute the future of democracy within Britain, are the focus of investigation for this chapter.

---

[*] Dr Janine Dermody. Reader in Consumer Psychology. CeReS. The Business School. University of Gloucestershire. The Park. Cheltenham. Gloucestershire. UK. GL50 2RH. Email: jdermody@glos.ac.uk.

[*] Dr Stuart Hanmer-Lloyd. Reader in Marketing. CeReS.The Business School. University of Gloucestershire. Email: shlloyd@glos.ac.uk

We begin with an in-depth review and analysis of youth voting behaviour within the UK, where evidence suggests that trust, cynicism, efficacy and alienation are key concepts in understanding youth electoral engagement. A discussion of the meaning of these concepts based on the extant literature follows. We then present the methodology employed in our unique, empirical large scale survey of 1134 British young people eligible to vote for the first time in the 2005 British general election. In presenting our results we concentrate on examining their levels of interest in the election, their voting behaviour and their levels of trust, cynicism and efficacy in relation to politicians, political parties and the political process. In conclusion we discuss the emergence of an engaged critical citizenry – through the vector of political sophistication – which gives voice to young peoples' politicisation and could reflect a new form of youth citizenship and their judicious engagement with politics in the future.

YOUTH ELECTORAL ENGAGEMENT: AN ANALYSIS OF EXISTING STUDIES

Can trust, distrust, cynicism and alienation be used to help explain young people's political attitudes and behaviour? Examining this question within the context of voting behaviour, there is clear evidence that the number of young British adults in Britain choosing not to vote at national, local and European elections is increasing (Bromley and Curtice 2002; Mori 2001; Mulgan and Wilkinson 1997; Park 1999; Russell et al 2002). The 2001 British general election saw the lowest voter turnout ever recorded – 59.4% overall, (Mori 2001), with approximately 61% of 18-24 year olds abstaining at this election and 63% in the 2005 election, compared with approximately 43% who abstained at the 1997 election (Mori figures) – indicating a downward trend. Ken Clarke talking about his Nottingham constituents during the 2001 election, commented: 'I have never known an election where so many sensible, intelligent young people would speak to me and make it quite clear they had no intention of taking part.' (Cited in Cockerell, 2003, 7).

It would therefore seem that with respect to voting behaviour, a significant proportion of younger people are alienated from electoral politics. And while abstention at elections is becoming more visible across all generations, it is feared that by failing to politically engage young people, they will be lost from the electoral process for the whole of their lives. As a result, the electorate as a body will not be renewed, thereby undermining the principles of western democratic governance.

Yet this seems a somewhat dramatic outcome of youth political disenchantment per se, particularly as their disenchantment can take a variety of forms, depending on its degree of intensity, mirroring Berman's (1997) mild to ardent cynicism. According to Park (1999), in a milder form, it may be a temporary lack of political interest and knowledge, resulting in a lack of party attachment and electoral indifference. This typically disappears as political policy has more of a direct consequence on their lives and they begin to judge the personal consequences on government policies. At its most extreme it may involve a longstanding alienation from and distrust in party politics– the kind of disenchantment that lasts for life. To what degree then are young people severely alienated from politics, and to what extent are they mildly disenchanted, where this is just a temporary phenomenon – a reflection of youth norms - that will fade as they take on the responsibilities of everyday life? To answer this question, we examine the evidence pertaining to political apathy and civic duty, and trust and cynicism.

POLITICAL APATHY

Young people's turnout at the 2001 and 2005 British elections reinforces the research of Pirie and Worcester (2000) who concluded that 16-24 year olds are more disinterested in politics than other age groups, and are less likely to vote or participate in mainstream political affairs than their elders – and that this is a behaviour they may not grow out of. The findings of the 2007 audit of political engagement in the UK concurs with this, namely that 18-24 year olds cited a lack of interest as a major factor in their non-political involvement; which itself was compounded by a direct relationship between lower educational attainment and lower political interest levels, (The Electoral Commission and The Hansard Society 2007). This lack of interest was also manifest in the research of White et al (2000) who implied that lower voter turnout among young people is due to their perceptions of politics as boring and irrelevant, and politicians as aggressive and dishonest – thereby feeding distrust, cynicism and alienation. Mulgan and Wilkinson (1997) maintain the evidence on young peoples' political attitudes and behaviour seems to suggest that either young people have not taken on the responsibilities of adulthood, or are more selfish and individually orientated than previous generations. This supports the conclusions of Putnam (2000) and Halpern (2003) on the increasingly suspicious nature of British society and reinforces Ken Clark's discussions with his young Nottingham constituents who maintained they had no intention of voting in the 2001 election. Mapping these attitudes on a 'disconnection index', where approximately 50% of 18-24 year olds feel alienated from British society, compared with fewer than 10% of 65+ year olds, Mulgan and Wilkinson (1997) conclude there is a whole generation of young people opting out of party politics. The proportion of young people who abstained in the 2001 and 2005 elections (61% and 63% respectively) adds credence to this perspective.

This political disinterest is reflected in the findings of the British social attitudes surveys. The 1994 survey found low political interest among teenagers (12-19 year olds) - with 27% of them expressing no interest in politics, compared with 8% of adults. The 1998 survey indicated the political interest of teenagers had continued to fall - with 34% of them expressing no interest in politics, compared with 11% of adults, (Park 1999). And while interest was higher amongst older teenagers than younger ones, it is among older teenagers that interest has fallen most sharply – from 45% in 1994 to 38% in 1998 (Park, 1999). So has this lack of interest extended into young adulthood? While interest among adult respondents (18+) has remained largely unchanged over this period, there is a widening gap between young adults (18-24 year olds) and the older adult population (25+ years), (Park, 1999). 1994-1996 witnessed significant gaps between them – in 1996 twice as many adults expressed a lot or quite a lot of interest in politics than did young adults, (Park, 1999). In 1998 this gap closed somewhat - with marginally higher degrees of disinterest on both sides (Park, 1999, 25). So while interest declined for young adults – this mirrored the increasing disinterest of the adult population as a whole – indicating a shift in public mood overall, as well as a generational trend.

The Electoral Commission's findings on young people and voter engagement, (Russell et al 2002), also found that the principle reason why 18-24 year olds abstained at the 2001 British general election was because they were disinterested in politics - approximately 23% - compared with only 5% of 25+ year olds. Those young people who did not vote were also more likely to believe voting is a worthless act – it would not make a difference, i.e. low efficacy, consequently undermining their civic duty. Further, even when young people are interested in elections, they are less likely to convert this into actually voting compared with their older peers. This is supported by the latest political engagement audit, (The Electoral Commission and The Hansard Society 2007). With respect to their wider political engagement, the findings from the Commission's study also indicated that young people were less likely to be interested in the 2001 election campaign, and any news about it, compared with the rest of the British electorate. This emphasises, that to some degree, young people's voting interest and intentions are dictated by the media, who report election campaigns very negatively – emphasising discord, hostility, voter apathy and the election as a non-event (Dermody and Scullion 2001, 2005; Dermody and Hanmer-Lloyd 2005) – all contributing to young people's perception that voting is a worthless act.

Pirie and Worcester, (1998), in their paper on the millennial generation, maintain that the falling political interest of young people can be explained by the classless, meritocratic society in which they live – where they lead independent, busy, mobile lives and have little knowledge of, or interest in parliamentary politics. This view is supported by the findings of Bromley et al, (2001), who found a reduced expectation, among young people, that governments can solve political issues, or create a society that guarantees them economic prosperity. This view is also echoed in the research of Dermody and Scullion (2003a, 2005) examining young people's attitudes towards political advertising. Essentially, then, a successful life is the responsibility of the individual, not government, while national governments have, themselves, become weakened by the tide of globalisation. Commenting, Michael Portillo maintains: 'Today, people are very aware of global forces which are beyond the control of national governments … yet those same governments seem too big and remote to deal with local issues. They can't arrange to get you an operation in the local hospital nor fix your local school. So there's a disenchantment with national governments: too puny to deal with global forces, and too remote to deal with local issues that really affect people.' (Cited in Cockerell, 2003, 7).

So, if younger people view the authority of national government to be undermined by today's global forces, it is not surprising that their apathy at elections and their cynicism of claims made by politicians have increased. However a distinction does need to be made between interest in party political issues, which the evidence suggests is declining, and "big" political issues, for example ecological degradation, animal rights, capitalism, globalisation, humanitarianism, which are stable, or growing, according to young people's membership of organisations like Greenpeace, coupled with activism like the May Day protests. Therefore, in judging young people's degree of political engagement, it is important to distinguish between party political and global political issues. What then of their attitudes towards civic duty?

Civic Duty

The concept of civic duty is central to any analysis of voter engagement, since a strong sense of civic duty facilitates positive political attitudes and voting behaviour. The trends in civic duty indicate no major shifts in public attitudes towards a duty to vote over a ten-year period. In 1991 68% of respondents maintained it is everyone's duty to vote, in 2001 this figure was 65% - a nominal change, (Bromley and Curtice 2002). An analysis of MORI data from the Hansard Society indicated that British youth have a strong sense of civic duty, even if this does not translate into voting behaviour. Unlike adults in general, the younger electorate are well below the norm of adult attitudes that voting is a civic duty, (Park 1999). Instead, approximately a third of them viewed it as a civic duty – well below the 65% adult norm and approximately half viewed voting as more of an instrumental act than a civic duty. This may well reflect 18-24 year olds belief that becoming involved in politics will have no significant impact on the way the UK is governed and their disposition of not wanting to express how it should be managed. In turn, this may relate to this age group possessing lower levels of knowledge about politics and parliament compared with older age groups, (The Electoral Commission and The Hansard Society 2007).

While the evidence suggests that civic-mindedness increases with age, for example an increase of 44% for 65+ year olds compared with young adults (Park 1999), a pattern also seems to be emerging of civic duty declining in two adjacent younger generations – 18-21 year olds and 26-29 years olds – suggesting the possibility that now as younger generations age they continue to remain politically disengaged. This reinforces the views of Pirie and Worcester (2000, 1998), Mulgan and Wilkinson (1997), Putnam (2000), and Halpern (2003) that, as young adults mature, fewer of them are 'growing out' of non-voting, nor taking on the responsibilities of adulthood. If this is true, then at a party political level, electoral turnout will decline as older generations of voters are replaced by younger generations of non-voters – or voting will become far more instrumental, with political offerings focusing more on the demands of particular segments, rather than the more holistic *"good for all"* philosophy of citizenship.

Political Trust and Cynicism

An analysis of levels of political trust, distrust and cynicism amongst British adults indicates trust has declined to an all time low, while cynicism, disenchantment and feelings of inefficacy have increased (Bromley and Curtice 2002). This indicates a trend of increasing disengagement from elections over the last decade. The young are typically considered to be the group who have lost the most faith in the political system, or who never had any. Yet according to the results of the British social attitude surveys, they are not as cynical as has been suggested, or any less trusting of governments than much older voters, or any more likely than older voters to believe it does not matter who is in power, or that voting in elections is a waste of time (Bromley and Curtice 2002; Park 1999). However, perhaps not surprisingly, cynicism is higher amongst teenagers who are politically disinterested and who have limited educational aspirations and lower among teenagers who are politically interested, have educational aspirations and come from higher income families, (Bromley and Curtice 2002; Park 1999).

Thus according to the British social attitudes results, the notion of an emerging cynical youth group in Britain does not appear as convincing as has been suggested – their degree of trust and cynicism broadly mirrors that of the total adult population. Yet, taking a more collective approach, the prior evidence presented in this paper, some of which originates from the social attitude studies, paints a different picture. Firstly turnout at elections is lower for 18-24 year olds than older voters, and, within this age group, it dropped by 18% at the 2001 election and 16% in the 2005 election compared with youth turnout at the 1997 election. Secondly young people are less interested in national political issues than older adults. Thirdly their failure to vote is due, in part, to their perceptions of politicians and governments as dishonest and inefficacious. Fourthly a significant number of young people feel alienated from British society, and are therefore not voting. Fifthly globalisation is undermining the credibility and authority of national governments, thereby destabilizing faith in a nation's elected officials and reinforcing electoral apathy among young people. Sixthly civic-mindedness is less strong in young people than it is in older adults, contributing to non-voting behaviour, or more instrumental, self-centred voting behaviour. There is, therefore, a clear gap between the attitudes and behaviour of young people compared with older adults. Our review of the political trust literature will stress that trust involves a positive evaluation of the performance of governments, parties and leaders, coupled with optimism and confidence in their intentions to do "good". The evidence presented here indicates that young people are not making a positive evaluation, and neither are they optimistic or confident about government/party/leader intentions. So viewing composite elements of trust and distrust together, the evidence suggests that young people are the most disengaged of all the electoral segments in Britain, albeit adults more generally appear to be becoming more distrustful too.

So what are the implications of increasing distrust and cynicism on turnout at elections? This is a highly contentious question. While some researchers argue it is reasonable to assume a relationship (Pattie and Johnson 1998; Wolfinger et al. 1999), others have argued this relationship only exists where the electorate have lost their faith in democracy overall. Klingemann, (1999), argues that where they have not lost their faith, but are distrustful and cynical, they are transformed into *'dissatisfied democrats'* who are strongly motivated to vote in order to show their dissatisfaction. Further, while previous studies have found that those with less trust and efficacy are sometimes less likely to vote, (Bromley et al 2001; Pattie and Johnson 2001; Russell et al 2002), this has not proven to be universally the case (Curtice and Jowell, 1995, 1997) – indicating that distrust, cynicism and inefficacy are not wholly responsible for electoral decline, but they are key contributors in its demise.

Findings from the Electoral Commission, (Russell et al. 2002), indicate that distrust directly influenced young people's voting abstention at the 2001 election, and was more influential for this generation, compared with older generations. Certainly political trust and voting are complex to disentangle, since it is typically anticipated that turnout will continue to decline among the untrusting electorate, but it is also declining among the trusting electorate too (Bromley and Curtice 2002). This suggests that 'diffuse support' (Heatherington 1998) - not specifically government, but politics generally - is being affected. An example of this diffuse support is evident in the findings of Dermody and Scullion (2003a, 2005) who investigated the attitudes of young people (18-22 year olds) towards the 2001 and 2005 general election advertising campaigns. Overall, credible communication is critical in building political trust, yet a large majority of the young people interviewed judged the advertising to be unhelpful, untrustworthy, *and* dishonest. Of particular importance here is the fact that so few respondents regarded the advertising as honest or trustworthy. These attributes may well act as barriers to successfully engage young people, since messages they believe to be dishonest and untrustworthy are unlikely to be fully processed and the message sources treated with suspicion – exacerbated by the negative media coverage of the election. (Dermody and Hanmer-Lloyd 2005a; Dermody and Scullion 2001, 2005). Given the evidence we have presented on young peoples' trust, distrust and cynicism, these judgments should not be surprising since they reflect wider political distrust. Dermody and Scullion (2003a,b, 2005) found confirmation that these negative ad evaluations were fuelling a greater distrust of party politics and politicians among young people. These findings are supported by the work of Ansolabehere and Iyengar (1995), Ansolabehere et al. (1999), Kahn and Kenney (1999) and Procter and Schenck-Hamlin (1996), who examined the consequences of negative advertising and its detrimental consequences on political trust and voter turnout. Overall these studies indicate that advertising campaigns in their current format contribute to a *'cycle of cynicism'* because they offer very few positive messages and very little hope for the future (Dermody and Hanmer-Lloyd 2005a; Dermody and Scullion 2001, 2003b, 2005). The issue of political communication failing to stimulate young people's voting behaviour is also evident in the findings from the British social attitude surveys, (Bromley et al. 2001; Bromley and Curtice 2002).

Table 1. Youth Political Attitude and Behaviour Studies

Youth Political Attitudes and Behaviour	Studies
Turnout at elections is lower for 18-24 year olds than older voters, and the drop in turnout indicates an increasing predisposition amongst this younger age group not to vote in elections.	Berman (1997); Bromley and Curtice (2002); Curtice and Jowell (1997); Mulgan and Wilkinson (1997); Park (1999); Russell et al. (2002).
Young people are less interested in national political issues than older adults; and they know less about the election process.	Bromley and Curtice (2002); Park (1999); Parry et al (1992); Pirie and Worcester (1998, 2000); Russell et al (2002); White et al. (2000).
Young people perceive politicians and governments as dishonest and inefficacious - contributing to their belief that voting is a 'worthless' act or creating anger resulting in the withholding of their vote.	Bromley and Curtice (2002); Dermody and Hanmer-Lloyd (fc); Mulgan and Wilkinson (1997); Park (1999); Parry et al. (1992); The Electoral Commission and The Hansard Society (2007): White et al. (2000).
A large proportion of young people feel alienated from British society, and are therefore not voting.	Dermody and Scullion (2005); Halpern (2003); Mulgan and Wilkinson (1997); Pirie and Worcester (1998, 2000); Putnam (2000); White et al. (2000).
Globalisation is undermining the credibility and authority of national governments - destabilizing faith in a nation's elected officials and reinforcing youth electoral apathy.	Bromley et al (2001); Dermody and Scullion (2005).
Electoral civic-mindedness is less strong in young people than it is in older adults, contributing to non-voting behaviour, or more self-centred voting behaviour.	Bromley and Curtice (2002); Halpern (2003); Mulgan and Wilkinson (1997); Park (1999); Pirie and Worcester (1998, 2000); White et al. (2000).

Table 1 summarises our analysis of the evidence on youth electoral engagement. Overall it can be seen that the causes of increasing youth disaffection are both multiple and complex – including distrust, disenchantment, cynicism, perceived lack of political efficacy, political disinterest, and a lack of civic duty.

We now move on to discuss the scholarship on political trust, cynicism and efficacy.

POLITICAL TRUST, CYNICISM AND EFFICACY: AN OVERVIEW OF THE LITERATURE

Political Trust

The issue of trust has increasingly been placed on the political agenda and particular concern has been voiced about links between younger people's voting behaviour and their level of trust in politicians and the political process, (Bromley and Curtice 2002; Cockerell 2003; Elliot and Quaintance 2003; Mulgan and Wilkinson 1997; Park 1999; Russell et al 2002; Schiffman et al 2002). Cockerell (2003) states, "Although Tony Blair pulverised William Hague in the 2001 [British] election, the big winner was apathy. The Labour vote fell by two million and three out of five young people stayed at home [did not vote]." While a number of explanations have been offered on why 61% of the younger electorate did not vote at the 2001 British general election, trust, distrust, cynicism and alienation feature strongly in them. Politicians do recognise the need to address public cynicism and distrust, indeed Tony Blair in the run up to the Labour party's landslide election victory in 1997 argued, "So low is public esteem for politicians and the system we operate that there is now little authority for us to use unless and until we first succeed in regaining it", (Blair 1996). Yet according to Cockerell (2003), "Among the politicians I talked to there was no unanimity about what might be done to counter public cynicism and mistrust [towards politicians]." Halpern (2003) maintains that as a nation we have become more suspicious of one another than ever before. His findings show that in the 1950's, 60% of the British population believed that other people could generally be trusted, by the early 1980's 44% believed this to be true, and currently it has declined still further to 29% and is predicted to continue to fall. Similarly, American voters have frequently been characterised as cynical, disillusioned and disengaged with respect to their views on politicians and the political process, (Berman 1997; Damico et al. 2000; Nye 1997; Putnam 2000), and according to Halpern (2003) are only fractionally less suspicious than the British public.

With the exception of upturns in the early 1980s and mid 1990s, trust in government has declined dramatically over the last thirty years (Rosenstone and Hansen 1993). Heatherington (1998) maintains that this decline has continued through the 1990s - even where decisive leadership and economic success have increased political trust (Citrin and Green 1986) – this effect has been temporary. The importance of political trust is best summed up by Hetherington (1998): "Without public support for solutions, problems will linger, will become more acute, and if not resolved will provide the foundation for renewed discontent." Thus a challenge to the whole democratic process can be envisaged as a result of dramatically reduced political trust.

So what do we mean by political trust? This involves a basic evaluative orientation towards the government, (Stokes 1962), founded on how well the government is operating according to people's normative expectations, (Miller 1974b), and individuals confidence in and optimistic expectations of the intentions and motives of political figures, (Deutsch 1958, 1960; Hosmer 1995; Mayer et al 1995; Mellinger 1956; Read 1962). Writers have argued that the evaluative element of political trust can take two forms: 'specific support' – satisfaction with Government outputs and the performance of political authorities – and 'diffuse support' – public attitudes towards regime-level objects, (e.g. values of a political party), regardless of their performance, (Citrin 1974; Citrin and Green 1986; Miller 1974[a][b]; Miller and Listhaug 1990). Because the delivery of policy is very visible, it is easier to generate 'specific trust' than 'diffuse trust'. 'Diffuse trust' is more difficult to generate because of questions associated with parties merging identities, sleaze and scandal – which are reflected in the British public's declining political trust and increasing political distrust. Consequently, if young people have low trust in a political party's values and integrity, regardless of their successful delivery of their election promises, trust of them will remain low, and, potentially, distrust of them will grow. Miller (1974a, b), and Miller and Listhaug (1990) maintain that sustained low trust ultimately challenges regime legitimacy – thereby establishing a connection between political trust and diffuse support. Heatherington, (1998), however, suggests that it is more appropriate to investigate whether political trust affects specific and diffuse support rather than vice versa. "Viewed in this way, political trust can have system-level import regardless of which type of support it effects." (Heatherington 1998, 792). Further, he argues, that if trust affects only specific support, this can have long-term implications for one regime. For example the distrust felt by Conservative party identifiers towards the Conservative government prior to the 1997 election was still being echoed for a number of years following the election, (Dermody and Scullion 2003a). However there is also evidence of much wider implications – with trust affecting diffuse support, since as Hetherington (1998, 792) points out, "trust has continued to erode despite frequent changes in political authorities." Overall, Hetherington's research highlights that it is declining political trust, rather than simply dissatisfaction with incumbents and institutions that is important, because declining political trust creates "an environment in which it is difficult for those in government to succeed." (Heatherington 1998, 791). Additionally, with the evidence indicating that political trust is continuing to fall, (Bromley and Curtice 2002; Bromley et al. 2001; Park 1999), the role of government, in theory, will become more difficult, which in turn will continue to feed distrust. This cycle is further compounded by those members of the British public who think it is easy for governments to deliver, and who are most likely to be disillusioned by their actual performance, (Bromley et al. 2001) – again feeding cynicism and distrust.

Further, political trust can vary in intensity, with individuals simultaneously trusting and distrusting politicians, parties and/or government (Miller 1974a; Lewicki et al 1998). The public's degree of trust appears to be a direct consequence of their approval of political leaders and the personal characteristics of these leaders (Citrin 1974; Citrin and Green 1986). Moreover, political trust varies with the perception of the government's ability to solve problems that are personally most important to individuals, (Miller et al 1979; Craig 1996). The degree of trust and distrust is also dependant on the distribution of positive and negative information people receive about the government (Patterson 1993; Hetherington 1998; Newman 1999a,b). Additionally the further away a person's position is from the government, the less trustful they are (Miller and Borrelli 1991). Fluctuating political trust can result from the positive or negative state of the economy, (Hetherington 1998). Finally, with respect to individual attributes, characteristics such as age, race, education, income and gender have some bearing on levels of trust (Abramson 1983; Kanter and Mirvis 1989; Schiffman et al 2002). Overall, higher trust translates into "warmer feelings" for both elected officials and political institutions, which in turn provides leaders with more freedom to govern effectively, (Hetherington 1998, 803).

In conclusion, political trust essentially involves a positive appraisal of the performance of governments, parties and leaders, combined with optimism and confidence in their intentions to do "good", (Citrin and Green 1986; Hosmer 1995; Miller 1974a,b; Mayer et al 1995). The negative political attitudes and behaviour of young people implies that their appraisals are not positive, and that they are not hopeful or certain of the intentions of governments, political parties and/or party leaders to do "good". This begins to explain why young peoples' trust in politicians and government is declining.

Political Cynicism, Efficacy and Alienation

If political trust is essentially an evaluative or affective orientation towards government, (Miller 1974a,b), then cynicism results from a negative orientation, since it is essentially a high degree of distrust. Cynicism therefore refers to the degree of negative affect towards the government, and is a statement of belief that the government is not functioning and producing outputs in accord with individual expectations. Berman (1997) takes a slightly different perspective with his view that cynicism results from low trust – a pervasive disbelief in the possibility of good in dealing with others, (Barber 1983; Damon 1995; Merton 1957). Clearly there is an issue here in terms of equating the intensities of high, low and moderate trust against high, low and moderate distrust.

Cynical attitudes towards government, then, typically focus on the integrity, purpose and effectiveness of government and its officials, (Durant 1995; Jurie 1988; O'Connell et al 1986; Starobin 1995). And furthermore, according to some scholars, cynicism, like trust, can also vary in intensity – from ardent cynicism to milder cynicism. Ardent cynicism is usually linked to ideological beliefs that are highly critical of government, where the beliefs running rife are encapsulated in *"the government is always out to get the ordinary citizen"* and *"authorities use smoke and mirrors to appease and mislead the masses"*, (Berman 1997). Ardent cynicism would seem to equate with high distrust. In contrast, milder expressions of cynicism are typically characterised by beliefs that are less hostile towards governments – they are less critical, less blaming and more evidence-based (i.e. facts are given greater weight). Because of this greater dependence on facts, milder cynicism may be more influenced by communicated reason – for example mediated communication from political parties, (Berman 1997). Consequently electoral segments characterised by mild cynicism (low trust) are potentially less of a problem than highly distrusting, ardently cynical electoral segments – a description typically applied to the younger electorate.

Yet according to Berman, (1997), it is not so much individual characteristics that determine electoral segments level of cynicism, rather it is their evaluation of the way in which government-citizen relations are managed that is critical to both the intensity and proportion of trust and cynicism within contemporary British society; and it is this evaluation that is influenced by both personal characteristics and economic and social conditions. With many young people claiming that they are ill-informed about the electoral process and parties' manifestos, there is a risk that their cynicism verges on paranoia concerning the intentions of governments, politicians and parties to "do good."

Political efficacy has been defined as *"the feeling that individual political action does have, or can have an impact on the political process"*. (Campbell et al, 1954, 187) According to Bandura (1986), efficacy develops through successful experiences that cultivate confidence and expertise, while unsuccessful experiences - for example the failure of the anti-war and anti-tuition fees protests - can decrease efficacy. Political efficacy has long been regarded as important to our understanding of public opinion, political behaviour and political systems (Campbell et al, 1954; Westholm and Niemi 1986). As Pinkleton et al (1998, 35) observe – *"...citizens are likely to participate in the political process to the extent that they feel their participation can make a difference."* In addition efficacy can help explain the development (or not) or civic culture (Almond and Verba 1963), and, in examining the importance of political efficacy to individuals, it can act as an indicator of "quality of life" (Campbell and Converse 1972). As with trust and cynicism, the nature of efficacy can vary. Political efficacy has two distinct perceptual dimensions – personal political competence (the citizen) and governmental responsiveness (the system) (Balch 1974; Westholm and Niemi 1986). Not only are these conceptually distinct, they also behave differently with respect to other variables. As Westholm and Niemi (1986, 61) observe: *"A feeling of personal political competence is correlated with an interest in politics, political knowledge and conventional political participation; perception of governmental responsiveness is not."*

What then is the relationship between cynicism and alienation – again another term used to describe the younger electorate? Miller (1974a) maintains that cynicism and efficacy are components of political alienation. Thus by increasing trust, cynicism is reduced, which in turn, combined with higher efficacy, will reduce political alienation. Given the decline in turnout at elections, it would seem that further understanding of this relationship is important in re-engaging the British electorate, particularly with the concerns that younger voters are becoming alienated from the political process, political parties, and political leaders. From a pragmatic perspective, Berman (1997) proposes three strategies to reduce political cynicism, thereby increasing trust and reducing alienation. Firstly, governments need to show citizens that they use their powers to help not harm them, and that it is not indifferent to the public's needs. Secondly citizen input needs to be formally integrated into public decision-making – so they are included, not excluded (they have some degree of efficacy). Thirdly, strategies are needed to enhance the reputation of government with respect to competency, efficiency and integrity. This requires both good performance and effective, believable communication of that performance. However, according to Bromley and Curtice, (2002), much of the communication preceding the 2001 British general election failed to persuade a vast proportion of the electorate that they needed to vote on election day – in part explaining the drop in turnout. This reinforces the argument put forward by Dermody and Scullion (2003[b]) that communication aiming to encourage people to vote needs to begin outside elections from non-party sources.

Exploring the Relationships between Trust, Cynicism and Efficacy and Engagement and Alienation

Figure 1 portrays *some* of the relationships between trust, distrust, cynicism and efficacy and engagement and alienation. For example, low trust, high distrust, high cynicism and low efficacy feed young peoples' feelings of alienation, (Aberbach 1969; Finifter 1970; Miller 1974a,b), thereby contributing to non-voting behaviour. Essentially they have no political hope, faith or confidence; they are politically sceptical, highly cynical, and ever wary and watchful of government, politicians and parties (Dermody and Hanmer-Lloyd 2005b).

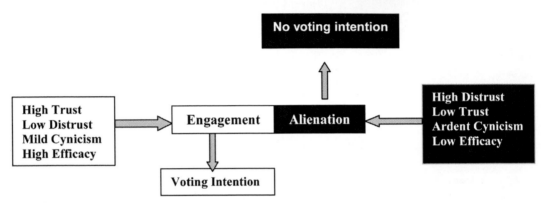

Source: J. Dermody and S. Hanmer-Lloyd, (2005), Safeguarding the Future of Democracy. 118.

Figure 1. Dimensions of Political Engagement and Alienation.

This representation concurs with a number of studies that indicate that the electorate, particularly young people, become caught in a cycle where their cynicism lowers their perceived efficacy, which in turn increases their cynicism and apathy still further (Bromley and Curtice 2002; Jennings and Niemi 1978; Lau and Erber 1985; Mulgan and Wilkinson 1997; Park 1999; Pinkleton et al 1998; White et al. 2000.

However, studies have also indicated that cynicism does not always prevent individuals from voting. Bandura (1986), Capella and Jamieson (1997), de Vrees (2005, 2004), Horn and Conway (1996), Lau (1982), Mishler and Rose (2001), Pinkleton and Austin (2002, 2001), Pinkleton et al. (1998), Shah et al (2002) and Zaller (1998) maintain that voters may participate, despite their cynicism, if their efficacy is high. Thus, it would seem that efficacy acts as a mediating variable in explaining cynics who still vote. Additionally, de Vrees (2005, 2004) and Capella and Jamieson (1997) note that individuals can be politically sophisticated (interested in and knowledgeable about politics) whilst being cynical and critical of government, politicians and parties. As a result, de Vrees (2005) questions whether cynicism may indicate an *"interested and critical citizenry."* To some extent, of course, this depends on the nature of the cynicism – the paranoia of ardent cynicism versus evidence-based milder cynicism.

In conclusion what emerges is that the relationships between trust, distrust, cynicism and efficacy and their effects on voting behaviour are complex. What appears to be pertinent, however, in understanding young peoples' electoral attitudes and behaviour, is the causality created by the combined rather than individual effects of trust, distrust, cynicism and efficacy.

Accordingly in order to examine these relationships, we will be evaluating three research questions in our analysis of our empirical work:

1) How 'involved'[1] were young, potential first-time voters (FTVs) in the 2005 British general election?
2) What degree of (a) cynicism, (b) trust, (c) efficacy (political sophistication), did young, potential FTVs possess during the 2005 British general election?
3) What relationships emerge between young, potential FTVs levels of (a) cynicism, (b) trust, (c) efficacy (political sophistication), and their 'involvement'[1] in the 2005 British general election?

Having established the conceptual foundations of youth electoral engagement and trust, cynicism and efficacy, we now move on to the empirical study itself, firstly presenting the methodology employed to investigate young, British first-time voters.

RESEARCH DESIGN

The empirical findings in this paper form part of a wider study examining youth attitudes to political advertising, set within the context of the advertising campaigns employed in the 2005 British General Election campaign, (see Dermody and Hanmer-Lloyd 2005, 2006).[2]

For this phase of the study, a quasi-random sampling approach was utilised for the survey. Filter questions were used to ensure all respondents were British Citizens aged between 18-22 - the interview was terminated if they did not satisfy these criteria. The survey involved street intercept interviews - using an interviewer-administered questionnaire - in principle towns in geographic regions throughout the UK, during the three-week period following the general election in May 2005. Once this time period ended all survey data collection ceased, giving a total of 1134 useable questionnaires. It is worth noting that while the sample criteria of 18-22 year old British first-time voters was satisfied, the respondent profile that has emerged contains over 60% of students and voters, which is double this age groups national pattern of approximately 30% students and 63% non-voters.

The survey questions were identical to the 2001 study,[3] with the exception of the trust, cynicism and efficacy attitude statements, which have been added for the first time in this study. The questions were checked against studies conducted since 2001 – to ensure they were still valid. As a result, some additional affective and cognitive measures [4] were added to the semantic differential scales assessing attitudes towards two specific adverts. The questionnaire was fully piloted and revised prior to the survey commencing.

The selection of trust, cynicism and efficacy statements used in this study are used in the British election studies, British social attitude studies and Mori's opinion polls as well as

---

[1] Involvement is measured via interest and voting behaviour.
[2] With the exception of the trust, cynicism and efficacy statements, this study repeats research carried out by Dermody and Scullion on the 2001 British general election (see Dermody and Scullion 2001, 2005; Scullion and Dermody 2005).
[3] The questions were based on key issues from the literature and previous research and 2 exploratory focus groups. (See, for example Dermody and Scullion 2001, 2005; Scullion and Dermody 2005).
[4] Derived from the work of Robideaux (2002) for the affective measure and Hill (1989) and Tinkham and Weaver-Larisy (1994) for the cognitive measures.

academic studies (see for example Austin and Pinkleton 1995; Citrin 1974; Craig et al. 1990; de Vreese 2005; Jennings and Niemi 1978; Pinkleton et al. 2002). The trust statements reflect diffuse trust – the extent to which the integrity of politicians, MPs, and the Prime Minster can be trusted. The cynicism statements include evaluations of the intentions and honesty of governments and politicians. The efficacy statements represent system and personal efficacy – voting's influence on government and the degree of political awareness. The statement of personal efficacy - *'I feel that I have a pretty good understanding of the important political issues facing our country'* – can also be used as a measure of political sophistication (de Vreese 2005). The actual statements used are listed in table 3. In all cases respondents were asked the extent to which they agreed or disagreed with each statement using a 7-point scale. The measure of involvement has its origins in the work of Citrin (1974), who used, inter alia, whether respondents voted in the election and their level of interest in the election campaign as evidence of political involvement. SPSS was used to analyse the survey data.

RESULTS

Youth Involvement in the 2005 Election

The majority of our respondents maintained they were interested or very interested in the 2005 general election (63%) and 61% claimed they voted – table 2. This indicates that the majority of our respondents were 'involved' – in varying degrees - in the election process.

Table 2. Level of Involvement in the 2005 Election

Interest	N	%	Voting	N	%	Voting	Interest[a]		Disinterest[b]	
							N	%	N	%
Very interested	138	12	Labour	263	23					
Interested	574	51	Conservative	173	15	Voter	549	83	126	37
Disinterested	284	25	LibDem	209	18	Non-voter	111	17	218	63
Very disinterested	106	9	Other	49	4	Total	660	100	344	100
Not sure	32	3	Subtotal	(694)	(61)	N = 1004 (excluding not sure)				
			Did not vote	335	30	Pearson Chi-Square = 224.061 Sig = .000 df = 2 Cramer's V = .467 0 cells <5				
			No answer	105	9					
Total	1134	100	Total	1134	100					

Note: a - Interest = interested + v interested. b - Disinterest = disinterested + v disinterested.

Of those who maintained they were interested, 83% claimed they voted compared with 17% who claimed they did not vote. Of those who maintained they were disinterested, 63% claimed they did not vote, while, interestingly, over a third (37%) claimed they did vote. These findings indicate a relationship between degree of interest and voting behaviour. Further analysis gives a Chi-square value of 224.061 with a significance level of p=.000 -

illustrating a highly statistically significant difference between voters and non-voters and their levels of interest in the general election. Cramer's value of .467 indicates a moderate strength of association between interest and voting behaviour.

Degrees of Trust, Cynicism and Efficacy – An Overview

Overall, as table 3 indicates, our respondents' political trust is low, their cynicism is high and their efficacy is moderately high.

Table 3. Degree of Trust, Cynicism and Efficacy

Statement	A	D	N	T
Trust:				
Most politicians are trustworthy	361 33%	638 57%	112 10%	1111
I trust those we elect as MPs to keep the promises they made during the election	486 44%	498 46%	110 10%	1094
I trust the intentions of the Prime Minister to always do what is right	345 32%	546 51%	184 17%	1075
Cynicism:				
Politicians loose touch with the people once elected	693 63%	251 24%	156 14%	1100
It seems our government is run by a few big interests who are just looking out for themselves	580 55%	257 24%	223 21%	1060
Politicians lie to the media and the public	778 71%	190 17%	136 12%	1104
Too many politicians only serve themselves or special interests	659 61%	180 16%	247 23%	1086
Candidates for office are only interested in people's votes, not their opinions	744 67%	175 16%	183 17%	1102
Efficacy:				
My vote makes a difference	687 63%	132 25%	271 12%	1090
I feel that I have a pretty good understanding of the important political issues facing our country	703 66%	196 18%	177 16%	1076
I have a real say in what the government does	301 28%	566 53%	198 19%	1065
Voting gives people an effective way to influence what the government does	748 68%	200 18%	151 14%	1099

Key: A=agreement. D=disagreement. N=neither. T=total (excludes not sure). Total N=1134.

The majority disagreed that 'Most politicians are trustworthy' (57%) and with the statement 'I trust the intentions of the Prime Minister to always do what is right' (51%). Their judgements surrounding 'MPs keeping their promises' were more mixed, with approximately half agreeing and half disagreeing. With respect to their cynicism, their levels of agreements with 'politicians lying to the media and public' (71%) and 'candidates are interested in votes not opinions' (67%) are particularly high. However they expressed less certainty in their evaluations of 'governments being run by a few big interests' and 'politicians serve themselves or special interests.' Their efficacy appears to be consistently high – with one exception – the majority did not believe or were unsure they influenced the behaviour of the government. However they did believe their 'vote made a difference' (63%) and that voting influences the behaviour of the government (68%). This indicates a difference between levels of personal and system efficacy.

Interest in the 2005 Election and Trust, Cynicism and Efficacy Levels

We were interested to examine whether respondents' degree of interest and disinterest in the election influenced their trust, cynicism, and efficacy. An independent-samples t-test was performed to examine the differences between those whose expressed an interest in the general election and their trust, cynicism and efficacy, with those who expressed disinterest in the general election and their trust, cynicism and efficacy – table 4.

Table 4. Interest in the Election x Degree of Trust, Cynicism and Efficacy (Independent t-test)

Statement: How strongly do you agree or disagree:[5]	Interested/ Disinterested?	N	Mean (M)	SD	t	df	Sig
Trust:							
Most politicians are trustworthy	Interested	708	-4.90	16.51	4.68	824.98	.000
	Disinterested	373	-9.54	14.94			
I trust those we elect as MPs to keep the promises they made during the election	Interested	693	-0.22	17.47	4.21	838.51	.000
	Disinterested	371	-4.61	15.48			
I trust the intentions of the Prime Minister to always do what is right	Interested	685	-3.04	16.34	3.23	757.29	.001
	Disinterested	361	-6.40	15.78			
Cynicism:							
Politicians loose touch with the people once elected	Interested	701	5.12	14.10	-5.01	761.15	.000
	Disinterested	367	9.59	13.72			
It seems our government is run by a few big interests who are just looking out for themselves	Interested	685	4.53	15.37	-4.60	718.91	.000
	Disinterested	349	9.08	14.92			
Politicians lie to the media and the public	Interested	698	9.34	14.48	-0.93	728.48	.351
	Disinterested	374	10.27				
Too many politicians only serve themselves or special interests	Interested	692	6.39	13.73	-4.26	771.69	.000
	Disinterested	365	10.05	13.09			

Statement: How strongly do you agree or disagree: [5]	Interested/ Disinterested ?	N	Mean (M)	SD	t	df	Sig
Candidates for office are only interested in people's votes, not their opinions	Interested Disinterested	697 374	8.22 10.56	13.85 13.83	-2.64	763.94	.009
Efficacy:							
My vote makes a difference	Interested Disinterested	699 363	10.53 -1.96	16.00 16.66	11.74	707.55	.000
I feel that I have a pretty good understanding of the important political issues facing our country	Interested Disinterested	687 359	12.05 1.62	13.35 15.49	10.84	639.56	.000
I have a real say in what the government does	Interested Disinterested	683 353	-4.82 -9.09	16.98 15.89	4.01	754.37	.000
Voting gives people an effective way to influence what the government does	Interested Disinterested	706 363	9.65 2.62	13.44 14.77	7.59	673.18	.000

The results show highly statistically significant differences between those who expressed an interest in the election and those who did not and their levels of trust, cynicism and efficacy in all cases except the cynicism statement - *'Politicians lie to the media and the public'* – which had the highest percentage of agreement from respondents (see table 3). The biggest differences occur with the efficacy statements *'My vote makes a difference'* - where M=10.53 for the interested group and M=-1.96 for the disinterested group - and *'I feel that I have a pretty good understanding of the important political issues facing our country'* - where M=12.05 for the interested group and M=1.62 for the disinterested group. Overall the mean values in table 4 indicate that neither interested nor disinterested respondents trusted politicians generally, MPs to keep their promises, nor the Prime Minister to do what is right, albeit the distrust levels of the interested group are slightly lower. Additionally, for those respondents who expressed an interest in the election, their cynicism is lower (although it is still quite high) and their efficacy is higher compared with those respondents who expressed disinterest in the election. Once again there are differences in levels of personal and system efficacy between interested and disinterested respondents.

---

(5) Table 4 - Agreement and disagreement are coded into positive and negative values: +10=slightly agree. +20=agree. +30 = strongly agree. −10=slightly disagree. −20=disagree. −30=strongly disagree.
(5) Table 4 - Agreement and disagreement are coded into positive and negative values: +10=slightly agree. +20=agree. +30 = strongly agree. −10=slightly disagree. −20=disagree. −30=strongly disagree.

(Non)Voting Behaviour in the 2005 Election and Trust, Cynicism and Efficacy Levels

Having established statistically significant differences between interest and disinterest and trust, cynicism, and efficacy, an independent-samples t-test was also performed to examine the differences between those who maintained they voted and their trust, cynicism and efficacy, compared with those who maintained they did not vote and their trust, cynicism and efficacy – table 5.

Table 5. Did You Vote in the Election x Degree of Trust, Cynicism and Efficacy (Independent t-test)

Statement: How strongly do you agree or disagree:	Voter or Non-Voter	N	Mean (M)	SD	t	df	Sig
Trust:							
Most politicians are trustworthy	Voter	685	-4.49	16.28	6.87	703.72	.000
	Non-Voter	325	-11.51	14.59			
I trust those we elect as MPs to keep the promises they made during the election	Voter	670	.716	16.99	7.63	676.01	.000
	Non-Voter	322	-7.67	15.82			
I trust the intentions of the Prime Minister to always do what is right	Voter	658	-2.87	16.12	4.21	970	.000
	Non-Voter	314	-7.55	16.40			
Cynicism:							
Politicians loose touch with the people once elected	Voter	680	6.10	13.65	-2.66	996	.008
	Non-Voter	318	8.65	14.89			
It seems our government is run by a few big interests who are just looking out for themselves	Voter		5.14		-3.17	958	.002
	Non-Voter	654	8.50	15.06			
		306		15.73			
Politicians lie to the media and the public	Voter	681	8.90	14.59	-2.97	1000	.003
	Non-Voter	321	11.84	14.71			
Too many politicians only serve themselves or special interests	Voter	670	7.42	13.19	-2.22	982	.027
	Non-Voter	314	9.46	13.96			
Candidates for office are only interested in people's votes, not their opinions	Voter	675	7.93	13.97	-4.70	999	.000
	Non-Voter	326	12.27	13.12			
Efficacy:							
My vote makes a difference	Voter	670	10.75	15.36	12.45	551.40	.000
	Non-Voter	317	-3.60	17.58			
I feel that I have a pretty good understanding of the important political issues facing our country	Voter	666	11.31	13.94	8.84	548.26	.000
	Non-Voter	312	2.11	15.69			
I have a real say in what the government does	Voter	654	-3.58	16.85	9.20	694.90	.000
	Non-Voter	310	-13.29	14.53			
Voting gives people an effective way to influence what the government does	Voter	679	10.10	13.18	9.56	545.22	.000
	Non-Voter	317	.57	15.21			

---

[6] Table 5 - Agreement and disagreement are coded into positive and negative values: +10=slightly agree. +20=agree. +30 = strongly agree. –10=slightly disagree. –20=disagree. –30=strongly disagree.

The results show highly statistically significant differences in all cases between claimed voters and non-voters and their levels of trust, cynicism and efficacy. Once again the biggest differences occur with the efficacy statements: *'My vote makes a difference'* - M=10.75 for voters and M=-3.60 for non-voters; *'I feel that I have a pretty good understanding of the important political issues facing our country'* - M=11.31 for voters and M=2.11 for non-voters; *'I have a real say in what the government does'* - M=-3.58 for voters and M=-13.29 for non-voters; and *'Voting gives people an effective way to influence what the government does'* - M= 10.10 for voters and M= .57 for non-voters. In addition there is also a notable difference between the means scores of one trust statement: *'Most politicians are trustworthy'* - M= -4.49 for voters and M= -11.51 for non-voters.

Overall the mean values in table 5 indicate that neither voters nor non-voters trusted politicians generally, MPs to keep their promises, nor the Prime Minister to do what is right, albeit the distrust levels of voters are slightly lower compared with non-voters. Additionally, voters' efficacy is higher and their cynicism is lower (albeit they are still quite cynical) compared with non-voters. Once again there are differences in levels of personal and system efficacy between claimed voters and non-voters.

Gender Differences in Trust, Cynicism and Efficacy Levels

Finally we were interested in any gender differences in interest levels, voting behaviour and levels of trust, cynicism, and efficacy. No statistically significant differences emerged between males and females and their interest levels or voting behaviour. However some statistically significant differences did emerge between male and female levels of trust, cynicism, and efficacy – table 6 – albeit the values of Cramer indicate a low strength of association between these attitudes and gender.

Comparing male and female levels of trust in the Prime Minister – Tony Blair – while both genders distrusted the Prime Minister, men distrusted him more. With respect to their cynicism - *'Too many politicians only serve themselves or special interests'* and *'Candidates for office are only interested in people's votes, not their opinions'* – cynicism is high for both genders. However, overall, men are more cynical than women, with more of them strongly agreeing or agreeing with these statements. This gender difference in cynicism levels was confirmed by an independent t-test, verifying that men are significantly more cynical than women (t=1.95, p=0.05). Exploring the efficacy results, the gender split is a little more complex. For *'My vote makes a difference'* – more women agreed than men, indicating a higher degree of female efficacy with respect to voting. However, for the statements *'I feel that I have a pretty good understanding of the important political issues facing our country'* and *'I have a real say in what the government does'*, more women disagreed with these statements than men, indicating that men have a higher level of efficacy in terms of their perceived knowledge levels and their 'influence' on government decision-making.

We now consider the implications of our findings for twenty first century youth and their political engagement – are they politically alienated or an engaged, critical citizenry?

Table 6. Gender Differences in Levels of Trust, Cynicism, and Efficacy

Statement: How strongly do you agree or disagree -								
Trust:	StA	A	SA	N	SD	D	StD	Total
I trust the intentions of the Prime Minister to always do what is right Pearson X^2= 15.033 df = 6 Sig = .020 0 cells <5 Cramer's V = .118								
Male N	14	64	84	109	109	118	64	562
%	2.5	11.4	14.9	19.4	19.4	21.0	11.4	52.3
Female N	11	67	105	75	121	83	51	513
%	2.1	13.1	20.5	14.6	23.6	16.2	9.9	47.7
Total N	25	131	189	184	230	201	115	1075
%	2.3	12.2	17.6	17.1	21.4	18.7	10.7	100.0
Cynicism:	StA	A	SA	N	SD	D	StD	Total
Too many politicians only serve themselves or special interests Pearson X^2= 13.943 df = 6 Sig = .030 1 cell <5 Cramer's V = .113								
Male N	77	108	172	125	55	33	7	577
%	13.3	18.7	29.8	21.7	9.5	5.7	1.2	53.0
Female N	35	101	166	122	54	28	3	509
%	6.9	19.8	32.6	24.0	10.6	5.5	0.6	47.0
Total N	112	209	338	247	109	61	10	1086
%	10.3	19.2	31.1	22.7	10.0	5.6	0.9	100.0
Candidates for office are only interested in people's votes, not their opinions Pearson X^2= 17.971 df = 6 Sig = .006 0 cells <5 Cramer's V = .128								
Male N	89	133	175	106	47	30	5	585
%	15.2	22.7	29.9	18.1	8.0	5.2	0.8	53.0
Female N	44	116	187	77	54	33	6	517
%	8.5	22.4	36.2	14.9	10.4	6.4	1.1	47.0
Total N	133	249	362	183	101	63	11	1102
%	12.1	22.6	32.9	16.6	9.2	5.7	1.0	100.0
Efficacy:	StA	A	SA	N	SD	D	StD	Total
My vote makes a difference Pearson X^2= 15.232 df = 6 Sig = .019 0 cells <5 Cramer's V = .118								
Male N	66	139	130	74	47	66	47	569
%	11.6	24.4	22.8	13.0	8.3	11.6	8.3	52.2
Female N	50	151	151	58	41	45	25	521
%	9.6	28.9	28.9	11.1	7.9	8.6	4.8	47.8
Total N	116	290	281	132	88	111	72	1090
%	10.6	26.6	25.8	12.1	8.1	10.2	6.6	100.0

Efficacy (Continued):	StA	A	SA	N	SD	D	StD	Total
I feel that I have a pretty good understanding of the important political issues facing our country Pearson X²= 18.439 df = 6 Sig = .005 0 cells <5 Cramer's V = .131								
Male N	67	176	142	92	43	25	14	559
%	12.0	31.5	25.4	16.5	7.7	4.5	2.5	52.0
Female N	35	143	140	85	53	43	18	517
%	6.8	27.7	27.1	16.4	10.2	8.3	3.5	48.0
Total N	102	319	282	177	96	68	32	1076
%	9.5	29.6	26.2	16.4	8.9	6.3	2.9	100.0
I have a real say in what the government does Pearson X²= 21.504 df = 6 Sig = .001 0 cells <5 Cramer's V = .142								
Male N	28	49	97	98	101	95	98	566
%	4.9	8.7	17.1	17.3	17.8	16.8	17.3	53.0
Female N	4	36	87	100	86	110	76	499
%	0.8	7.2	17.4	20.0	17.2	22.0	15.2	47.0
Total N	32	85	184	198	187	205	174	1065
%	3.0	7.9	17.3	18.6	17.6	19.3	16.3	100.0

ANALYSIS – ALIENATED YOUTH OR AN ENGAGED CRITICAL CITIZENRY?

Reflecting on the youth political attitudes and behaviour presented in table one, our respondents do appear to be more politically involved than these studies suggest. This may well be explained by the nature of our sample. However, there is also consistency with previous research with respect to their distrusting and cynical attitudes, (Bromley and Curtice 2002; Diplock 2001; Mulgan and Wilkinson 1997; Park 1999; Parry et al. 1992; White et al. 2000). Our respondents, overall, expressed distrustful and cynical attitudes towards politicians' trustworthiness, their integrity and their good intentions, and as we would have expected, this was strongest among the disinterested, non-voting group. To some degree, then, our findings support figure one – distrust and cynicism can lead to feelings of political alienation, (Aberbach 1969; Dermody and Scullion 2005; Finifter 1970; Halpern 2003; Miller 1974a,b Mulgan and Wilkinson 1997; Pirie and Worcester 1998, 2000; Putnam 2000; White et al. 2000).

Our findings also indicate that while young people can be highly distrusting and cynical, they can also be interested in the election and vote. This 'paradox' can partially be explained through their personal efficacy levels - political sophistication (de Vresse 2005). Thus two groups emerge – those with high political sophistication and those with low political sophistication. For those who perceive themselves to have high political sophistication, whilst they remain distrusting of politicians, and highly cynical of them, they retain a much stronger sense of personal efficacy – where they believe they are knowledgeable about political issues and are interested in elections. Consequently they do not feel as politically alienated as those with lower personal efficacy (low political sophistication). Accordingly, for those with high political sophistication, their cynicism and distrust does not act as barrier to them voting – supporting the findings of Bandura (1986), Capella and Jamieson (1997), de Vrees (2005, 2004), Lau (1982), Mishler and Rose (2001), Pinkleton and Austin (2002, 2001), Pinkleton et al. (1998), Shah et al. (2002), Westholm and Niemi (1986) and Zaller (1998). These relationships are illustrated in figure 2.

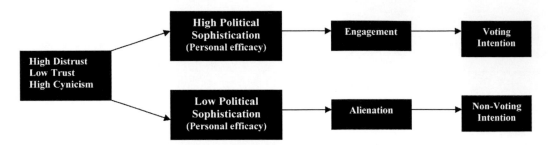

Figure 2. Political Sophistication and Voting Behaviour.

Hence, while previous research has suggested that high political cynicism and low trust can be both detrimental to political participation (Patterson 2002) and *not* detrimental to political participation (Lesher and Thorson 2000; de Vreese and Semetko 2002), this contradiction can be explained through the mediating variable of personal efficacy – political sophistication. Those with high political sophistication, then, can be described as 'an interested and critical citizenry' (de Vrees 2005) – they have the capacity to be politically involved and knowledgeable voters while at the same time remaining critical and disparaging about the integrity of politicians and their performance. This appears to be particularly true for our male respondents, who were highly cynical with a stronger sense of personal efficacy.

The concept of political sophistication is therefore important in aiding our understanding of youth political engagement as critical citizens. Not only does it contribute to our appreciation of young peoples' expression of electoral participation, it also offers us insight into their more fluid and modern engagement with civic society, for example interaction with interest groups, social causes and protests such as boycotts and buycotts. A notable new expression of this is the phenomenon of political consumerism (Anderson and Tobiasen 2004; Mitchelletti et al. 2004). Thus the concept of political sophistication enables us to examine more widespread and manifold forms of the political participation of young people as 'critical citizens', most notably their political behaviour as politicised consumers. Educated young people are one group whose consumption choices are informed by political and ethical issues, (Anderson and Tobiasen 2004; Shah et al. 2007), which reflects key elements of citizenship – responsibility, justice, equality and the 'common good'. As our earlier analysis of youth electoral engagement indicates this group have little trust in the ability of government to solve political issues (Bromley et al. 2001), and accordingly some are relying on their power in the marketplace to take on this more citizenly responsibility as politicised consumers (Beck 1997; Mitchellette et al. 2004; Schudson 2007; Shapiro and Hader-Cordon 1999; Shaw 2006; Stolle and Hooghe 2004).

Consequently while we have seen some alarming forecasts for the future of electoral engagement and thus democracy, this politicisation, which is transforming young people into citizen-consumers, is changing and strengthening the nature of political engagement, broadening it beyond the traditional establishment of democracy via voting for politicians and political parties in elections, towards much more cosmopolitan, young citizen consumers who are using the 'supremacy' of the marketplace to actively engage in promoting human, social, environmental and economic capital. It is worth remembering that *"good citizens are made, not born."* (Galston 2001, 217). Furthermore, when these young critical citizens do engage at election time, they participate as 'new' floating voters – interested, educated and non-party loyal – who choose their candidate(s) based on their critical analysis of these individuals contribution to this more citizenly agenda. As Follesdal (2006, 19) reminds us, *Political consumerism allows individuals, living under conditions of globalization beyond control of accountable governments, to express their sense of justice as citizens of the world."* The increasing politicisation of young people is thus critical in helping to create and nurture civic engagement – in all its forms - in the future. Can we therefore hypothesise that this is the new face of citizenship in the twenty-first century – young, cynical and politicised?

In conclusion, it has been argued that the decline of trust in politicians and parties should not be seen as a dangerous for political stability, but rather as an indication of these traditional institutions reaching maturity, where politicians must embrace critical citizens' constant scrutiny of them (Inglehart, 1997; Norris 1999, 2002; Welzel and Inglehart, 1999). While this will be challenging for politicians, evidence indicates that these younger, critical citizens strongly support democracy (Inglehart 1997), particularly more cosmopolitan political engagement, for example protests through politicised consumption. However, reflecting on the varying intensity of cynicism, we add a note of caution. When does cynicism become so potent, it destroys young people's strength of personal efficacy and thus their agency as critical citizens? This question is particularly pertinent when we consider the prevalence of low trust, high distrust, high cynicism and low personal efficacy within our data. Accordingly, while the presence of a young, critical citizenry offers hope for the future health of civic society in Britain, we need to be cognisant of the impact of cynicism given *"Cynicism increases social distance and diminishes the public spirit"* (Gore 1994).

REFERENCES

Aberbach, J.D. (1969). Alienation and Political Behaviour. *American Political Science Review,* Vol.63, (March), 36-99.

Abramson, P.R. (1983). Political Attitudes in America: Formation and Change. San Francisco: Freeman.

Almond, G. and Verber, S. (1963). The Civic Culture. Princeton NJ: Princeton University Press.

Anderson, J.G. and Tobiasen, M. (2004). Who are these Political Consumers Anyway? in Micheletti, M., Follesdal , A. and Stolle, D., (Eds.). *Politics, Products and Markets. Exploring Political Consumerism Past and Present.* London: Transaction Publishers. 203-222.

Ansolabehere, S., and Iyengar, S. (1995). *Going Negative: How Political Advertisements Shrink and Polarize the Electorate*. New York: Free Press.

Ansolabehere, S.D., Iyenger, S., and Smith, A. (1999). Replicating Experiments Using Aggregate and Survey Data: The Case of Negative Advertising and Turnout. *American Political Science Review,* Vol.93 No.4 (December).

Austin, E.W. and Pinkleton, B.E. (1995). Positive and Negative Effects of Political Disaffection on the Less Experienced Voter. *Journal of Broadcasting and Electronic Media.* Vol. 39. 1-21.

Balch, G.I. (1974). Multiple Indicators in Survey Research: The Concept 'Sense of the Political Efficacy.' *Political Methodology.* Vol. 1. 1-44.

Bandura, A. (1986). *Social Foundations of Thought and Action: A Social Cognitive Theory.* Englewood Cliffs, NJ: Prentice Hall.

Barber, B. (1983). *The Logic and Limits of Trust,* New Brunswick, N. J: Rutgers University Press.

Beck, U. (1997). *The Reinvention of Politics: Rethinking Modernity in the Global Social Order.* Cambridge: Polity Press.

Berman, E. M. (1997). 'Dealing with Cynical Citizens', Public Administration Review, Vol. 57, No. 2. 105-112.

Blair, A., (1996), Democracy's Second Age, The Economist, 14th September.

Bromley, C., and Curtice, J. (2002). Where Have All The Voters Gone?, in A. Park, J. Curtice, K. Thomson, L. Jarvis, and C. Bromley, (Eds.), *British Social Attitudes. The 19th Report.* (National Centre for Social Research). London: Sage. Chapter 7.

Bromley, C., Curtice, J., and Seyd, B. (2001). Political Engagement, Trust and Constituitional Reform, in A. Park, J. Curtice, K. Thomson, L. Jarvis, and C. Bromley, (Eds.), *British Social Attitudes. The 18th Report: Public Policy, Social Ties.* (National Centre for Social Research). London: Sage. Chapter 9.

Campbell, A. and Converse, P.E. (Eds). (1972). *The Human Meaning of Social Change.* New York: Russell Sage Foundation.

Campbell, A. Gurin, G. and Miller, W. (1954). *The Voter Decides.* Evanston, Il: Row, Peterson.

Capella, J.N. and Jamieson, K.H. (1997). *Spiral of Cynicism: The Press and the Public Good.* NY:Oxford University Press.

Citrin, J. (1974). Comment: The Political Relevance of Trust in Government. *American Political Science Review.* Vol. 68, September. 973-988.

Citrin, J. and Green D. P. (1986). Presidential Leadership and the Resurgence of Trust in Government. *British Journal of Political Science.* Vol. 16, October. 431-453.

Cockerell, M. (2003). Are These Men to Blame for Making us Sick of Politics? *The Guardian,* G2 section, 4th Feb. 7.

Craig, S.C. (1996). Change and the American Electorate. in S.C. Craig (Ed.). *Broken Contract: Changing Relationships Between Americans and Their Government, Boulder,* CO: Westview, 1-20.

Craig, S.C., Niemi, R.G. and Silver, G.E. (1990). Political Efficacy and Trust: A Report on the NES Pilot Study Items. *Political Behaviour.* Vol. 12. 289-314.

Curtice, J. and Jowell, R. (1997). Trust in the Political System. in R. Jowell, J. Curtice, A. Park, L. Brook, K. Thomson, L. Jarvis, and C. Bryson (Eds.). *British Social Attitudes.*

The 14th Report. The End of Conservative Values? (National Centre for Social Research). Aldershot: Ashgate. Chapter 5.

Dalton, R.J. and Wattenberg, M.P. (2000). *Parties without Partisans.* Oxford: Oxford University Press.

Damico, A.J., Conway, M.M., and Damico, S.B. (2000). Patterns of Political Trust and Mistrust: Three Moments in the Lives of Democratic Citizens. *Polity.* Vol.32. 377-400.

Damon, W. (1995). *Greater Expectations.* NY: Free Press.

De Vreese C.H. and Semetko, H.A. (2002). Cynical and Engaged: Strategic Campaign Coverage, Public Opinion and Mobilization in a Referendum. *Communication Research.* Vol. 29. No. 6. 614-641.

De Vreese, C.H. (2004). The Effects of Strategic News on Political Cynicism, Issue Evaluations and Policy Support: A Two-Wave Experiment. *Mass Communication and Society.* Vol. 7. No. 2. 191-215.

De Vreese, C.H. (2005). The Spiral of Cynicism Reconsidered. *European Journal of Communication.* Vol. 20. No. 3. 283-301.

Dermody, J. and Hanmer-Lloyd, S. (2005a). Promoting Distrust? A Chronicle of the 2005 British General Election Advertising Campaigns. *Journal of Marketing Management* (special edition: The Marketing Campaign: The 2005 British General Election).

Dermody, J. and Hanmer-Lloyd, S. (2005b). Safeguarding the Future of Democracy: (Re)Building Young People's Trust in Parliamentary Politics. *Journal of Political Marketing.* Vol.4. No. 2/3.115-134.

Dermody, J. and Hanmer-Lloyd, S. (2006). A Marketing Analysis of the 2005 General Election Advertising Campaigns. in D. Lilleker, N.A. Jackson and R. Scullion (Eds.). *The Marketing of Political Parties. Political Marketing at the 2005 British General Election.* Manchester University Press. (Chapter 5).

Dermody, J. and Hanmer-Lloyd, S. (fc). Consuming Elections? An Analysis of Youth (Non)Voting Behaviour. in Lilleker, D. and Scullion, R. (Eds.) *Consumers or Citizens: Analysing the Contemporary Electorate.* Manchester: Manchester University Press.

Dermody, J., and Scullion, R. (2001). An Exploration of the Advertising Ambitions and Strategies of the 2001 British General Election. *Journal of Marketing Management.* (special edition: The Marketing Campaign: The 2001 British General Election). Vol.17. No. 9-10, 969-987.

Dermody, J., and Scullion, R. (2003a). Facing the Future: Young People's Awareness of the 2001 British General Election Advertising Campaigns. *Journal of Public Affairs.* Vol.3, No.2. (May). 152-165.

Dermody, J and Scullion, R. (2003b). Exploring the Consequences of Negative Political Advertising for Liberal Democracy. *Journal of Political Marketing.* Vol.2. No. 1. 77-100.

Dermody, J and Scullion, R. (2005). Young People's Attitudes Towards British Political Advertising: Nurturing or Impeding Voter Engagement? *Journal of Nonprofit and Public Sector Marketing.* Vol.14. No. 1/2. 129-149.

Deutsch, M. (1958). Trust and Suspicion. *Journal of Conflict Resolution.* Vol.2. 265-279.

Deutsch, M. (1960). The Effect of Motivational Orientation upon Trust and Suspicion. *Human Relations.* Vol.13. 123-139.

Diplock, S. (2001). *None of the Above.* London: Hansard Society.

Durant, R.F. (1995). The Democratic Deficit in America. *Paper presented at the 56th Annual Research Conference of the American Society for Public Administration.* 22-26th July, San Antonio.

Elliot, J. and Quaintance, L. (2003). Britain is Getting More Suspicious. *The Sunday Times.* May 18th. 5.

Finifter, A. W. (1970). 'Dimensions of Political Alienation'. *American Political Science Review.* Vol. 64. June. 389-410.

Follesdal , A. (2006). Political Consumerism as Chance and Challenge. in Micheletti, M., Follesdal , A. and Stolle, D., (Eds.). Politics, Products and Markets. Exploring Political Consumerism Past and Present. London: Transaction Publishers. 3-20.

Galston, W.A. (2001). Political Knowledge, Political Engagement and Civic Education. *Annual Review of Political Science.* Vol. 4. 217-234.

Govier, T. (1994). Is It A Jungle Out There? Trust, Distrust and the Construction of Social Reality. *Dialogue.* Vol.33. 237-252.

Halpern, D. (2003). Downing Street advisor, University of Cambridge, in Elliot, J. and Quaintance, L. Britain is Getting More Suspicious. *The Sunday Times.* May 18th 2003, 5.

Hetherington, M. J. (1998). The Political Relevance of Trust. *American Political Science Review.* Vol. 92. No. 4. 791-808.

Hill, R.P. (1989). An Exploration of Voter Response to Political Advertisements. *Journal of Advertising.* Vol. 18. No. 4. 14-22.

Horn, R.C and Conway, M.M. (1996). Public Judgement and Political Engagement in the 1992 Election. in S.C. Craig (Ed.), Broken Contract? *Changing Relationships between Americans and their Government.* Boulder, CO: Westview Press. 110-126.

Hosmer, L.T. (1995). Trust: The Connecting Link between Organizational Theory and Philisophical Ethics. *Academy of Management Review.* Vol.20. 379-403.

Inglehart, R.J. (1997). *Modernization and Postmodernization.* Princeton, NJ: Princeton University Press.

Jennings, M.K. and Niemi, R.G. (1978). The Persistence of Political Orientations: An Over-time Analysis of Two Generations. *British Journal of Political Science.* Vol. 8. 333-363.

Jurie, J. (1988). Bureaucracy and Higher Education: The Redefinition of Relevance. *Scholar and Educator.* Vol.12 (Fall). 80-91.

Kahn, K.F. and Kenney, P.J. (1999). Do Campaigns Mobilize or Suppress Turnout? Clarifying the Relationship Between Negativity and Participation. *American Political Science Review.* Vol.93. No.4 (December). 877-89.

Kanter, D.L., and Mirvis, P.H. (1989). The Cynical Americans: Living and Working in an Age of Discontent and Disillusion. San Francisco: Josey-Bass.

Klingemann, H. (1999). Mapping Political Support in the 1990's: A Global Analysis. in P. Norris, (Ed.) *Critical Citizens: Global Support for Democratic Governance.* Oxford: Oxford University Press.

Knight, B. and Stokes, P. (1996). The Deficit in Civil Society in the United Kingdom. Foundation for Civic Society. Working paper No. 1.

Lau, R.R. (1982). Negativity in Political Perception. *Political Behaviour.* Vol. 4. 353-377.

Lesher, G. and Thorson, E. (2000). Overreporting Voting: Campaign Media, Public Mood, and the Vote. *Political Communication.* Vol. 17. No. 3. 263-278.

Lewicki, R.J., McAllister, D.J., and Bies R.J. (1998). Trust and Distrust: New Relationships and Realities. *Academy of Management Review.* Vol.23. No.3. 438-458.

Mayer, R.C., Davis, J.H., and Schoorman, F.D. (1995). An Integrative Model of Organizational Trust. *Academy of Management Review.* Vol.20. 709-734.

McClelland, D.C. (1985). Human Motivation. Glenview, IL: Scott Foresman.

Mellinger, G.D.. (1956). Interpersonal Trust as a Factor in Communication. *Journal of Abnormal Social Psychology.* Vol.52. 304-309.

Merton, R.K. (1957). Social Theory and Social Structure. Glencoe IL: Free Press.

Micheletti, M., Follesdal , A. and Stolle, D., (Eds.). Politics, Products and Markets. Exploring Political Consumerism Past and Present. London: Transaction Publishers.

Miller, A. H. (1974b), Rejoinder to 'Comment' by Jack Citrin: Political Discontent or Ritualism?, *The American Political Science Review,* Vol. 68, September, pp. 989-1001.

Miller, A. H. (1974a). Political Issues and Trust in Government: 1964-1970. *The American Political Science Review.* Vol. 68. September. 951-972.

Miller, A. H., and Borrelli, S. (1991). Confidence in Government During the 1980s. *American Politics Quarterly.* Vol.19. April. 147-173.

Miller, A. H., and Listhaug, O. (1990). Political Parties and Confidence in Government: A Comparison of Norway, Sweden and the United States. *British Journal of Political Science.* Vol. 20. July. 357-386.

Miller, A. H., Goldenberg, E., and Erbring, L. (1979). Typset Politics: Impact of Newspapers on Public Confidence. *The American Political Science Review.* Vol.73. March. 67-84.

Mishler, W. and Rose, R. (2001). What are the Origins of Political Trust? Testing Institutional and Cultural in Post-Communist Societies. *Comparative Political Studies.* Vol. 34. No. 1. 30-62.

MORI, (2001). British Public Opinion. June, XXIV, (3/4).

MORI, (2005). General Election 2005. MORI Final Aggregate Analysis. http//www.mori.com/polls/2005/election-aggregate.shtml

Mulgan, G. and Wilkinson, H. (1997). Freedom's Children and the Rise of Generational Politics. in G. Mulgan (Ed), Life After Politics: New Thinking for the Twenty-First Century. London: Fontana.

Newman, B.I. (Ed.). (1999a). Handbook of Political Marketing. *Thousand Oaks,* CA: Sage.

Newman, B.I. (Ed.). (1999b). The Mass Marketing of Politics, *Thousand Oaks,* CA: Sage.

Norris, P. (2002). Democratic Phoenix: Reinventing Political Activism. Cambridge: Cambridge University Press.

Norris, P. (Ed.). (1999). Critical Citizens: Global Support for Democratic Government. Oxford: Oxford University Press.

Nye, J., Zelikow, P., and King, D. (1997). Why People Don't Trust Government. Cambridge, MA: Harvard University Press.

Nye, J.S., Jr. (1997). In Government We Don't Trust. *Foreign Policy.* 99-111.

O'Connell, B.J., Holzman, H., and Armandi, B.R. (1986) Police Cynicism and the Modes of Adaptation. *Journal of Police Science and Administration.* Vol.14. September. 307-313.

Park, A. (1999). Young People and Political Apathy. in R. Jowell, J. Curtice, A. Park, K. Thomson, L. Jarvis, C. Bromley, and N. Stratford, (Eds.). *British Social Attitudes. The 16th Report. Who Shares New Labour Values?,* (National Centre for Social Research). Aldershot: Ashgate. Chapter 2.

Parry, G., Moyser, G., and Day, N. (1992). Political Participation and Democracy in Britain. Cambridge: Cambridge University Press.

Patterson, T. (1993). Out of Order. New York: Knopf.

Pattie C. and Johnston, R. (2001). A Low Turnout Landslide: Abstention at the British General Election of 1997. *Political Studies.* Vol.49. No. 2. 286-305.

Pattie, C., Seyd, P., and Whitely, P. (2004). Citizenship in Britain. Values, Participation and Democracy. Cambridge: Cambridge University Press.

Pinkleton, B.E. and Austin, E.W . (2001). Individual Motivations, Perceived Media Importance and Political Disaffection. *Political Communication.* Vol. 18. 321-334.

Pinkleton, B.E., and Austin, E.W. (2002). Exploring Relationships Among Media Use Frequency, Perceived Media Importance and Media Satisfaction in Political Disaffection and Efficacy. *Mass Communication and Society.* Vol. 5. 113-40.

Pinkleton, B.E., Austin, E.W and Portman, K.J. (1998). Relationships of Media Use and Political Dissaffection to Political Efficacy and Voting Behaviour. *Journal of Broadcasting and Electronic Media.* Vol. 42. 34-49.

Pirie, M. and Worcester, R.M. (2000). The Big Turn-Off: Attitudes of Young People to Government, Citizenship and Community. Adam Smith Institute. http://www.adamsmith.org.uk/

Pirie, M. and Worcester, R.M. (1998). The Millennial Generation. Adam Smith Institute. London.

Procter, D.E. and Schenck-Hamilton, W.J. (1996). *Form and Variations in Negative Political Advertising. Communication Research Reports.* Vol.13. 1-10.

Putman, R. (2000). Bowling Alone. The Collapse and Revival of American Community. New York: Simon and Schuster.

Read, W.H. (1962). Upward Communication in Industrial Hierarchies. *Human Relations.* Vol.15. No.3. 3-15.

Robideaux, D.R. (2002). Party Affiliation and Ad Attitude towards Political Ads. *Journal of Marketing Theory and Practice.* Vol. 10. No. 1 (Winter). 36-45.

Rosenstone, S. J. and Hansen, M. (1993). Mobilization, Participation and Democracy in America.New York: Macmillan.

Russell, A., Fieldhouse, E., Purdam, K., and Kalra, V. (2002). Voter Engagement and Young People. The Electoral Commission, London, UK. www.electoralcommission.org.uk

Schiffman, L. G., Sherman, E. and Kirpalani, N. (2002). Trusting Souls: A Segmentation of the Voting Public. *Psychology and Marketing.* Vol. 19. No. 12. 993-1007.

Schudson, M. (2007). Citizens, Consumers and the Good Society. in D.V. Shah, L. Friedland, D.M. McLeod and M.R. Nelson, (Eds.). The Politics of Consumption/The Consumption of Politics. *The Annals of the American Academy of Political and Social Science.* Vol. 611. May. 236-249.

Scullion, R. and Dermody, J. (2005). The Value of Party Election Broadcasts for Electoral Engagement. A Content Analysis of the 2001 British General Election Campaign. *International Journal of Advertising.* Vol. 24. No. 3. 345-372.

Shah, D., Watts M.D., Domke, D. and Fan, D. (2002). News Framing and Cueing of Issue Regimes: Explaining Clinton's Public Approval in Spite of Scandal. *Public Opinion Quarterly.* Vol. 66. 339-370.

Shapiro, I. and Hacker-Cordon, C. (1999). Democracy's Edges. Cambridge: Cambridge University Press.

Shaw, D., Newholm, T. and Dickinson, R. (2006). Consumption as Voting: an Exploration of Consumer Empowerment. *European Journal of Marketing.* Vol. 40. No. 9/10. 1049-1067.

Sheppard, B.H. (1995). Negotiating in Long-Term Mutually Interdependent Relationships Among Relative Equals. in R.J. Bies, R.J. Lewicki, and B.H. Sheppard, (Eds.). *Research on Negotiation in Organizations.* Greenwich, CT: JAI Press. Vol.5. 3-44,

Starobin, P. (1995). A Generation of Vipers: Journalists and the New Cynicism. Columbia *Journalism Review.* Vol.33. March/April. 25-33.

Stokes. D.E. (1962). Popular Evaluations of Government: An Empirical Assessment. in H. Cleveland and H.D. Lasswell, (Eds.). Ethics and Bigness: Scientific, Academic, Religious, Political, and Military. NewYork: Harper and Brothers. 61-72.

Stolle, D. and Hooghe, M. (2004). Consumers as Political Participants? Shifts in Political Action Repertoires in Western Socities. in Micheletti, M., Follesdal , A. and Stolle, D., (Eds.). *Politics, Products and Markets. Exploring Political Consumerism Past and Present.* London: Transaction Publishers. 265-288.

The Electoral Commission and The Hansard Society. (2007). An Audit of Political Engagement 4. March. www.electoralcommission.org.uk www.hansardsociety.org.uk

Tinkham, S.F. and Weaver-Larisy, R.A. (1994). Ethical Judgements of Political Television Commercials as Predictors of Attitude Towards the *Ad. Journal of Advertising.* Vol. 13. No. 3. 43-57.

Westholme, A. and Niemi, R.G. (1986). Youth Unemployment and Political Alienation. Youth and Society. Vol. 18. No. 1. 58-80.

Wezel, C. and Inglehart, R. (1999). Analyzing Democratic Change and Stability. Berlin: Wissenschaftszentrum Berlin.

White, C., Bruce, S., and Ritchie, J. (2000). Young Peoples Politics. Political Interest and Engagement Amongst 14-24 Year Olds. Joseph Rowntree Foundation. York Publishing Services.

Whitely, P.F. and Seyd, P. (2002). High-Intensity Participation: The Dynamics of Party Activism in Britain. Ann Arbour: University of Michigan Press.

Wolfinger, R., Glass, D., and Squire P. (1990). Predictors of Electoral Turnout: An International Comparison. *Policy Studies Review.* Vol.9. 551-574.

Zaller, J.R. (1998). Monica Lewinsky's Contribution to Political Science. *Political Science and Politics.* Vol. 31. No. 2. 182-189.

In: Citizenship in the 21st Century   ISBN: 978-1-60456-401-3
Editors: L. T. Kane and M. R. Poweller, pp.185-204   © 2008 Nova Science Publishers, Inc.

Chapter 6

CITIZENSHIP AND GOVERNMENTALITY: PEOPLE WITH INTELLECTUAL DISABILITY AS NEW CITIZENS OF THE 21ST CENTURY

Tony Gilbert[1] and Jason L. Powell[2]

[1] Faculty of Health and Social Work, University of Plymouth, Plymouth, UK. PL4 8AA
[2] Department of Sociology, Social policy and Social Work Studies, University of Liverpool, Liverpool, UK. L69 7ZA

INTRODUCTION

This chapter focuses on the emergence as citizens of a group of people previously excluded from this qualification due to their perceived intellectual impairment. Using the United Kingdom as an example of trends across the developed world where people with intellectual disability, once the targets of policies of exclusion and dependency, have emerged at the advent of the twenty-first century [C21] as citizens in their own right (Kings Fund, 1999; DH 2001; Stainton, 2005; Redley and Weinberg, 2007). However, while it is possible to see this trend within a humanitarian perspective with the newly enlightened populace able and willing to accept into it's mist a group of people previously disenfranchised; this position somewhat underplays the significance of what has occurred and complex nature of the processes that underpin this shift. Drawing on range of theories of citizenship the discussion locates these developments within the 'governmentality thesis' originally described by the French Philosopher Michel Foucault. Reasons for choosing this perspective relate to the way that Foucault, in contrast with many other writers, focussed on how particular configurations of knowledge [discourse] and associated practices underpinned the management of populations. In this process, he highlighted the key role of social institutions, particularly those of health and social work. These institutions, which embed a range of professional expertise, have particular significance for people with intellectual disabilities as these institutions play a central role in both the management of this section of the population and consequentially in the realization of their citizenship.

A deal of space in the chapter is devoted to theoretical debates that identify citizenship as a complex, dynamic and contested idea that is subject to constant but subtle revision due to changes in social policy. Consequentially, individuals reliant upon a myriad of social supports to exercise citizenship are particularly vulnerable to any revisions particularly where these influence welfare provision. In addition, citizenship is a prominent idea in contemporary British social policy with notions of work, obligation, community and social inclusion providing core concepts in the dynamic relationship between the state and individuals. People with intellectual disability provide a special group within this process as previously they fell outside of entitlements as citizens rather; they held a secondary position as welfare subjects. However, the turn of the C21 sees older discourses of care, support and normalisation rearticulated within a liberal discourse of citizenship (Redley and Weinberg, 2007). In turn, revising the social positions for individuals with intellectual disability who are no longer perceived as passive and dependent but constructed as having the capacity to make choices in a market orientated welfare system and therefore active citizens in their own right. However, this newly acquired status is conditional; citizenship rights bring responsibilities and obligations for individuals. In response, social provision deploys a range of risk management technologies to differentiate between individuals who can be 'empowered' to become responsible citizens and those who fail to meet these criteria. The latter, identified as 'risky' individuals and managed accordingly, thus providing different trajectories for those concerned.

There are four stages to this discussion. The first is to identify citizenship, as an ambiguous concept with changing and contested meanings while the second stage is to establish citizenship as a tactic of government through a discussion of Foucault's governmentality thesis. The third stage explores four themes linked to the citizenship of disabled people in general that also have significance for people with intellectual disabilities drawn from a thematic review of the literature and empirical work involving a range of providers of supports to people with intellectual disability. Themes of work, participation, community and consumption, suggest the principle discourses that underpin the citizenship of this section of the population. This is not to underplay the significance of standard social variables such as class, gender, race, ethnicity etc. that continue to cross cut the experience of individuals; rather it identifies the common experience of intellectual disability as the core variable. Evaluation of the interplay of these themes and the practices provides the final section, which highlights confusion over what citizenship entails and the observation that the organisations that provide support to people with intellectual disability continue to mediate their experience of citizenship.

THE CONCEPT OF CITIZENSHIP

Citizenship relates to the experience of 'belonging' in a society and having the opportunity to contribute is the exercise of rights to citizenship. Importantly, discussions of citizenship related to socially marginalized groups, frequently occur in terms of responsibilities and obligations while failing to highlight society's reciprocal responsibility to recognise the claims of these groups as citizens. Defining citizenship as the principle of equal membership in a nation based on a set of publicly recognised rights and responsibilities, equality of citizenship is a formal equality, which may or may not result in substantive equality. It ranges from being restricted to a single dimension of citizenship, such as equality before the law to including equal rights on a broad range of political and social dimensions. Citizenship rights and responsibilities are, on occasions, imposed from above or alternatively achieved through the struggles of excluded groups (Phillipson, 1998). Citizenship and the contests over rights and equality can engender a sense of national identity and a stronger commitment to the welfare of fellow-citizens than to non-citizens, depending on the distribution of benefits of citizenship. However, both identity and commitment to the state may be stronger for some groups than for others due to locality or regionally based conflicts over resources. Other conflicts over citizenship involve individuals and groups who are members of a territorially bounded state for example, relations between different age stage groups or different groups of welfare users. Consequently, the content of citizenship varies between nations and has varied historically as different groups have struggled to be included in particular rights or to gain new rights (Phillipson, 1998). Embedding and enmeshing Citizenship, no less than the economy, is in the specific histories and workings of social institutions (Powell, 2006).

This perspective on citizenship has several linked implications for understanding of disability as it involves identities, norms, and practices, never easily abandoned or taken up. Social relationships embed the civil, legal, political, and social rights of citizenship in everyday activities and thus an integral part of the way people see and cope with the world. For example, the state plays a crucial role in promoting perceptions of disabled people within a given society. From the point of view of social role, the 'state' performs the function of facilitating general economic activity, maintaining law and order and ensuring the legitimacy of social order. However, one of the transformations which has been taking place since 1979 to the present in the UK and elsewhere has been one in which 'citizenship' is changing its form from 'rights holder' to 'responsible consumer'. This is a point we return to later first, we explore the conceptual basis of citizenship in more depth.

Denise Riley (1992) uses Wittgenstein's notion of a cluster concept to identify the complexity of citizenship, which she argues has no single, fixed or even agreed meaning. Rather, citizenship is a problematic concept, the meeting place of a diverse set of positions and claims (van Steenbergen, 1994). In the context of this discussion, citizenship is a point of articulation for a number of competing discourses and a site for the interplay of power relations produced by practices underpinned by these discourses. Conceptually, citizenship is central to a diverse range of philosophical positions; Social-Democratic, Conservative and Reformist (Riley, 1992) or; Liberal, Communitarian, Republican and Neo-Republican (van Gunsteren, 1994); each producing very different outcomes for the 'citizen'. Turner (1990; 1994) places these different positions into a model developed along two axes, active – passive and public – private. The first axis represents radical and bottom-up movements while the latter conservative or top-down movements. Paradoxically, both liberal and communitarian models of citizenship conclude that the increasing consolidation of government undermines citizenship, which occurs as managerial governance, substitutes for popular control (Lowery *et al*. 1992).

In addition, citizenship takes historically and culturally specific forms varying systematically both between societies (Turner, 1990) and within the same society (Lewis, 1998). Culturally, in western society, notions of citizenship articulate discourses of capitalism, nationalism and patriarchy (Humphries, 1996; Riley, 1992; Turner, 1994; van

Steenbergen, 1994). Producing a situation that establishes instrumental equality between citizens while inequalities and exclusions persist based around social variables such as class, race, culture, age, gender and disability (Taylor, 1996b). In the context of intellectual disability, eugenic discourses reinforce the affect of these social variables with ideas of fitness, dangerousness and charity (Shakespeare, 1998; Gilbert, 1998). Nevertheless, the attraction of citizenship lies in its potential to unite those whom the market inevitably divides (Alcock, 1989).

Lewis (1998) suggests that debates over citizenship involve three elements. First, they are a way of conceptualising the relationship between the state and the individual. Second, they raise questions of inclusion and exclusion and finally they relate to a particular social status and entitlements. Tensions in debates over citizenship arise from distinctions between the 'rights of individuals' and the 'duties of the citizen'. Conceptually, 'the civil' describes the rights of the 'private' individual associated with liberal notions of freedom, the market and a rejection of egalitarianism; in contrast, the 'civic' relates to the duties of the citizen associated with communitarian notions of intervention, solidarity and egalitarianism (Silverman, 1996). For people with intellectual disabilities, this distinction produces further ambiguity for the civic and the civil are not clearly delineated.

T. H. Marshall's classic 1950 essay 'Citizen and Social Class' (1996), is often taken as the start point for discussions of the foundations of modern British citizenship. The post war British State extended citizenship rights beyond political and civil rights by the addition of social rights encapsulated within the framework of the welfare state; thus providing mechanisms that mediate between the formal equality of citizens and the inequalities of class, socializing both hardship and security against hardship (Rose, 1996). However, Marshall never considered material equality as the desired outcome of citizenship rather; he saw a measure of inequality as motivational. Citizenship therefore rested on equality of [social] status. Vincent locates this 'status' with contradictions inherent in British citizenship that arise from its development within a framework of capitalist social relations; a position that compromises the citizenship of the poor and others excluded from participation in a common civilisation:

"Equal rights to suffrage and social rights to welfare exist in an uneasy relationship with the material inadequacies and class structure of capitalist society". (Vincent, 1992: 710).

Historically, the advent of a welfare state meant that populations in a society such as 'the old or disabled' had services devised in order to meet their needs. For example, after 1945 in the UK, a welfare apparatus was set up to offer education, health care and pensions. By the 1970's the state was 'in crises' due to a world economic recession. Consequently, in most advanced capitalist societies, the allocation of services and benefits became selective. When a neo-liberal Conservative government took power in the UK in 1979, the emphasis was not on 'citizen rights' but the efficiency concerns of the state. Responsibility for well-being thus shifted from the state to the individual. Significantly, this equality of status is rearticulated within neo-liberal discourse to become 'equality of opportunity' now deployed in 'New Labour's' policy platform (Lister, 1998; 2003; Jordan 2005). In addition, this model of social citizenship perpetuates moral discourse of rights and duties that contribute to a second-class citizenship for individuals reliant upon the welfare state for their continuing existence.

Producing a subordinated position of 'welfare subject' that includes particular groups of disabled people (Lewis, 1998) for whom this second-class citizenship has social, material and psychological implications:

"People who enjoy 'social citizenship' get 'social rights' not 'handouts'. This means not only that they enjoy guarantees of help in forms that maintain their status as full members of society entitled to 'equal respect'. It also means that they share a common set of institutions and services designed for all citizens, the use of which constitutes the practice of social citizenship: for example, public schools, public parks, universal social insurance, public health services." Fraser and Gordon (1994: 91).

Discourses of citizenship have thus shifted away from the rights of the citizen. Instead, there is the view that citizens are best portrayed as 'consumers' of social services and the role of the state is but to facilitate this consumption preferably through the use of private providers. Accompanying this view, greater emphasis is placed on the 'responsibilities' of citizens to maintain their communities and to pay for their own health care and social provision. This has enormous implications for how the state has responded to disabled people who have not been able to 'consume' the right way, to 'be responsible' in the appropriate manner and to accept their duty as citizens to ensure the maintenance of good order in society. This signals a turn towards personal, individual responsibility for one's actions regardless of wider social context. Hence, this holds as a threat to basic democratic principles and human rights that impinges on their welfare.

Furthermore, this tension raises questions about welfare and its relationship to conditions of exclusion for it is quite possible for individuals to survive physically but not socially in society (van Steenbergen, 1994). For example, Vogel (1994) points to the way in which women have been included in citizenship not as individual citizens but as the subjects of citizens [men] while Yuval-Davis (1994) notes the way legal and cultural processes target women separately. In addition, Lewis (1998) points to the differential experience of people from different racial and ethnic backgrounds. Moreover, for people with intellectual disabilities, functional integration is quite possible without being socially integrated (Harris 1995). Alternatively, as Gilbert et al. (2005) point out, integration may occur as a secondary condition of support provided by a particular organisation i.e. as subjects of that organisation. Contemporary British social policy also makes much of notions of 'active citizenship' (All Party Commission on Citizenship, 1990) interpreted as an obligation to contribute through taxation, charitable giving and active volunteering. Compounding differential experiences of marginalised groups such disabled people, due to the way 'active citizenship' reinforces the identity of welfare subjects by confusing social needs. Rather than a standard of social participation, active citizenship becomes associated with individual choice to give freely of goods, money or time with particular consequences for the targets of charity as it confirms their different social role and status:

"As it is presently conceived it is likely that active citizenship will require passive non-citizens to receive the bounty of such volunteering." (Walmsley, 1993: 259)

In further criticisms, Barton (1993) points out that active citizenship contains a conception of the individual as essentially private. Consequentially, it is not possible to transfer or delegate the felt responsibility of one individual for another to a third party such as the state; legitimatizing what he describes as the abrogation of responsibility by the state. In this situation, socially disadvantaged individuals and groups such as people with intellectual disability provide a kind of conscience fodder for the self-esteem of respectable citizens. Furthermore, Spiker (1990) claims that discourses of active citizenship contain echoes of the Poor Law perpetuated by the idea that persons are unable to be both beneficiaries of government and able to exercise control over it.

CITIZENSHIP AND GOVERNMENTALITY

The purpose of this section is to construct the links between citizenship and governmentality that stands at the centre of this proposition that people with intellectual disability emerge as newly franchised citizens at the advent of the C21. Misztal (1996) and Lewis (1998) highlight the significance of citizenship as a means of governance; they argue that citizenship is a response of the state to the problem of social cohesion. The longer-term enhancement of social solidarity requires the means to overcome social tensions and social conflicts, which involves more than the institutionalisation of political and legal rights. However, Misztal observes that social cohesion is uneven and there continues to be a lack of solidarity, mutuality and trust in public spaces such as hospitals, schools and workplaces, suggesting that the penetration of the discourses of citizenship is less than complete. A condition that requires policy interventions to promote the institutional arrangements that sustain and re-build trust as social capital and in so doing guide autonomous individuals into the practice of citizenship. Such programmes and technologies, institutionalized under the umbrella of the welfare state, operate to regulate behaviour, while at the same time locating individuals within a network of personal obligations to themselves, to their family and friends, and to the community. Central to this 'conduct of conduct' rest discourses of morality and responsibility that reciprocate with the conferring of citizenship rights. In this sense, we can move very quickly from the rights of citizenship to the duties of citizenship with the associated dangers of victim blaming (Osborne, 1997). Sachs makes the following observation:

"Without these local arenas of duty to others, we would never acquire the sense of responsibility necessary for citizenship." (Sachs, 1997: 170)

It is to Foucault's notion of governmentality we now turn to explore this relationship between citizenship and the management of populations. Central to Foucault's analysis of governmentality is the proposition that modern forms of government have largely dispensed with coercion and operate through the deployment of a range of techniques and technologies that aim to manage the 'conduct of conduct' by producing self-managing individuals. At the core of this process is the relationship between power – knowledge - truth and discipline (Foucault, 1980). Foucault proposed a particularly modern form of power had developed since C17 described as 'bio-politics'; a 'politics of the population' that operates through two modalities, 'totalizing' and 'individualizing'; to produce what Miller (1993) describes as a two way process between the subject as a private individual [consumer] and the subject as a public citizen. These modalities produce interplay of knowledge and power located on the body and provides the basis for the development of specific disciplines such as medicine and psychology, which in turn provides historically and culturally specific versions of 'truth' (Dreyfus and Rabinow, 1982). Individuals have a dual orientation towards these knowledges [discourses] as they both formed by and forming of these discourses (Miller, 1993). In addition, tensions between the totalizing and individualizing affects produce an ethical incompleteness on which the techniques of self-management operate. Moreover, truth is subject to constant political and economic demands and surveillance; it is commodified and the focus of conflict and struggle (Foucault, 1984). Furthermore, no essential relationship between truth and science persists as political and commercial interests have compromised such potential (Petersen, 1997).

Another important insight from Foucault's conceptualization is the notion of power as productive. Power induces pleasure, forms knowledges and produces discourse. At the same time, discourses are neither fixed nor stable but possible of transformation. Discontinuity identified in the way certain discourses have broken with previously configurations of discourses or 'orders of discourse' to form completely new ways of 'speaking and seeing' and in so doing producing new 'conditions of possibility'. In this sense the emergence of ideas of citizenship and intellectual disability represents a discontinuity of older configurations of discourses such as eugenics, psychology, medicine, fitness and morality and the establishment of a new configuration drawing some of these discourses [psychology, medicine, morality] into contact with discourses of citizenship, usefulness and social inclusion. These two modalities of bio-power, the politics of the body and the politics of the population, give rise to the calculation implicit in modern forms of 'good and legitimate' Government; that is the Government of the people must be, 'of all and of each'.

Fundamental to contemporary debates over citizenship is the notion of the 'self managing individual' which Miller (1993) argues is produced by the deployment of an ethic of the self that works on the 'ethical incompleteness' noted earlier. This establishes a reflexive process focused on the tension between private desire and public obligation. Miller, following Foucault, argues that the aim of government is to structure the possible field of action of others, which he describes in the following way:

> "The process of formulating this ethical incompleteness works through the operation of technologies of governance, which are a means of managing the public by having it manage itself. This is achieved through the material inscription of discourse into politics and programmes of the cultural-capitalist state". (Miller, 1993: xiii).

Such technologies of governance draw on a range of disciplinary process to produce the modern subject as docile, productive and willing to participate in their own management. To achieve this aim, power/knowledge works to separate, analyse and differentiate groups of people from other groups, to divide individuals from other individuals finally creating components within individual subjectivity:

> "Foucault discerns three methods of manufacturing such subjects. First, the human sciences produce subjects by pronouncing the conditions and operation of speech, of material productiveness and of physical morphology. Second, various practices divide the subject within itself and divide it from others in terms of healthiness and appropriateness of conduct. Finally, the subject identifies as a subject. It works on itself in order to perform these classificatory operations and then to recognise itself within one or several of them". (Miller, 1993: xvi).

Neo-liberal rule involves the shifting of responsibilities away from the state onto individuals who as noted above are self-managing. For disabled people, including those with intellectual disability, this has seen two developments in the latter half of the C20. First deinstitutionalization, underpinned by discourses of normalization (Wolfensberger, 1973; 1983), saw the closure of a range of state sponsored institutions for people considered dependant or dangerous with the subsequent dispersal of this population across the social landscape in a strategy of social [re]engineering. The second rearticulated these discourses of normalization within a neo-liberal framework. Now, the mere categorization of people as disabled is no longer justification for welfare. Rather, the aim was to reduce dependence through establishing the norms of society in the shape of responsibility to take care of oneself and the obligation to work. The critical issue here is that citizenship is a means of structuring the relationship between the State and individuals it governs. However, this relationship is not purely instrumental; discourses of citizenship are active in the production of particular identities emotionally and cognitively committed to particular categories of belonging, which at the same time provide conduits for political and social intervention (Lewis, 1998). This brings to the fore the question of how programmes and technologies of citizenship become tactics of governmentality in relation to people with intellectual disabilities i.e. what categories and identities created through social policy enable people with intellectual disability to recognise themselves and affiliate to that lifestyle; a point we develop further in the next section.

To return to Miller's earlier point about the tension between these two critical forms of post-modern subjectivity: the citizen and the consumer. The political importance of these two forms is that their fusion has the potential to produce a well ordered rather than a disordered liberal democracy. Self and society become one in the form of the citizen. However, there is not a single unified identity produced in this fusion for the tension between the civil and the civic continues, resulting in the need for the state to promote two forms of subjectivity: the selfless active citizen and the selfish active consumer. Miller parallels Marshall's analysis of the development of citizenship by arguing that the classical position gave citizens representation via the state, later added to by a guarantee of basic social conditions through the welfare state. Ironically, the emergence of the post-modern condition has produced the need to re-assert the sovereignty of the public to discipline the organisations of the welfare state. Thus giving rise to a particularly post-modern citizenship through the subject position and identity of the citizen-consumer who draws on a variety of techniques such as charters, standards and guarantees to exert [limited] power over the provision of public services. Nevertheless, the implications of this post-modern condition for people reliant upon welfare services for daily support, such as many people with intellectual disability, require analysis in their very specific context. This brings to the analysis questions of where and how do people with intellectual disability act as consumers and make market based choices and/or under what conditions do they engage in forms of participation; it also raises questions over consequences of these activities for those involved.

Questions concerning government of the marginalised and recognition of the extent to which people are included or excluded from citizenship, are identified by the different strategies employed to govern the marginalised in contrast to the affiliated. Rose (1996) argues that the included need constantly to demonstrate their affiliation through active choice and the maintenance of an accredited lifestyle. While the marginalised, whose ability to be actively involved in choices is incapacitated or alternatively, individuals and groups who do not share the same value base, become the focus for risk management. Petersen (1997) describes this new subtle form of social control as one, which works to assign different destinies to individuals based on their potential to respond to the requirements of a market philosophy. Moreover, Taylor-Gooby (1993) identifies potential for different groups to experience citizenship in different ways. He argues that changes in the organisation of work, mirrored in welfare, produce a core and periphery model with central co-ordination and the contracting out of other activities. Leading to the conclusion, that welfare citizenship may develop simultaneously in different directions for different groups. For marginalised groups the insecurity of opportunities may be such that the alternative to the dependency culture is a captivity culture that brings with it a sense of isolation and humiliation.

CITIZENSHIP: DISCOURSE AND PEOPLE WITH INTELLECTUAL DISABILITY

This section draws on a thematic review of literature and empirical work involving eighteen providers of community based services to people with intellectual disability. Before moving on it is useful to explore a little further the notion of the citizen-consumer noted above. In the context of the proposition that people with intellectual disability represent a 'new citizens of the C21', this idea of the citizen-consumer has specific relevance. Prior to the advent of the C21, many adults with intellectual disability were reliant on support provided 'in kind' through organisations paid by the state to provide particular services. Block payments made to organisations rarely identified entitlements of specific individuals or gave them rights over space, property or access. Even where some mapping of resources against needs took place, individuals concerned had no right to claim that money. Control rested with the organisation. This was particularly evident in residential homes where residents had no rights over the space they occupied with providers able to move people from their homes with little warning or enter the rooms at a whim. The critical shift occurred almost by accident as some providers looking for alternative models of financing projects moved away from using community care budgets managed by local health and social services departments. Instead, they began claiming unemployment and housing benefits on behalf of named people with intellectual disability from budgets designated for use by the general population. To achieve this position service providers had to give people legally binding tenancy agreements. Thus providing people with intellectual disability a new status, that of the citizen-tenant (Gilbert *et al.* 2005), and an instrumental equality with other citizens similarly unemployed and in need of housing.

We continue this discussion by focussing on four areas of discourse related to citizenship. Taylor-Gooby (1993) suggests that the analysis of social citizenship involves two themes; first, who participates in the exercise of power and second, who gets what in the competition over resources. In addition, Harrison (1991) argues that the analysis of patterns of consumption is essential if citizenship is to move away from a purely idealistic debate to one that focuses upon material differences, while Sachs (1997) focuses upon the relationship between the individual and their community. These four areas concern the relationship between individuals and the world of work, the extent to which people are engaged in managing their own lives (self-management), the extent to which people are able to contribute to the development of their community and patterns of consumption in which they engage.

Citizenship and Work

One of the central problems facing people with intellectual disabilities is that their exclusion from employment frustrates their status as adults and as citizens (Jenkins, 1989). Similarly, Croft and Beresford (1996) argue that in the confused language of rights and responsibilities, that surrounds citizenship, employment is an obligation that excludes many disabled people. This has particular consequences for the excluded as this leaves only the subordinate role of welfare subject and related identity (Lewis, 1998). Van Steenbergen (1994) points out that citizenship is primarily about social participation and to this end possibly the most important integrating factor is work. This relationship between work and citizenship continues at the core of contemporary social policy (Lister, 1998; 2003; DSS, 1999; Clarke, 2005; Jordan, 2005). Work or the participation in waged labour is therefore pivotal in the way in which the discourses of rights and responsibilities operate to construct the categories of deserving and undeserving. Dahrendorf (1994) describes those not having a regular and guaranteed access to labour markets as an 'underclass' or 'victims', who are particularly powerless in defending themselves. He suggests that these 'victims' require help in order to escape their situation. However, this has to be part of a social contract not as the objects of charity (Fraser and Gordon, 1994), for the association with charity continues to compromise the citizenship of disabled people (Oliver, 1990; Drake, 1996).

Fieldwork involving a range of providers of services for people with intellectual disability (Gilbert et al. 2005) highlighted issues of fundamental importance to the citizenship of people in this social group due to the somewhat ambiguous relationship between the labour market, work, wages and benefits. Due to the rules related to welfare benefits the majority of the people in 'employment' did not receive wages in the conventional sense as receipt of wages over a very low financial threshold resulted in the loss of the whole benefit package which was invariably worth considerably more than the wage afforded by that employment. In addition, much of this 'work' was undertaken in a voluntary capacity even thought it was structured to mirror waged labour. Moreover, niche markets in which the social firms operate i.e. with charitable status produced a contradictory theme fixing people at once as both voluntary worker and the object of charity. However, at the same time the potential of work as both an integrating factor and a source of identity and self-esteem is recognised. A number of providers noted that people wanted real jobs.

Citizenship and Participation

Participation and the struggles of groups for inclusion have been central to the analysis and evaluation of citizenship (Held, 1991; Taylor-Gooby, 1993). Taylor (1996a) suggests that participation gives rise to three questions. These concern the nature of inclusion, the appropriate strategies that enable participation to occur and the means through which the entitlement to participate is promoted. Taylor observes a tension in debates over citizenship and participation between a universalistic position which concerns a rights-based defence of the welfare state and a particularistic position that is associated with needs-based arguments concerning self-advocacy and new social movements, although these two positions need not be mutuality exclusive. He also identifies a further tension between essentially passive notions of participation such as consumerism and active participation such as collective self-advocacy.

Calls for more a political form of participation have arisen alongside evidence of the 'significantly poorer standard of living' of disabled people linked to institutional discrimination (Barnes, 1996; Oliver, 1990; 1996; 1997). Such issues provide the basis and motivation for political movements and campaigns that include achievement of anti-discrimination legislation such as the Disability Discrimination Acts (1995; 2000) and legislation that support independent living such as the Direct Payment Act (1996), which aim to ensure the meaningful integration of disabled people into mainstream social and economic life (Morris, 1997). Participation in service delivery has been a significant area of development however; critics argue that many examples of user-involvement involve tokenism and non-participation (Croft and Beresford, 1996; Beresford, 2001). Although in the context of intellectual disability, the potential for user-involvement to be an embryonic political movement is noted (Crawley, 1988). Nevertheless, Dowson (1990) suggests that service providers have used 'self advocacy' as a means of controlling people with learning disabilities.

Croft and Beresford (1996) argue that to promote participation two components are critical: first, access (physical and participatory) to the political structures at both local and national levels; and second, support (self-esteem, skill development and practical support for individuals and groups) to address the imbalances in power and to enable effective participation to occur. Support of disabled people needs to take account of the level of energy involved in participation as many disabled people use their total personal and financial resources in a daily struggle for survival. Beresford (2001) also notes that many disabled people feel 'consulted fatigue' through constant pressures to get involved in policy development and service delivery. Dahrendorf (1994) offers the following observation:

> "Basic human and civil rights have little meaning for people who for reasons outside
> of their control are unable to make use of them. They therefore lead to a series of needs
> of empowerment which may also acquire the quality of rights." (Dahrendorf, 1994: 14).

Using Taylor's distinction between passive and active forms of participation, fieldwork (Gilbert et al.2005) highlighted the prominence of consumerist approaches to participation in professional discourse with much emphasis given to participation through the use of local shops and leisure facilities. Choice making was very much in terms of market-based choices, which fits with the notion of the citizen-consumer noted earlier. In contrast, while people with intellectual disabilities who were involved in active forms of participation such as advocacy groups were able to gain time and resources to participate this activity; such participation did not register as embryonic political activity rather it became part of the care plan. Furthermore, potential impact on the organisation was low as often the focus of this participation was external to the organisation however; benefits to organisations were high as this promoted their overall image as modern support systems. In addition, there was evidence that some service providers used advocacy as an organisational tool either to provide feedback to managers or as a means of resolving conflicts between the organisation, service users and carers.

Citizenship and Community

The idea of community, as discussed here, contains at lease two alternative perspectives of community. The first relates to the community of identity that transcends physical environments with the potential to be national or global in membership. In this sense, a global community of disabled people has formed over the past thirty years or so. Croft and Beresford (1996) discuss the development of participation and citizenship of disabled people by creating a distinction between new social movements and new social welfare movements; linking the concerns of Black, Gay, and Feminist movements with groups of users of traditional welfare services but caution that the latter contains a tendency to identify people based on services. Nevertheless, both forms of user movement have to resist tendencies to draw them into the administrative structures of the welfare bureaucracies (Beresford, *et al.* 1997).

However, fieldwork (Gilbert *et al.* 2005) suggested problems with the proposition that people labelled as intellectually disabled identify either with each other on a local or international basis. There were examples of people involved in national advocacy groups such as 'People First' [see above] but there were more examples of managers reporting that people had expressed desire not to be included with other people with intellectual disability. Furthermore, there was little evidence to suggest that the wider community of disabled people considers people with intellectual disability to be part of the same movement of identity. This links with the observations of other critics (Harris, 1995; Biklen and Mosley, 1988; Duckett, 1998). Nevertheless, weakness of this identification may have something to do with the influence of normalisation theories (Wolfensberger 1972; 1983) in professional discourse, which saw identification of people with intellectual disability with each other as contributing to devaluing imagery.

The second meaning of community to consider here is in relation to the physical and social environment where a person lives. Earlier, Sachs (1997) identified the reciprocal relationship that links individual identity, a felt responsibility for others and a local area. However, this connection to the 'local' may mean that the conflicts that produced at a more abstract or impersonal level play out in the personal relationships of local communities; consequentially, producing new patterns of social fragmentation with advances for some and losses for others (Harrison, 1991). Walmsley (1993) for example, notes the paradox in informal care where the liberation of women carers may result in the institutionalisation of the dependent relative. In contrast, Phillipson (1994) points out that many dependent elders, fearing that dependency may adversely affect relationships, indicate that they preferred state rather than family care. Likewise, Ungerson (1997) notes that outcomes of the Direct Payments Act may be liberating for some disabled people but it may further marginalising many care workers, whose already vulnerable situation may be worsened due to the impact of the act impact on the labour market.

Fieldwork (Gilbert *et al.* 2005) highlighted a number of instances where organisations looked to become involved in their local communities often through the voluntary activity of the people with intellectual disability mediated by the organisation. This 'felt responsibility' was explained through the metaphor of a 'gift' freely given in exchange for an imaginary 'something' provided by community. At the same time, this produced 'obligations' on the part of people with intellectual disability towards people living in the area and a 'felt responsibility' for that area; producing an ambiguous citizenship bringing together elements related to citizenship, charity, belonging and dependence.

Citizenship and Consumption

Michael Harrison (1991) makes a very useful distinction between normative and material aspects of citizenship pointing to the importance of patterns of consumption and the need to evaluate citizenship on empirical rather than idealistic terms. He also provides a comparative basis for the evaluation of groups such as people with intellectual disability. This involves an analysis of the material basis that constructs relationships between citizens as unequal and on which notions of the deserving and undeserving are built. Harrison points to the significance of property rights, which he cautions, need to be included in the analysis of citizenship:

"In modern western societies property rights and political participation can be bound up closely together, and private property need not necessarily be counterpoised either to welfare or to full participation in politics". (Harrison, 1991: 213).

Harrison links the concepts of incorporation and citizenship as both relate to stratification, state activities and the relative status achieved by various groups. He then employs the terms 'differential incorporation' and 'differential citizenship' to explore the experiences of social and private consumption by social groups distinguished by class, gender, race, and ethnicity. Central to this analysis is the relationship between group membership and the world of work as the status conferred by work communicates into so many other settings. In addition, this critique of citizenship develops by relating it to the social division of welfare, which provides a link between organised consumption outside of direct wages, the division of labour and the division of welfare. Harrison claims this develops a comprehensive model of state activity based upon an analysis of the state and its associated institutions in the management of dependency, welfare and consumption. This thesis holds that welfare arrangements occur through a diverse range of structures and methods located within distinctive fiscal, public and occupational systems. Divisions relate to consumption based social cleavages or particular social patterns in consumption analysis of which highlight the role of the state in the organisation of large parts of the consumption process through an array of public and private institutions.

Harrison's concept of social cleavages is particularly significant when discussing people with intellectual disability especially those with high support needs. In financial terms, levels of consumption are high while levels of participation are low contradicting the classical model of incorporation and citizenship where low participation corresponds with low levels of consumption and a marginalised citizenship. However, social cleavages allow the potential to separate and evaluate this group in their very specific context. In the context of the fieldwork, many of the people supported by the organisations had packages that included leisure and recreational activity providing a marked contrast to people ordinarily unemployed and in receipt of benefits.

EVALUATING CITIZENSHIP: ISSUES OF INCLUSION AND EXCLUSION

As 'New citizens of the C21', questions arise over the progress of people with intellectual disability towards full citizenship. It would be churlish to expect the rectification of over a century of exclusion, segregation and denial of citizenship in the short time since the advent of the new century although; we might identify the origins of this process with a much longer trajectory. However, it has only been recently that configurations of discourse have enabled practices to move beyond a dependant relationship between the state and people with intellectual disability. Nevertheless, questions remain over the symbolic and material affects of these shifts and it would be helpful to remind ourselves of Lewis's (1998) proposal that citizenship relates to three elements; the relationship between the individual and the state, issues of inclusion and exclusion and finally, the social status of the individual and the entitlements this brings.

Regarding the relationship between individuals and the state, the concept of governmentality enables analysis in terms of techniques for managing populations and the role of professionals in working on individuals with intellectual disability to move them along a continuum towards self-management with the objective of establishing the 'reflexive self managing individual' central to neo-liberal government. However, Clarke (2005) cautions that this perspective can produce a rather pessimistic view of change nevertheless, it provides a framework to understand power relations and strategies of government. Central to this link between citizenship and governmentality is the requirement for individuals to make choices in a market orientated welfare system and the status of the citizen-consumer reproduced here as the citizen-tenant. These shifts produce a paradox where the state assumes responsibility for promoting the normative citizenship of people with intellectual disability while also distancing itself from material responsibility for the same group. Intellectual disability, in itself, no longer provides a status that demands entitlement to support and therefore the state is no longer obligated to provide care unless people meet certain criteria. Effectively severing one set of ties that kept people with intellectual disability as dependants separated from the general population while also producing an instrumental equality through the status of citizen-tenant. However, this shift also has the effect of reducing the visibility of individuals in this group by merging them with others reliant on benefits.

Analysis of governmentality suggests further potential of citizenship for lowering visibility. Redley and Weinberg (2007) while encouraged by the shift towards inclusion and citizenship highlight dangers inherent in the process. They argue that incongruity between liberal conceptions of citizenship formulated on voice, ability and independence, and the position of a section of the population, who individually and as a group often find it difficult to exercise these qualities without support; may result in the loss or denial of entitlements base on inability. Declining visibility and increasing restrictions to eligibility could lead to a loss of protected resources for the specific support needs of this section of the population. In addition, governmentality enables us to explore the tactics formulated for those individuals with intellectual disability unable or unwilling to accept the obligations and responsibilities of this newly acquired status. In such instances, citizenship is denied and less favourable circumstances wait. Strategies of risk management deployed alongside an array of professional expertise: psychiatrists, psychologists, social workers etc, beckon these individuals towards segregated and oppressive services that continue to display the characteristics of institutional detention.

The second area noted by Lewis, issues of inclusion and exclusion, produced four areas related to citizenship: work, participation, community and consumption. Riley's (1992) observation that citizenship is an ambiguous and contested concept is bourn out in the discussion of ways services were developing as identified through fieldwork. Paid work produces particularly difficult challenges, as it remains central to government agendas concerning citizenship and inclusion (Lister, 2003) but the forms of work available lack the full range of characteristics expected of adult employment such as the exchange of labour for wages. In addition, such work tends to be either on the fringes of markets or work-like discipline reproduced in a voluntary context, consequentially, producing a new form of segregation with a contradictory status as neither worker or volunteer.

Participation or voice is central to liberal conceptions of citizenship however; this is generally limited to passive forms via consumerist activity. Where active forms of participation occurred, there was a tendency for organisational imperatives to take over frustrating embryonic political potential. Consequentially, running the danger noted by Armstrong (2002) that where people with intellectual disability are included in decision making but not allowed to make the final decision this compounds their exclusion and reinforces their secondary status. Indeed, commentators suggest that despite 'self advocacy' being one of the most significant developments over the last quarter of a century. Organisations promoting self-advocacy remain uncoordinated, under resourced and reliant on untrained and unpaid volunteers (Atkinson, 1999; Walmsley and Johnson, 2003) a partial exception to this being the parliament for People with Learning Disabilities described by Redley and Weinberg (2007).

Community identifies some organisations structuring relationships with local communities in moves that create a 'felt responsibility' and sense of obligation often through work like activity. However, this produces contradictions for it is unclear who it is that is engaged in civic duty – the organisation or the individuals that organisation supports. In addition, as with the discussion of participation above, the benefits to the organisations delivering support through developing community trust, potentially outweigh benefits for individuals involved. Moreover, choice is limited to options that organisations deem appropriate. Turning to consumption again there is ambiguity. As noted earlier, the classical position that matches low participation with low levels of consumption to a marginalised citizenship strictly does not hold in the context of people with intellectual disability, due to the high level of consumption associated with their support needs. Use of Direct Payments [money provided so that individuals can meet their own support needs] further complicates the analysis as it means that it is not easy to separate disposable income from overall income.

This brings the discussion to the final element in Lewis's framework: status. Discussion above highlights some of the contradictions and ambiguities that emerge when people with intellectual disability look to exercise their newly acquired citizenship. However, this new status as citizens is a much more optimistic status than the dependency and segregation previously afforded people with intellectual disability. Nevertheless, this new status of citizen-consumer/citizen-tenant has particular hazards especially that of a new form of social isolation as highlighted by Redley and Weinberg's (2007). Congruence emerges here with Taylor-Gooby's (1993) distinction between dependency and captivity cultures, for despite instrumental equality with other citizens through sharing the same benefit platform; people with intellectual disability remain largely unable to escape this basic level of subsistence because work opportunities continue to locate them in niche sectors of the labour market where rewards are low. In addition, Stainton's (2005: 291 - 292) notes the continuing importance of support if this citizenship is going to produce anything other than a new form of exclusion. Commenting on similar movements of choice, rights and citizenship for people with intellectual disability observed in the UK, North America and Australasia. He identifies four elements essential to resolve tensions between theoretical notions of citizenship and the production of a meaningful experience of citizenship these are: support for people to articulate their claims; support for people to identify, obtain and manage supports necessary to actualize these claims, providing control over resources and governance.

Nevertheless, despite this complexity, there are moves to bring some clarity to the context. Duffy (2003) developed a model specifically designed to capture the social context of people with intellectual disability described as the 'Six Keys to Citizenship'. Capturing many of the core issues discussed in the preceding sections this model identifies: self-determination, direction, money, home, support and community life as features of a modern citizenship thus providing a framework to guide all those concerned. Nevertheless, in reducing complexity the model fails to give adequate recognition to the contradictions, tensions and ambiguities surrounding the citizenship of people with intellectual disability many of which emanate from beyond this social group. In particular, power relations identified through the analysis of governmentality evaporate. Presenting a benign situation that reduces hazards to the decisions of individuals.

CONCLUSION

Arriving at the advent of the C21 with the newly acquired status as citizens, people with intellectual disability can claim considerable achievement. For as a group they have travelled a more torturous journey than many other marginalized groups. Moreover, this new status offers a more optimistic future than at any time in the previous hundred years or more. Nevertheless, as the analysis of governmentality shows, this shift is conditional. It matches broader movements in the relationship between the state and the population, where debates concerning citizenship once conceived in terms of rights now highlight individual responsibility and obligation. Central to this revision is the 'autonomous, reflexive and self managing individual' of neo-liberal rule. In addition to these responsibilities and obligations, there is the loss or reduction of entitlements to automatic support based on intellectual disability alone. In many ways this is a positive move as stigmatizing payments or services 'in kind' designed for a segregated minority fall away to be replaced by the same supports accessed by the general population.

Nevertheless, the complex and ambiguous position inhabited by people with intellectual disability amongst the contradictory and contested discourses of citizenship retains certain hazards. In the first place, ongoing need for support in the exercise of citizenship produces dangers that new forms of dependency arise. Organizational priorities can lead to a situation where choices and supports offered further the aims of the organisations more than the personal ambitions of individuals with intellectual disability. In addition, the need for support maintains dependence either on organisations or on particular forms of expertise for access to social life. Furthermore, ongoing failure to resolve the problem of work and reward maintains a deep division between the included and the excluded in society as work remains the central mechanism in contemporary social policy for social inclusion. A secondary affect of this exclusion is that it will continue to frustrate the aspirations of this group for full status as adults and citizens.

Finally, there is the danger of invisibility. Segregation that occurred under earlier regimes hid people with intellectual disability from view and ensured their stigmatization as a group and that of the services with which they associated. However, campaigns around human rights and deinstitutionalization since the 1970s raised their profile and ensured that once in the public view they retained visibility although not always for the right reasons. Achieving citizenship has established instrumental equality with fellow citizens but possibly at a cost to their visibility. This is not to argue for a return to the previous non-citizen status and there is much benefit in the removal of facets that attract stigma. Nevertheless, the dispersal of the claims of people with intellectual disability among the claims of a complex range of welfare recipients' risks new forms of invisibility that lack the moral purpose, which attracted campaigns in the past. Moreover, as noted earlier a liberal citizenship based on ability immediately places claims underpinned by inability at a disadvantage.

Therefore, despite the complexity of citizenship both as a concept and as experience we caution against adopting simple models that purport to map the core elements in an unproblematic way. The attractiveness of simple frameworks is clear and they may have some utility when shaping service delivery. However, this needs reinforcement by a vigilant and critical debate or else run the risk that simple frameworks and uncritical humanitarian perspectives enable this very particular struggle to dissolve into history. Thus leaving people with intellectual disability in new circumstances of disenfranchisement through a failure to address both governmentality and the contradictions inherent in a liberal citizenship based on ability and the needs of a group that require support.

REFERENCES

Alcock P. (1989) Why citizen and welfare rights offer new hope for new welfare in Britain. *Critical Social Policy*. 26: 32-43.

Armstrong, D (2002) The politics of self-advocacy and people with learning disability, *Policy and Politics,* 30: 333 – 345.

Atkinson, D (1999) *Advocacy: A review,* York: Joseph Rowntree Foundation.

Barnes, C. (1996b). Institutional discrimination against disabled people and the campaign for anti-discrimination legislation, in Taylor, D (ed.) *Critical Social Policy – A Reader, Social Policy and Social Relations*. London: Sage.

Barton L. (1993). The struggle for citizenship: The case of disabled people. *Disability, Handicap and Society*, 8(3): 235-248.

Beresford, P. (2001) Service Users, social policy and the future of welfare. *Critical Social Policy,* 21(4): 494 – 512.

Beresford, P., Croft, S., Evans, C. and Harding, T. (1997). Quality in personal social services: The developing role of user involvement in the U.K. In Evers, A., Haverinen, R.,

Leichsenring, K. and Winstow, G. (eds.) *Developing Quality in Personal Social Services: A European Perspective*. Aldershot: Ashgate.

Biklen, S, K. and Mosley, C, R. (1998). "Are you retarded?" "No, I'm Catholic": Qualitative methods in the study of people with severe handicaps. *Journal of the Association for Persons with Severe Handicaps*. 13(3): 155-162.

Clarke, J. (2005) New Labour's citizens: activated, empowered, responsibilized, abandoned? *Critical Social Policy,* 25(4): 447 – 463.

Crawley, B. (1988). *The Growing Voice: A survey of self-advocacy groups in adult training centres and hospitals*. London: CMH.

Croft, S. and Beresford, P. (1996). The politics of participation, in Taylor, D. (ed.). *Critical Social Policy – A Reader, Social Policy and Social Relations*. London: Sage.

Dahrendorf, R. (1994). The Changing Quality of Citizenship, in van Steenbergen.B. (ed.). *The Condition of Citizenship*. London: Sage.

Department of Health (2001) *Valuing People: A new strategy for people with learning disabilities for the 2!st Century*. London: Stationery Office.

Department of Health. (1999). *National Service Framework for Mental Health. London*: The Stationery Office.

Dowson, S. (1990). *Keeping it Safe: Self-advocacy by people with learning difficulties and the professional response*. London: Values into Action.

Drake, R, F. (1996). A critique of the role of traditional charities, in Barton, L. (ed.) *Disability and Society: Emerging Issues and Insights*. Harlow: Longman.

Dreyfus, H, L. and Rabinow, P. (1982). *Michel Foucault: Beyond Structuralism and Hermeneutics*. Brighton: Harvester.

Duckett, P, S. (1998). What are you doing here? 'Non disabled' people and the disability movement: a response to Fran Branfield. *Disability and Society*. 13(4): 625-628.

Duffy, S. (2003). *Keys to Citizenship: A guide to getting good support for people with learning difficulties*. Birkenhead: Paradigm.

Foucault, M. (1980). Truth and Power, in Gordon, C. (eds.) *Power/Knowledge, Selected Interviews and Other Writings 1972-1977*. London: Harvester Press.

Foucault, M. (1984). The History of Sexuality Volume 1; Right of death and power over life, in Rabinow, P. (eds.) *The Foucault Reader*. Harmondsworth: Penguin.

Fraser. N. and Gordon, L. (1994). Civil citizenship against social citizenship? On the ideology of contract-versus-charity, in van Steenbergen.B. (ed.). *The Condition of Citizenship*. London: Sage.

Gilbert T., Cochrane A. and Greenwell S. (2005) Citizenship: locating people with learning disabilities. *International Journal of Social Welfare*, 14: 287 – 296.

Gilbert, T. (1995). Nursing: Empowerment and the problem of power. *Journal of Advanced Nursing*. Vol. 21. 865-871.

Gilbert, T. (1998). Sexual health and people with learning disabilities. In Morrissey, M. (ed.) *Sexual Health: a human dilemma*. Wiltshire: Mark Allen.

Harris, P. (1995). Who am I? Concepts of disability and their implications for people with learning difficulties. *Disability and Society*. 10(3): 341-351.

Harrison, M. L. (1991). Citizenship, consumption, and rights: A comment on B S Turner's theory of citizenship. *Sociology*. May, 25(2): 209-213.

Held D. (1991). Between state and civil society, in Andrews G, (ed.) *Citizenship*. London: Lawrence and Wishart.

HM Government (1995) Disability Discrimination Act. London: Stationery Office.

HM Government (1996) Direct Payments Act. London: Stationery Office.

HM Government (2000) Disability Discrimination [amendment] Act. London: Stationery Office.

Humphries, B. (1996). Preface, in Humphries, B. (ed.). *Critical Perspectives on Empowerment*. Birmingham: Venture Press.

Jordan, B. (2005) New Labour: Choice and Values. *Critical Social Policy*, 25(4): 427 – 446.

Kings Fund (1999). *Learning Disabilities: From Care to Citizenship: A Kings Fund Position Paper*. London: The Kings Fund.

Lewis, G. (1998). Citizenship, in Hughes, G. (ed.) *Imagining Welfare Futures*. London: Routledge/Open University Press.

Lister, R (2003). Investing in the citizen-workers of the future: transformations in citizenship and the state under New Labour. *Social Policy and Administration*, 37: 427 – 443.

Lister, R. (1998). From equality to social inclusion: New Labour and the welfare state. *Critical Social Policy*. 18(2): 215-225.

Lowery, D., Hoogland De Hoog, R. and Lyons, W. (1992). Citizenship in the empowered locality: An elaboration, a critique, and a partial test. *Urban Affairs Quarterly*, 28(1): 69-103.

Marshall, T, H. (1996). Citizen and social class, in Marshall, T, H., and Bottomore, T. (eds.) *Citizenship and Social Class*. London: Pluto.

Miller, T. (1993). *The Well-Tempered Self: Citizenship, Culture and the Postmodern Subject*. Baltimore: John Hopkins University Press.

Misztal, B, A. (1996). *Trust in Modern Societies*. Cambridge: Polity Press.

Morris, J. (1997). Care or empowerment: a disability rights perspective. *Social Policy and Administration*. March, 31(1), 54-60.

Oliver, M. (1990). *The Politics of Disablement*. Basingstoke: Macmillan.

Oliver, M. (1996). A sociology of disability or a disabalist sociology? In Barton, L., (ed.) *Disability and Society: Emerging issues and insights*. Harlow: Longman.

Oliver, M. (1997). Emancipatory research: Realistic goal or impossible dream? in Barnes, C., and Mercer, G. (eds.) *Doing Disability Research*. Leeds: The Disability Press.

Osborne, T. (1997). Of health and statecraft, in Petersen, A. and Bunton, R. (eds.) *Foucault: Health and Medicine*. London: Routledge.

Petersen, A. (1997). Risk, governance and the new public health, in Petersen, A. and Bunton, R. (eds.) *Foucault: Health and Medicine*. London: Routledge.

Phillipson, C (1998) *Reconstructing Old Age*, Sage: London.

Phillipson, C. (1994). Community care and the social construction of citizenship. *Journal of Social Work Practice*. 6(2), 103-112.

Powell, J (2006). *Social Theory and Aging*. Rowman and Littlefield: New York, NY .

Redley, M. and Weinberg, D. (2007). Learning Disability and the limits of liberal citizenship: interactional impediments to political empowerment. *Sociology of Health and Illness*, 29(5): 767 – 786.

Riley, D. (1992). Citizenship and the welfare State, in Allen, J., Braham, P., and Lewis, P. (eds.). *Political and Economic Forms of Modernity*. Cambridge: Polity Press in association with the Open University.

Rose, N. (1996). The death of the social? Re-figuring the territory of government. *Economy and Society*. 25(3), 327-356.

Sachs, J. (1997). *The Politics of Hope*. London: Jonathon Cape.

Shakespeare, T. (1998). Choices and Rights: eugenics, genetics and disability equality. *Disability and Society*. 13(5): 665-681.

Silverman, M. (1996). The revenge of civil society: state, nation and society in France. In Cesarani, D. and Fulbrook, M. (eds) *Citizenship, Nationality and Migration in Europe*. London: Routledge.

Spiker, P. (1990). Mental handicap and citizenship. *Journal of Applied Philosophy*. 2(7): 139-151.

Stainton, T (2005). Empowerment and the architecture of rights based social policy. *Journal of Intellectual Disabilities*, 9: 289 – 298.

Taylor D. (1996a). Citizenship, needs and participation: Introduction, in Taylor, D. (ed.) *Critical Social Policy – A Reader, Social Policy and Social Relations*. London: Sage.

Taylor D. (1996b). Citizenship and social power, in Taylor, D (ed.) *Critical Social Policy – A Reader, Social Policy and Social Relations*. London: Sage.

Taylor Gooby, P. (1993). Citizenship, dependency and the welfare mix: Problems of inclusion and exclusion. *International Journal of Health Services*. 23(3): 455-474.

Turner, B, S. (1990). Outline of a theory of citizenship. *Sociology*. May, 24(2): 189-217.

Ungerson, C. (1997). Give them the money: Is cash a route to empowerment? *Social Policy and Administration*. March, 31(1): 45-54.

Van Gunsteren, H. (1994). Four Conceptions of Citizenship, in van Steenbergen, B. (ed.) *The Condition of Citizenship*. London: Sage.

Van Steenbergen, B. (1994). The condition of citizenship: An introduction, in van Steenbergen, B. (ed.) *The Condition of Citizenship*. London: Sage.

Vincent, A. (1992). Citizenship, poverty and real will. *The Sociological Review*. 40(4): 702-725.

Vogel, U. (1994). Marriage and the boundaries of citizenship, in van Steenbergen.B. (ed.) *The Condition of Citizenship*. London: Sage.

Walmsley, J and Johnson, K (2003) *Inclusive Research with People with Learning Disabilities: Past, present and Future*. London: Jessica kingsley.

Walmsley, J. (1993). Talking to top people: Some issues relating to the citizenship of people with learning difficulties, in Swain J., Finklestein V., French S. and Oliver M. (eds.) *Disabling Barriers - Enabling Environments*. London: Sage.

Wolfensberger, W. (1972) *The Principle of Normalisation in Human Services*. Toronto: National Institute on Mental Retardation.

Wolfensberger, W. (1983). Social role valorisation: a proposed new term for the principle of normalisation, *Mental Retardation,* 21(6): 234-239.

Yuval-Davis, N. (1994). Women, ethnicity and empowerment, in Bhavnani, K. K., and Phoenix, A. (eds) *Shifting Identities Shifting Racisms*. London: Sage.

In: Citizenship in the 21ˢᵗ Century   ISBN: 978-1-60456-401-3
Editors: L. T. Kane and M. R. Poweller, pp. 205-220   © 2008 Nova Science Publishers, Inc.

Chapter 7

ASSESSING CITIZENSHIP AMONG FRENCH EMPLOYEES: DIMENSIONALITY OF ORGANIZATIONAL CITIZENSHIP BEHAVIOR AND LINK WITH SOME ATTITUDES

Pascal Paillé

Univeristy of Laval, Quebec, Canada

ABSTRACT

For a dozen years now, organizational citizenship behaviour has been a subject of continually increasing interest in academic managerial literature. While most current research comes from the United States, several scholars have argued for the need for global data. As Podsakoff, MacKensie, Paine and Bachrach (2000, p. 556) insist, "cultural context may affect a) the forms of citizenship behaviour observed in organizations and b) the strengths of relationships between citizenship behaviour and its antecedents and consequences." To date, little research has been done in the French context and existing research does not sufficiently take conceptual advances into account in the French context. Furthermore, new targets of commitment (commitment to the supervisor and to the workgroup) have appeared. New forms of citizenship (civic virtue and sportsmanship) may be added to these. Empirical relations between various targets of commitment and these new forms of citizenship remain to be clarified in the French context. This chapter proposes to examine dimensionality of citizenship behaviour and explore empirical links between attitudes (targets of affective commitment to the organization, one's supervisor and colleagues), job satisfaction, and job involvement and citizenship oriented towards the organization and individuals to determine which attitude explains which forms of citizenship.

INTRODUCTION

The theme of citizenship in the workplace is currently very popular in the organizational behaviour and human resource management literature. The study of organizational citizenship behaviour (OCB) has a long history. As Organ (1988) and Podsakoff, MacKensie, Paine and

Bachrach (2000) remind us, the theme of citizenship in the workplace has roots in "the desire to cooperate" described by Barnard in his classic work The Function of the Executive. It is developed in the writings of Roethlisberger and Dickson (1939), in the experiments of Elton Mayo, and then in the work of Katz and Khan (1978). During the last twenty years, various forms of OCB have been identified. In less than that time, the number of related concepts has increased threefold. Already in the mid-1980s, Brief and Motowidlo (1986) were able to distinguish thirteen different constructs. In their critical review of the literature, Podsakoff, MacKensie, Paine and Bachrach (2000) recognized thirty different forms. Several years later, LePine, Erez and Johnson (2002), in turn, listed forty-odd concepts. Furthermore, in a recent publication on the nature, causes and consequences of OCB, Organ, Podsakoff and MacKensie (2006) present eleven different conceptualizations, themselves combining a number of forms of OCB (See particularly pp. 243-297).

In this chapter, the approach adopted to examine OCB is consistent with the developments of Organ et al. (Bateman and Organ, 1983; Organ, 1988; and Smith, Organ and Near, 1983). In this, OCB is: "discretionary individual conduct, not directly or explicitly recognized by the formal system of compensation contributing to the general good functioning of the organization that does not arise from the prescribed role or tasks of the job, in other words, the specific terms of a contract between employees and organizations; this behaviour arises rather from personal choices, in such that its omission is not generally understood as punishable"(Organ, 1988, p.4.).

Since those first developments of Organ et al., variations have been suggested. Early research focused on altruism and conscientiousness. Altruism "is the act of helping others on work-related matters." Conscientiousness refers to "the willingness to perform beyond the minimal requirement in the areas of attendance, taking breaks, and working overtime." Several years later, Organ (1988) introduced civic virtue and sportsmanship as forms of OCB to consider. Civic virtue refers to behaviour promoting the organization's image, reputation, high profile, etc. It also relates to an employee's attitude towards wishing to participate to varying degrees and in different ways in the firm's governance. Finally, sportsmanship is defined by Organ (1990, p. 96) as "willingness of the employee to tolerate less than ideal circumstances without complaining." Subsequently, Podsakoff and MacKensie (1994) recommend dropping conscientiousness which can no longer be seen as discretionary behaviour because their results show that managers see this as expected in the workplace. Studying OCB requires consideration of these various adjustments. Nowadays, research based on Organ's model most often examines citizenship in the workplace through helping behaviour, sportsmanship and civic virtue, though certain researchers continue to use the original forms of OCB (for example, Cohen, 2006; Schappe, 1998).

Long widespread in U.S. research, interest in studying OCB is now conspicuous in other cultural contexts. In the French cultural context, the OCB craze is recent. While a number of studies have been published using samples of French employees (Vontrhon and Dagot, 2003; Grima, 2007; Paillé, 2004), the possible influence of cultural context on 1) citizenship structure and 2) the impact of attitudes at work has been neglected. The goal of the current research is twofold. First, we propose to examine the dimensionality of citizenship at work on French employees to determine the salient forms of OCB. Secondly, we propose to examine possible links with a number of workplace attitudes. Finally, our intention is to collect data to determine which workplace attitudes explain which forms of OCB in the French context.

OCB Structure and Dimensions

On the whole, up until the end of the 1990s, OCB was primarily studied in North America. Helping behaviour, sportsmanship and civic virtue are the three principal forms of OCB studied by researchers following in Organ's footsteps. Research on American employees focuses on different forms of OCB in varying combinations. To date, we note four types of configuration.

- Certain researchers choose to examine citizenship as a whole (for example, Chen, Hui and Sego, 1998; Hui et al., 2004; MacKensie et al., 1998; Thau et al., 2004). There is no distinction between helping behaviour, sportsmanship and civic virtue. In this case, items on the three subscales (helping behaviour, sportsmanship and civic virtue) are blended into a single scale.
- Certain researchers (for example, Chen and Francesco, 2003; Cohen, 2006; Schappe, 1998), in studying OCB, distinguish between citizenship behaviours towards individuals and those towards the organization.
- Other researchers (for example, Podsakoff and MacKensie, 1994; Yoon and Suh, 2003) examine citizenship by adopting a three-factor model distinguishing between helping behaviour, sportsmanship and civic virtue. In this third configuration, items measuring helping behaviour are grouped into the same single dimension. As there is no distinction between different facets of OCB (for example, courtesy, altruism, etc.), helping behaviour is thus defined as a latent second-order construct.
- Finally, certain researchers (for example, Diefendorff, Brown, Kamin, and Lord 2002; Lievens and Anseel, 2004; Tansky, 1993) employ a five-factor structure to study OCB (courtesy, altruism, peacemaking, sportsmanship, and civic virtue).

For several years now, OCB research has been done outside of U.S. context. For example, empirical data have been provided on Chinese employees (Chen and Francesco, 2003), Australians (Feather and Rauter, 2004), Germans (Thau, Bennett, Stahlberg and Werner, 2004), Malaysians (Coyne and Ong, 2007), Africans (Ehigie and Otukoya, 2005), Arabs (Shaw, Delery and Abdulla, 2003), Dutch and Belgians (Lievens and Anseel, 2004), Israelis (Cohen, 2006), and English (Coyle-Shapiro, 2002). The fact that this list continues to grow shows that the existence of behaviours related to OCB is no longer questioned by researchers around the world. At the same time, a consensus is emerging around the notion of the possible impact of cultural context on OCBs. A number of researchers (Lievens and Ansel, 2004; Motowidlo, 2000; Paine and Organ, 2000; Podsakoff et al., 2000) believe that the cultural context could influence the structure of OCBs. Nonetheless, it is astounding to observe that cultural context as an influential factor is often ignored. In fact, we frequently find research outside of North America adopting models tested in the U.S. context, while neglecting any possible influence of the cultural context in which the research is being conducted. Therefore, there is a great risk of reaching flawed conclusions. As mentioned earlier, a number of empirical studies have used samples of French employees (Dagot and Vontrhon, 2003; Grima, 2007; Paillé, 2007; Paillé, 2004). The theme of citizenship in the French cultural context is, thus, not new. Yet further research is necessary because none of the research on French employees has systematically investigated the factorial structure of OCBs, as recommended by Lievens and Anseel. For their part, Dagot and Vonhron (2003) and Paillé (2004) studied citizenship as a whole without a rigorous analysis of the structure. More recently, Grima (2007) studied OCBs with a three-factor model (civic virtue, sportsmanship and helping behaviour) without a prior structural analysis. To date, only one study has examined OCB structure. Using the CFA technique, Paillé (2007) obtained a structure in 4 dimensions (altruism, helping, civic virtue and sportsmanship).

Satisfaction, Commitment, Involvement and Citizenship in the Workplace

One of the present study's objectives is to examine the possible influence of a number of attitudes on OCBs in the French cultural context. In the following sections, we focus on job satisfaction, multiple targets of commitment and job involvement.

Job Satisfaction

Job satisfaction is one of the most studied attitudes in the organizational context (Dorfmann and Zapf, 2001; and Lease, 1998). The current literature has reached a consensus on considering job satisfaction the result of an employee's evaluation of his or her work (for example, Judge, Bono and Locke, 2000; Testa, 2001; Weiss, 2002). Consistent with this orientation, we could say that the state of satisfaction is merely the result of an evaluation process through which employees value or are dismissive of their work. A negative evaluation of the workplace environment engenders employee dissatisfaction. On the other hand, a positive evaluation leads to a feeling of satisfaction. In the latter case, employees express gratitude towards the organization and feel the need to build a lasting relationship, partially based on the desire for reciprocity (MacKensie et al., 1998). This context of mutual exchange encourages employees to develop OCBs. Analysis of the relationships between job satisfaction and OCBs has generated a considerable volume of empirical work (for example, Bateman and Organ, 1983; MacKensie, Podsakoff and Ahearne, 1998; Rioux and Penner, 2001; Schappe, 1998; Smith, Organ and Near, 1983; Tansky, 1993; Williams and Anderson, 1991). In the current state of knowledge, relations are more often positive (for example, Podsakoff et al., 2000), or sometimes nonexistent (for example, Konovsky and Organ, 1989; Schappe, 1998; Williams and Anderson, 1991), but they are never negative. These results were obtained with altruism and conscientiousness, two forms of OCB operationalized by Smith, Organ and Near (1983).The broader approach of Organ (1988) allows us to evaluate a greater number of links with job satisfaction. Incorporating the older approach of Smith, Organ and Near (1983), studies are introducing other forms of citizenship (for example, courtesy, civic virtue, and sportsmanship). Tansky (1993) conducted one of the earliest studies to test the association of this new approach to job satisfaction. The data the researcher collected on a sample of managers show that job satisfaction is empirically and positively correlated to courtesy and civic virtue. In contrast, no significant correlation was obtained to altruism, sportsmanship or peacemaking. More recently, Yoon and Suh (2003) studied only three relationships with job satisfaction. Their results reveal that job satisfaction is linked to sportsmanship and civic virtue and is not associated with altruism. The findings in this section demonstrate that satisfied employees tend to develop OCB. We currently lack empirical data allowing us to determine whether this is true of French employees. It thus strikes us as reasonable to pursue the current trends in the literature.

Hypothesis 1: In the French workplace, job satisfaction and OCB are positively correlated.

Employee Commitment

Affective commitment to the organization refers to individuals identifying with the organization's values, accepting its goals and making significant efforts at work (Meyer and Herscovitch, 2001). Affective commitment to the organization is a major determinant of OCBs (for example, LePine, Erez and Johnson, 2002; Podsakoff et al., 2000). Sharing values and organizational goals is accompanied by an employee's higher affective commitment to the organization which encourages tendencies towards efficient behaviour at work. The relationship between OCBs and affective commitment to the organization was explored in the 1980s (O'Reilly and Chatman, 1986), only a few years after the first works on the association with job satisfaction (Bateman and Organ, 1983; Smith, Organ and Near, 1983), such that, from our perspective, the interest generated by affective commitment to the organization in the field of OCBs is no more recent than that of job satisfaction. Only the amount of empirical research in the 1980s differentiates them, since job satisfaction is the attitude most studied as a determinant (Schappe, 1998). However, it was really only at the start of the 1990s that affective commitment to the organization became a topic of significant research interest. A review of the literature reveals that most knowledge on the relation between affective commitment to the organization and OCB concerns the aspects touching altruism and conscientiousness. The vast majority of empirical relations are positive and significant (for example, Bishop, Scott and Burroughs, 2000; Chen and Francesco, 2003; Schappe, 1998). Certain findings provide data that contradict this tendency since an absence of a relationship is sometimes observed (Shore et al., 2000; Williamson and Anderson, 1991). Researchers who used Organ's expanded taxonomy shed no greater light on the issue (for example, Rioux and Penner, 2001; Tansky, 1993; Yoon and Suh, 2003). Tansky (1993) finds no significant correlation between affective commitment to the organization and altruism, conscientiousness, courtesy, civic virtue and sportsmanship. The researcher attributes this result to the possible influence of other variables, without, however, naming them. Rioux and Penner (2001) find positive relationships with altruism, civic virtue and sportsmanship. These data are partially confirmed in the most recent research of Yoon and Suh (2003), since the latter show that only civic virtue and sportsmanship correlate with affective commitment to the organization. While certain research sometimes finds no correlation, in most cases, the association between affective commitment to the organization and OCB is positive. Based on the results of the literature discussed in this section, it seems feasible to postulate positive, significant relationships. Consequently,

Hypothesis 2a: In the French workplace, affective commitment to the organization and OCB are positively correlated

Recently, the academic literature has admitted the existence of other targets and it now regularly provides empirical data demonstrating the utility of associating them in studying employee commitment. This extension of the research framework is based on the critical analysis of Reichers (1985) and various empirical works of Becker et al. (Becker, 1992; Becker, Billings, 1993; Becker, Billings, Eveleth, and Gilbert, 1996). In this approach, the organization is a target of commitment, much like the profession chosen (Meyer, Allen and

Smith, 1993), the supervisor (Stinglhamber, Bentein and Vandenberghe, 2002) or even the work team (Bishop, Scott and Burroughs, 2000). Up to now, little research has focused on the effects of the multiplicity of targets of commitment on OCB. A few results are currently available (Becker, 1992; Bentein, Stinghlamber and Vandenberghe, 2002; Bishop, Scott and Burroughs, 2000). Becker (1992) shows that introducing complementary targets of commitment (for example, towards top management, supervisor and colleagues) alongside affective commitment to the organization significantly raises the variance of two of these three forms of OCB analysed in the research. Indeed, unlike altruism and conscientiousness, idleness seems less sensitive to the multiplication of targets of commitment. For their part, Bishop, Scott and Burroughs (2000) have shown that the outcome of modelling a structural equation is that commitment to the organization and commitment to the team influence OCB, studied as a single dimension, simultaneously and positively. More recently, Bentein, Stinghlamber and Vandenberghe (2002) examined relations between commitment and OCB by looking at these two concepts for three targets, the superior, the workgroup, and the organization. Three researchers' results show, on one hand, that employees are affectively closer to the "workgroup" and more distant from the entities of "the organization" and "the supervisor" and, on the other hand, that this proximity has the effect of improving OCB prediction. The preliminary results suggest positive correlations between OCB and commitment to the colleagues and commitment to the supervisor. Consequently:

Hypothesis 2b: In the French workplace, commitment to the colleagues and OCB are positively correlated

Hypothesis 2c: In the French workplace, commitment to the supervisor and OCB are positively correlated

Job Involvement

Job involvement refers to a cognitive belief state of psychological identification with one's job (Brown and Leigh, 1996). Only recently have the empirical relationships between job involvement and OCB been studied. Indeed, neither the literature review of Podsakoff et al. (2000), nor the recent work of Organ, Podsakoff and MacKensie (2006), mentions the existence of data allowing for clarification of the association between job involvement and OCB. Job involvement remains an important topic of debate in recent literature. Indeed, it is a considerable factor in job satisfaction (Brown, 1996). Job involvement also turns out to be a determining factor in organizational efficacy (Pfeffer, 1994). The most up-to-date definitions consider job involvement as the measure of the degree to which individuals see their professional activity as central, meaningful and important (Mortimer and Lorence, 1989), or even as the psychological identification with work (Lodahl and Kejner 1965; Lawler and Hall, 1970; Kanungo, 1982; Rabinowitz 1981). Diefendorff, Brown, Kamin and Lord (2002) were the first to be interested in the relationship between job involvement and OCB. On the whole, these early findings systematically display a positive correlation between job involvement and OCB (Cohen, 2006; Diefendorff et al., 2002). Thus:

Hypothesis 3: In the French workplace, job involvement and OCB are positively correlated.

METHOD

Participants

The participants were 355 working adults. The sample included 182 women and 173 men with a mean age of 30.6 (ranging from 21 to 60 years old) of age. The average professional experience is 7 years (ranging from 1 year to 37).

Measures

All measures employed in this research have been used on numerous occasions in the anglophone context. They have also been used a number of times in the francophone context. All our scales were subject to a process of double translation (from English to French and French to English) in order to maximize the psychometric properties of certain of our measurement scales.

1. OCB. Organizational citizenship behaviours were measured with scales developed by Podsakoff and MacKensie (1994) in the U.S. context and validated in French by Paillé (2007). A first scale (whose scores must be reversed during the data recording) measures sportsmanship (4 items), a second scale civic virtue (3 items) and a third helping behaviour (6 items).
2. Employee commitment. Three targets of commitment (affective commitment to one's supervisor, affective commitment to colleagues and affective commitment to the organization) were measured with scales developed and validated in French by Stinglhamber, Bentein and Vandenberghe (2002).
3. Job satisfaction was measured with the three-item scale of Hackman and Oldham (1975). These were validated in French by Paillé (in press).
4. Job involvement was measured with a selection of three items arising from the abbreviated scale of Lodhal and Kelner (1965), especially focused on relationships to work (Paillé, 2000). These three items were validated in French by Neveu (1996).

Age and tenure were chosen as control variables because they can be linked to OCB (Organ and Ryan, 1995; Wagner and Rush, 2000). Finally, items were measured on a five point Likert-type scale, ranging from 1 (disagree completely) to 5 (agree completely).

Procedure

The goal of the present research is to 1) evaluate the factorial structure of citizenship in the workplace and 2) examine the relative contribution of a number of attitudes at work to variance in OCB forms. The following section describes the procedure employed to attain these two objectives.

Using confirmatory factor analysis, preliminary research on French employees (Paillé, 2007) provides results suggesting a four-factor structure (civic virtue, sportsmanship, helping and altruism). These first results represent a particularly useful benchmark. In the present research, the four-factor structure was evaluated with the Amos 5.0 program (Arbuckle, 2003). A number of statistical indices are used to examine the findings. The larger and more significant the value for the test of Chi-squared, the more the model differs from perfect adjustment. Other indices are also employed, including the root mean square error of approximation (RMSEA), whose expected value must ideally be less than .05 (Schermelleh-Engel, Moosbrugger and Müller, 2003); the Comparative Fit Index (CFI); the Good Fit Index (GFI); and the Adjusted Good Fit Index (AGFI). The rules concerning the threshold of acceptability for certain indices vary according to the source. Some researchers recommend values greater than .90 (Medsker, Williams and Holahan, 1994), while others set the threshold at .95 (Hu and Bentler, 1999). We choose to consider the adjustment acceptable if the values fall between .90 and .95. Finally the χ^2/df ratio was also calculated. Values between 1 and 3 indicate a good fit.

Hierarchical regressions were performed to analyse relative contributions of attitudes to forms of OCB. In stage 1, age and professional experience were introduced as control variables. In stage 2, attitudes were introduced.

RESULTS

The first stage was to evaluate the factorial structure discovered by Paillé (2007) for French employees. In the current research, we test this structure. The four-factor structure offers a good adjustment χ^2 (61) = 112, 58, p < .000, CFI = .934, GFI = .955, RMSEA = .049. Consistent with the present research's methodology, the four-factor model was compared to the most popular model on organizational citizenship behaviour in the literature. The goal was to confirm the eventual presence of nested models.

As with the four-factor model, adjustment to the five-factor model is good (table 1). Nonetheless, after an examination of the Chi-square difference (Bentler and Bonnett, 1980), the five-factor model offers no significant improvement over the four-factor model [$\Delta\chi^2$ (1) = 3.36 ns]. Bentler and Bonnett recommend ignoring an alternative model that provides no improvement in Chi-squared even if the values of the adjustment indices are greater. Therefore, the four-factor model is retained, rather than the five-factor one. In short, the initial findings of our research confirm those obtained previously by Paillé (2007). In summary, in the French cultural context, citizenship is structured in four dimensions: altruism, sportsmanship, civic virtue and helping others.

Table 1. Overall fit indices for the models

Models	X²	df	χ²/df	RMSEA	CFI	GFI	TLI
Nullmodel	2301***	91	25.28	-	-	-	-
Model 1	504.15***	65	7.75	.138	.441	.833	.329
Model 2	192.73***	53	3.62	.086	.741	.918	.678
Model 3	139.72***	51	2.74	.070	.836	.940	.788
Model 4	112.58***	61	1.85	.049	.934	.955	.916
Model 5	109.22***	60	1.82	.048	.937	.957	.919

Notes. Model 1: Citizenship as a whole. Model 2: 2 dimensions (behaviour oriented towards individuals and citizenship behaviour oriented towards the organization). Model 3: 3 dimensions (helping, civic virtue and sportsmanship). Model 4: 4 dimensions (altruism, helping, civic virtue and sportsmanship). Model 5: 5 dimensions (altruism, peacekeeping, courtesy, civic virtue and sportsmanship).
*** $p < .000$.

The means, standard deviations, internal consistencies and correlations are presented in table 2. Internal consistencies are depicted on the diagonal. They were calculated with Cronbach's alpha. Nunally and Bernstein (1994) recommend values above .70. The alphas range from .66 (altruism) to .91 (affective commitment to one's supervisor).

Table 2. Correlation Matrix

Variables	1.	2.	3.	4.	5.	6.	7	8	9
1.Altruism	(66)								
2.Helping	27**	(73)							
3.Civic virtue	05	17**	(69)						
4.Sportsmanship	02	01	03	(75)					
5. AE-org	01	21**	35**	33**	(82)				
6. AE-sup	02	01	14**	30**	37**	(91)			
7.AE-coll	11*	25**	33**	17**	56**	31**	(79)		
8.Job satisfaction	01	10	17**	37**	58**	44**	36**	(.77)	
9.Job Involvement	10*	04	20**	04	34**	05	18**	15**	80)

AE-Org: Affective commitment to organization; AE-Sup: Affective commitment to supervisor; AE-coll: Affective commitment to colleague.
** $p < .01$; * $p < .05$.

Table 3 presents the results of hierarchical regression. The introduction of control variables at stage 1 shows that age and professional experience do not contribute to altruism ($R^2 = .004$), helping behaviour ($R^2 = .006$), civic virtue ($R^2 = .003$) and sportsmanship ($R^2 = .009$).

Table 3. Regression Results

Variables	Altruism	Helping others	Civic virtue	Sportsmanship
Step 1				
Age	.083	-.009	.142	.148
Tenure	-.135	.086	-.117	-.062
	$R^2 = .004$	$R^2 = .006$	$R^2 = .003$	$R^2 = .009$
Step 2				
Age	.077	.000	.175	.123
Tenure	-.104	.066	-.167	-.044
Job satisfaction	.023	-.019	-.059	.214**
Job involvement	-.107*	-.045	.096*	-.153**
AE-Org	-.097	.146*	.229**	.229**
AE-Sup	-.015	-.079	.013	.156**
AE-Coll	.183**	.222**	.202**	-.053
	$R^2 = .037$	$R^2 = .089$	$R^2 = .159$	$R^2 = .211$

AE-Org: Affective commitment to organization; AE-Sup: Affective commitment to supervisor; AE-coll: Affective commitment to colleague.
*** $p < .000$ ** $p < .005$ * $p < .01$

Attitudes at work are introduced in stage 2. As seen in Table 2, attitudes at work contribute to the change in variance of altruism ($\Delta R^2 = .033$, $p < .042$), helping ($\Delta R^2 = .083$, $p < .000$), civic virtue ($\Delta R^2 = .156$, $p < .000$), and sportsmanship ($\Delta R^2 = .202$, $p < .000$).

- Hypothesis 1 is supported since the relationship between sportsmanship and job satisfaction is positive ($\beta = .214$, $p < .005$).
- Hypotheses 2a, 2b, and 2c are supported. The correlation is positive between affective commitment to the organization and civic virtue ($\beta = .229$, $p < .005$) and sportsmanship ($\beta = .229$, $p < .005$). The correlation is positive between affective commitment to colleagues and altruism ($\beta = 183$, $p < .005$), and civic virtue ($\beta = .202$, $p < .005$). It is also positive between sportsmanship and affective commitment to one's supervisor ($\beta = .156$, $p < .005$).
- Hypothesis 3 is partially supported. There is a positive association between job involvement and civic virtue ($\beta = .096$, $p < .075$) but a negative one between job involvement and altruism ($\beta = -.107$, $p < .075$) and sportsmanship ($\beta = -.153$, $p < .005$).

DISCUSSION

The goals of this research were to evaluate the structure of organizational citizenship on French employees, and to study the possible role of a number if attitudes at work (for example, targets of commitment, job satisfaction and involvement at work) on dimensions of organizational citizenship. Our research findings serve to advance the literature on OCBs. First, the research provides data on OCBs in a still largely unexplored cultural context. Second, the research has examined possible associations between OCB and a number of attitudes at work (job satisfaction, job involvement and several targets of commitment).

The present research provides results that should contribute to the literature on citizenship in the French workplace. Until now, research with samples of French employees has been consistent with observations of North American employees. Thus, Dagot and Vonthron (2003) and Paillé (2004) studied citizenship as a whole. More recently, Grima (2007) examined a three-factor model (helping behaviour, civic virtue and sportsmanship). These investigations did not follow common practices. (Paine and Organ, 2000; Lievens and Anseel, 2004) which suggest a thorough examination of the structure to verify any possible influence of cultural context. Such an examination was neglected in the research of Dagot and Vonthron, of Paillé and of Grima. There were two problems with this early research. First, the models used do not consider the cultural context's possible influence on citizenship structure. Secondly, such research data may overstate the correlation of forms of citizenship and the variables studied by French researchers. In this regard, the present research offers results allowing us to improve future research on French employees' citizenship behaviour, in particular. This research shows both divergences and convergences with the OCB literature. As in other cultural contexts, the items of civic virtue and sportsmanship respectively, are weakly correlated factors. This is consistent with US samples. On this point, French employees clearly reveal different dimensions related to civic virtue and sportsmanship. In addition the cultural context's influence is determinant for helping behaviour. Research in the US context shows the items of altruism, peacemaking and courtesy load the same factor interpreted as helping behaviour. For the two samples of the present research, the altruism items load a different factor while the four other items of helping behaviour load the same factor. This seems to suggest that French employees consider altruism as part of their work. Further research using the model developed by Hofstede (1984) could enhance our understanding of the impact of OCB dimensions observed in the French context.

One of the interesting contributions of this study is the analysis of empirical relationships between a number of attitudes at work and forms of organizational citizenship. While subtle distinctions are observed, on the whole, the data collected on French employees suggest results comparable to research in other cultural contexts. Job satisfaction is certainly the attitude at work that has been most extensively employed in research on determinants of OCBs. Based on the most common findings, we expected significant, positive correlations. On this point, our research offers comparable findings to earlier research (Yoon and Suh, 2003). Another contribution concerns the correlations between multiple targets of commitment and forms of citizenship. Our study confirms the propositions of a number of researchers (Becker, 1992; Becker et al. 1996) on the utility of multiplying the targets of commitment to study behaviour at work, and especially the study of organizational citizenship. In the conclusion of their article, Bishop et al. (2000) encourage future researchers to collect data allowing for greater exploration of the nature of relations between employees' targets of commitment and citizenship behaviour. Data collected on French employees suggest: 1) the influence of commitment to the colleagues on altruism, helping behaviour and civic virtue; 2) the influence of the commitment to the supervisor on sportsmanship; and 3) the influence of commitment to the organization on helping behaviour, civic virtue and sportsmanship. Another contribution of the research concerns analysis of the impact of involvement at work. As indicated earlier, while empirical research has recently explored the links between involvement at work and OCBs, the role of involvement at work is still relatively unknown. Previous research shows positive correlations or no correlations but never negative correlations. From this viewpoint, our findings are surprising. Indeed, the relationships are negative with regard to altruism and sportsmanship, positive for civic virtue and nonexistent for helping others. This is the first time that significant negative associations have been observed. Such findings may be related to the cultural context.

Our findings provide a practical benchmark, of use to managers working in firms established in France or those who are supervising French employees elsewhere in the world. As OCBs contribute to organizational efficiency (Organ, Podsakoff and MacKensie, 2006), it is important to understand which attitudes of French employees towards work affect OCBs. Therefore, our research results offer valuable information for managers.

While making a number of contributions to the literature on organizational citizenship, there are also certain limitations to our research that cannot be ignored. First, we have chosen to treat the predictors in a similar fashion so as to determine their relative contribution. Certain of these predictors reflect a reaction related to the evaluation of the context (job satisfaction), while others are characteristic of a psychological state (involvement and targets of commitment). This could explain why job satisfaction remained inactive for most forms of organizational citizenship. Furthermore, our research was mainly focused on the citizenship model developed by Organ et al., with the findings partially conditioned by this choice. Perhaps a different model of citizenship, notably that developed by Graham (1991), would have led to different conclusions. Another limitation arises from our use of self-reported responses to measure citizenship. Nevertheless, we observe that the difficulties associated with data acquisition are perceived differently. Some researchers (for example, Organ and Ryan, 1995) believe that this choice somewhat biases the results and they encourage the use of responses reported by a third party to avoid interference from the respondent's subjectivity. Others (for example, Turnipsseed, 2002) believe the self-report is justified when the investigation is centred on examining links between psychological variables. The choice to collect data with self-reported measures may, nonetheless, result in a common variance bias likely to overestimate research findings (Spector, 1987). Finally, our results, as discussed, arise from a research design favouring a single measure.

In conclusion, this chapter had two principal objectives. The first was to study the structure of organizational citizenship in the French workplace. An original four-factor structure was discovered. Secondly, there was the goal of analysing possible relations between attitudes and forms of organizational citizenship. Research reveals a positive impact of job satisfaction, commitment to the organization, commitment to the colleagues and commitment to the supervisor. At the same time, the research displays a negative impact of involvement at work. This study contributes to the literature on OCBs through exploring a previously neglected cultural context. While making a number of contributions to the literature on OCBs, further research is necessary to deepen our knowledge of OCB in the French context.

REFERENCES

Arbuckle, J.L. (2003). *Amos 5.0. Update to the Amos. User's Guide*. Chicago. IL, SmallWaters Corporation.

Bateman, T., and Organ, D. (1983). Job satisfaction and the good soldier : the relationship between affect and employee citizenship. *Academy of Management Journal*, 26, 4, 586-595.

Bentler, P.M., and Bonnett, D.C. (1980). Significance tests and goodness of fit in the analysis of covariance structures. *Psychological Bulletin*, 80, 588-506.

Becker, T. (1992). Foci and bases of commitment: Are they distinctions worth making? *Academy of Management Journal*, 35, 1, 232-244.

Becker T.S. and Billings R.S. (1993). Profiles of commitments: an empirical test. *Journal of Organizational Behavior*, 14, 177-190.

Becker, T., Billings, R.S., Eveleth D.M., and Gilbert N. L. (1996). Foci and bases of employee commitment: Implications for job performance. *Academy of Management Journal*, 39, 464-482.

Bentein, K, Stinghlamber, F., and Vandenberghe, C. (2002). Organization-, supervisor-, and workgroup-directed commitments and citizenship behaviours: A comparison of models. *European Journal of Work and Organizational Psychology*, 11, 3, 341-362.

Bishop, J., Scott, K., and Burroughs, S. (2000). Support, Commitment, and Employee Outcomes in a Team Environment. *Journal of Management*, 26, 6, 1113-1132.

Brief A. and Motowidlo S. (1986). Prosocial Organizational Behaviors. *Academy of Management Review*, 11, 4, 710-725.

Brown, S. (1996). A Meta-Analysis and Review of Organizational Research on Job Involvement. *Psychological Bulletin*, 120, 235-255.

Brown, S.P., and Leigh, T.W. (1996). A New Look at Psychological Climate and Its Relationship to Job Involvement, Effort, and Performance. *Journal of Applied Psychology*, Vol. 81, No. 4, 358-368.

Chen, X.-P., Hui, C., and Sego, D.J. (1998). The Role of Organizational Citizenship Behavior in Turnover: Conceptualization and Preliminary Tests of Key Hypotheses. *Journal of Applied Psychology*, 83, 6, 922-931.

Chen, Z.X., and Francesco, A.-M., (2003). The relationship between the three components of commitment and employee performance in China. *Journal of Vocational Behavior* 62, 490-510.

Cohen, A. (2006). The relationship between multiple commitments and organizational citizenship behavior in Arab and Jewish Culture. *Journal of Vocational Behavior*, 69 1, 105-118.

Cohen, J. (1975). *Applied Multiple Regression Correlation Analysis for the Behavioral Sciences*. Hillsdale, NJ: Lawrence Erlbaum.

Coyle-Shapiro, J. (2002). A psychological contract perspective on organizational citizenship behavior. *Journal of organizational Behavior*, 23, 927-946.

Coyne, I., and Ong, T. (2007). Organizational citizenship behaviour and turnover intention: a cross-cultural study. *International Journal of Human Resource Management*, 18, 6, 1085-1097.

Dagot, L., and Vonthron, A.-M. (2003). Comportements de citoyenneté organisationnelle et anticipation de la performance professionnelle : une approche expérimentale. *Psychologie du Travail et des Organisations*, 9, 1-2, 69-88.

Diefendorff, J., Brown, D., Kamin, A., and Lord, R. (2002). Examining the roles of job involvement and work centrality in predicting organizational citizenship behaviors and job performance. *Journal of Organizational Behavior*, 23, 93-108.

Ehigie, B.O., and Otukoya, O.W. (2005). Antecedents of organizational citizenship behaviour in a government-owned enterprise in Nigeria. *European Journal of Work and Organizational Psychology*, 14 (4), 389–399.

Feather, N.T., and Rauter, K. (2004). Organizational citizenship behaviours in relation to job status, job insecurity, organizational commitment, and identification, job satisfaction and Work values. *Journal of Occupational and Organizational Psychology*, 77, 81-94.

Graham, J.W. (1991). An essay on organizational citizenship behavior. *Employee Responsabilities and Rights Journal*, 4, 4, 249-270.

Grima, F. (2007). Le rôle des comportements citoyens dans l'intention de partir des commerciaux. *Revue de Gestion des Ressources Humaines*, 63, 28-41.

Hackman, J.R., and Oldham, G.R. (1975). Development of the job diagnostic survey. *Journal of Applied Psychology*, 60, 159-170.

Hofstede G. (1984). *Culture's Consequences. International Differences in Work-Related Values*. Sage Publications: London.

Hu, L.T., and Bentler, P.M. (1999). Cutoff criteria for fit indices in covariance structure analysis: conventional criteria versus new alternatives. *Structural Equation Modeling*, 6, 1-55.

Hui, C., Lee, C. and Rousseau, D. (2004). Employment Relationships in China: Do Workers Relate to the Organization or to People ? *Organization Science*, 15, 2, 232-240.

Judge, T., Bono, J. and Locke, E. (2000). Personality and Job Satisfaction : The mediating Role of Job Characteristics. *Journal of Applied Psychology*, 85, 2, 237-249.

Kanungo, R. (1982). Measurement of job and work involvement. *Journal of Applied Psychology*, 67, 341-349.

Katz, D., and Khan, R.L., (1978). The social psychology of organizations (2nd ed.). New York: Wiley.

Lawler, E.E., and Hall, D.T. (1970). Relationship of Job Characteristics to Job Involvement, Satisfaction, and Intrinsic Motivation. *Journal of Applied Psychology*, 54, 305-312.

LePine, J., Erez, A., and Johnson, D. (2002). The Nature and Dimensionality of Organizational Citizenship Behavior: A Critical Review and Meta-Analysis. *Journal of Applied Psychology*, 87, 1, 52-65.

Lievens, F., and Anseel, F. (2004). Confirmatory factor analysis and invariance of an organizational citizenship behaviour measure across samples in a Dutch-speaking context. *Journal of Occupational and Organizational Psychology*, 77, 299-306.

Lodhal, T., and Kejner, M. (1965). The definition and measurement of job involvement. *Journal of Applied Psychology*, 49, 1, 24-33.

MacKensie, S., Podsakoff, P., and Ahearne, M. (1998). Some Possible Antecedents and Consequences of In-Role and Extra-Role Salesperson Performance. *Journal of Marketing*, 62, 87-98.

Medsker, G.J., Williams, L.J. and Holahan, P.J. (1994). A review of current practices for evaluating causal models in organizational behavior and human resources management research. *Journal of Management*, 20, 439-464.

Meyer J.P., Allen N.J. and Smith C.A. (1993) Commitment to Organizations and Occupations: Extension and test of a Three-Component Conceptualization. *Journal of Applied Psychology*, 78, 4, 538-551.

Meyer, J. P., and Herscovitch, L. (2001). Commitment in the workplace: Toward a general model. Human Resource Management Review, 11, 299–326.

Motowidlo, S. J. (2000). Some basic issues related to contextual performance and organizational citizenship behavior in human resource management. *Human Resource Management Review*, 10, 1, 115-126.

Mortimer J.T. and Lorence J. (1989).Satisfaction and Involvement: Disentangling a Deceptively Simple Relationship. *Social Psychology Quaterly*, 52,4,249-265.

Neveu, J.-P. (1996). *La démission du cadre d'entreprise*. Economica, Paris.

Nunnally, J.C., and Bernstein, I.H. (1994). *Psychometric theory*. New York: McGraw-Hill.

O'Reillly, C., et Chatman, J. (1986). Organizational Commitment and Psychological Attachment : The Effects of *Compliance*, Identification, and Internalization on Prosocial Behavior. *Journal of Applied Psychology*, 71, 3, 492-499.

Organ, D. (1988). *Organizational citizenship behavior: The good soldier syndrome*. Lexington, MA: Lexington books.

Organ, D., (1990). *The motivational basis of Organizational Citizenship Behavior*. In : Staw, B. M. and Cummings, L.L., Eds. Research in Organizational Behavior. (pp. 43-72). Greenwich CT, JAI Press.,

Organ, D.W. Podsakoff P.M., and MacKensie S.B. (2006). *Organizational Citizenship Behavior. Its Nature, Antecedents, and Consequences*. Sage Publication : Thousands Oaks.

Organ, D.W., and Konovsky, M. (1989). Cognitive versus affective determinants of organizational citizenship behaviour. *Journal of Applied Psychology*, 74, 1, 157-164.

Organ, D., and and Ryan K. (1995). A Meta-analytic review of attitudinal and dispositional predictors of organizational citizenship behavior. *Personnel Psychology*, 48, 775-802.

Paillé P. (2000). Facteurs de l'engagement dans l'emploi à l'issue d'un changement organisationnel. *Le Travail Humain*, 63, 2, 153-169.

Paillé, P. (2004). Engagement organisationnel, intention de retrait et comportements citoyens : l'influence de la satisfaction au travail. *Revue de Gestion des Ressources Humaines*, 53, 37-46.

Paillé, P. (2007). La citoyenneté dans les organisations : validation française des échelles de mesure de Podsakoff et MacKensie (1994). *Cahiers Internationaux de Psychologie Sociale*, 74, 59-66.

Paillé, P. (2008). Les comportements de citoyenneté organisationnelle : une étude empirique sur les relations avec l'engagement affcctif, la satisfaction au travail et l'implication au travail. *Le Travail Humain*. 71, 1, 22-42.

Paine, J., and Organ, D. (2000). The cultural matrix of organizational citizenship behavior: some preliminary conceptual and empirical observations. *Human Resource Management Review*, 10, 1, 45-59.

Pfeffer J. (1994). *Competitive advantage Though People*: Unleashing the Power of the work Force. Harvard Business School Press: Boston.

Podsakoff, P. and MacKensie, S. (1994). Organizational Citizenship Behaviors and Sales Unit Effectiveness. *Journal of Marketing Research*, 31, 351-363.

Podsakoff, P., MacKensie, S., Paine, J. and Bachrach D. (2000). Organizational Citizenship Behaviors: A Critical Review of the Theoretical and Empirical Literature and Suggestions for Future Research. *Journal of Management*, 26, 3, 513-563.

Rabinowitz S. (1981). Towards a developmental model of job involvement. *International Review of Applied Psychology*, 30, 31-50.

Reichers, A. (1985). A Review and Reconceptualization of Organizational Commitment. *Academy of Management Review*, 10, 3, 465-476.

Rioux, S., and Penner, L. (2000). The Causes of Organizational Citizenship Behavior: A Motivational analysis. *Journal of Applied Psychology*, 86, 6, 1306-1314.

Roethlisberger, F.J., and Dickson, W.J. (1939). *Management and the worker*. Cambridge, MA: Harvard University Press.

Schappe, S. (1998). The influence of Job Satisfaction, Organizational Commitment, and Fairness Perceptions on Organizational Citizenship Behavior. *The Journal of Psychology*, 132, 3, 277-290.

Schermelleh-Engel, K., Moosbrugger, H., and Müller, H. (2003). Evaluating the Fit of Structural Equation Models : Tests of Significance and Descriptive Goodness-of-Fit Measures. *Methods of Psychological Research Online*, 8, 2, 23-74.

Smith, C., Organ, D., and Near, J. (1983). Organizational Citizenship Behavior: Its nature and antecedents. *Journal of Applied Psychology*, 68, 653-663.

Shaw, J.D., Delery, J.E., and Abdulla, M. (2003). Organizational commitment and performance among guest workers and citizens of Arab country. *Journal of Business Research*, 56, 1021-1030.

Somech, A., and Drach-Zahary, A. (2004). Exploring organizational citizenship behaviour from an organizational perspective: The relationship between organizational learning and Organizational citizenship behaviour. *Journal of Occupational and Organizational Psychology*, 77, 281-298.

Smith, C., Organ, D. and Near, J. (1983). Organizational Citizenship Behavior: Its nature and antecedents. *Journal of Applied Psychology*, 68, 653-663.

Spector, P.E. (1987). Method variance as an artefact in self-reported affect and perceptions at work: Myth or significant problem? *Journal of Applied Psychology*, Vol. 86, N° 1, pp. 114-121.

Stinglhamber, F. Bentein, K. and Vandenberghe, C. (2002). Extension of the three-component model of commitment to five foci: development of measures and substantive test. *European Journal of Psychological Assessment*, 18, 123-138.

Testa, M. (2001). Organizational Commitment, Job Satisfaction, and Efforts in the Service Environment. *The Journal of Psychology*, 135, 2, 226-236.

Tansky, J. (1993). Justice and organizational citizenship behavior: What is the relationship? *Employee Responsabilities and Rights Journal*, 6, 195-207.

Thau, S., Bennett, R.J., Stahlberg, D., and Werner, J.M. (2004). Why should I be generous when have valued and accessible alternatives? Alternative exchange partners and OCB. *Journal of Organizational Behavior*, 25, 607-626.

Wagner, S.L., and Rush, M.C. (2000). Altruistic organizational citizenship behavior: Context, disposition, and age. The Journal of Social Psychology, 140, 3, 379-391.

Weiss, H. (2002). Deconstructing job satisfaction. Separating evaluations, beliefs and affective experiences. *Human Resource Management Review*, 12, 173-194.

Williams, L., and Anderson, S. (1991). Job satisfaction and organizational commitment as predictors of Organizational citizenship and in-role behaviors. *Journal of Management*, 17, 601-617.

Yoon, M.H., and Suh, J. (2003). Organizational citizenship behaviors and service quality as external effectiveness of contact employees. *Journal of Business Research*, 56, 597-611.

INDEX

D

E

F

G

M

T

U

V